Debates in Economic History

Edited by Peter Mathias

Revisions in Mercantilism

Revisions in Mercantilism

edited with an introduction by
D. C. COLEMAN

METHUEN & CO LTD
11 NEW FETTER LANE LONDON EC4

First published 1969 *by Methuen & Co Ltd*
Introduction © *by D. C. Coleman*
Printed in Great Britain by
Richard Clay (The Chaucer Press), Ltd,
Bungay, Suffolk

SBN (casebound) 416 48090 X
SBN (paperback) 416 48120 5

Distributed in the U.S.A.
by Barnes & Noble Inc.

Contents

Preface

Mercantilism, as a topic for a volume in this series, is different in kind from those preceding it (though, as a concept, the Industrial Revolution raises certain methodological parallels). 'Mercantilism' never enjoyed historical reality of the same order as agriculture, or the export of capital, or Venice – and, indeed, as a concept it is very much more recent than some of the historical phenomena, many centuries old, which it purports to embrace. Whenever a term representing some highly abstract, conceptualized scheme, such as mercantilism, begins to enjoy wide currency, academic commentators customarily reach for their blue pencils. Popularization usually brings with it a widening of the original terms of reference of the idea, a decline in discrimination. This, in turn, creates confusion about the original significance which a concept had for its users. At a certain point in the debate, therefore, terms have to be defined again; the different meanings and assumptions (some of them, perhaps, unspecified or unselfconscious) which have found shelter under the same linguistic form have to be sorted out. They must then be judged anew in the light of their own different assumptions. New questions will then be asked about the traditional assumptions themselves.

'Mercantilism' is now passing through such a sequence, to which the present volume bears witness. This is not to resolve the confusions by producing the 'right' answer. The inter-relations between economic thought and public policy – subject to so many time-lags and differing rhythms of change – with the realities of the historical situation of their context are infinitely complex. Here there really *is* a debate, and a necessarily continuing one. All this Dr Coleman's masterly introduction makes clear.

The lesson of the confusion created by this too casual adoption of a convenient label will doubtless be underlined by the contribution which the experience of the present century is all too likely to add to the currency of the term mercantilism. The revival of policies of 'economic nationalism' – high tariff walls to foster industry, trade rivalries, the search to maximize exports and minimize imports, the obsession (for good reason) about the balance of trade and the level of gold reserves (with Germany now, as Holland in the seventeenth century, less obsessed than others for equally good reason) has inevitably been dubbed 'neo-mercantilist' or 'the new mercantilism'. At first glance these horses do, indeed, seem to be from the same stable. Doubtless the underlying problems giving rise to these incursions of the state on – it seems – an ever-widening front in twentieth-century economies have given new insights into some of the constraints influencing the reactions of merchants and legislators in the seventeenth century. Certain aspects of the present context of international economic rivalries have their historical analogues; but the present world is none the less a very different place from that of Colbert and Thomas Mun, and historians are now shifting the whole debate about mercantilism into new ground by insisting on relating economic ideas to policy in its immediate executive context of particular problems of markets, costs, interest groups, fiscal necessities, and the like. This salutary exercise, to say the least, is throwing up more diversity than homogeneity compared with the older academic pursuit of placing ideas in logical sequence with their precursors and successors to form a smooth evolutionary sequence uncomplicated by the problem of trying to relate them to their 'external' context. The history of science faces a similar methodological crux. It is time the history of the concept of 'imperialism' passed under the harrow of the same historical discipline.

Another issue of wider significance in the methodology of economic history is raised by the debate about mercantilism. For a concept to remain useful as an explanatory device, a tool of analysis for marshalling data – even to remain meaningful in analytical terms – its embrace must not become too wide. To universalize a concept is to disembowel it of any *particular* significance. Mercantilism has suffered just such a fate (so, more recently, has the term 'imperialism'). When it purports to characterize or 'explain' economic policy as a whole over the whole of Europe for some centuries the diversity of historical experience this contains is too great to be usefully crammed into the confines of a single concept. This is the classical trap of conceptualization in the social sciences for the historian. The more universalistic a concept becomes in its claims, then the necessarily more abstract, the more remote from specific areas of historical experience, and the necessarily less useful as a tool of analysis for understanding them. In the end historians must demand that the conceptual apparatus born of the social sciences, however fertile for suggesting new relationships, be subject to the stubborn test of the empirical.

PETER MATHIAS

Acknowledgements

The editor and publishers wish to thank the following for permission to reproduce the articles listed below:

Professor Ingomar Bog for 'Mercantilism in Germany' (translated by George Hammersley from 'Der Merkantilismus in Deutschland' in *Jahrbücher für Nationalökonomie und Statistik*, Vol. CLXXIII, 1961); the Economic History Association for 'French Views on Wealth and Taxes from the Middle Ages to the Old Régime', by Professor Martin Wolfe (*Journal of Economic History*, Vol. XXVI, 4, 1966); His Excellency Gunnar Heckscher for 'Revisions in Economic History: Mercantilism', by Professor Eli Heckscher (*Economic History Review*, Vol. VII, 1, 1936–7); Professor Jacob van Klaveren for 'Fiscalism, Mercantilism and Corruption' (translated by George Hammersley from 'Fiskalismus-Merkantilismus-Korruption' in *Vierteljahrschrift für Sozial- und Wirtschaftsgeschichte*, Vol. XLVII, 3, 1960); the Royal Historical Society for 'The Idea of a Mercantile State', by Professor A. V. Judges (*Transactions of the Royal Historical Society*, 4th series, Vol. XXI, 1939), and 'The Other Face of Mercantilism', by Professor C. H. Wilson (*Transactions of the Royal Historical Society*, 5th series, Vol. IX, 1959); the Scandinavian Economic History Review for 'Eli Heckscher and the Idea of Mercantilism', by Dr D. C. Coleman (*The Scandinavian Economic History Review*, Vol. V, 1, 1957, and World Politics for 'Power Versus Plenty as Objectives of Foreign Policy in the Seventeenth and Eighteenth Centuries', by Professor Jacob Viner (*World Politics*, Vol. 1, 1948).

Editor's Introduction

*. . . That, my dear Algy, is the whole truth pure and simple.
. . . The truth is rarely pure and never simple. Modern life
would be very tedious if it were either . . .*
                    Oscar Wilde, The Importance of being Earnest

Such notions as mercantilism, the inventions of scholars, are
designed to simplify the infinite complexity of the past. They
usually end up by adding to the confusion of the present. But
there is no other way: without simplification we cannot
understand; without signposts we are lost. History shorn of
ideas is a bore; and ideas, fortunately, change. From time to
time, therefore, we have to take a fresh look at the invented
signpost, to wonder whether it is not in fact pointing in several
directions at once, or guiding the traveller towards a waste-
land. The curious may look into the *Oxford English Dictionary*
and discover that via 'mercantilism' he is heading towards 'the
system of economic doctrine and legislative policy based on the
principle that money alone is wealth'. Today, this definition
seems merely to stand as a tribute to the confidence of a past
age in its own economic beliefs; it is patently inadequate and
unacceptable. So now UNESCO's *Dictionary of the Social
Sciences* begins its definition thus:

> The term *mercantilism* denotes the principles of the mer-
> cantile system, sometimes understood as the identification of
> wealth with money; but more generally, the belief that the
> economic welfare of the state can only be secured by govern-
> ment regulation of a nationalist character.

The vast conceptual gap is obvious. The rest of the entry provides a necessarily brief, though admirably lucid, survey of how
the gap came to be.[1] Yet, confronted by such diversity under
one name, the traveller's doubts about the signpost may
legitimately still persist.

A Dictionary of the Social Sciences, ed. Julius Gould and William L. Kolb
(UNESCO, 1964), pp. 423–4. The definition is by Charles Wilson.

The debate about the nature of mercantilism as illustrated in the articles reprinted in this volume stretches over roughly the last thirty years. It is confined to that period for two simple reasons. First, it was earlier not so much a matter of discussion as of basic formulations. The first of these was Adam Smith's *Wealth of Nations* (1776), especially Book IV, in which he set out what he considered to be the principles of the mercantile system. The term was not of his invention,[1] but the systematic exposition was. The chapter from Gustav Schmoller's *Studien über die wirtschaftliche Politik Friedrich des Grossens* (1884), which contains the major elaboration of a new and much wider concept of mercantilism, i.e. as state-building, was translated into English (as *The Mercantile System and its Historical Significance*) in 1895; and English readers were offered a substantial application to English history of this expanded version of mercantilism in W. Cunningham's *Growth of English Industry and Commerce* (1882, and especially the editions of 1892 and 1903). Finally, there appeared, between 1931 and 1935, the Swedish, German, and English versions of the outstanding work on the subject, Eli Heckscher's *Mercantilism*. The second reason follows from this: although disagreement with Cunningham had been expressed by various writers, notably Hewins and Unwin, the debate about mercantilism achieved a new and more vigorous life with the publication of Heckscher's two massive and masterly volumes.

It is perhaps worth emphasizing at this point what is and is not the aim of the particular sample of articles here reproduced. The selection is designed neither to provide an exposition or explanation of mercantilism as a phase in the history of economic thought nor to offer a set of examples of mercantilism in practice. Of course, these ends are served, in part and in passing, by some of the articles. Heckscher's offers a commentary on his own treatment set out at length in his book; and Judges' a demolition of the whole concept as developed. In the course of demonstrating some affinities between the German cameralists and an English variant of what has been called 'social mercantilism', Charles Wilson's article examines a specific aspect of thought and action; so, too, does Ingomar Bog in his

[1] See below, p. 37.

exposition of what he sees as 'imperial mercantilism' at work in Germany. But these are all in the nature of illustrations, variations on a larger theme. All manner of books and articles exist on specific aspects of mercantilism, on particular phases of policy or thought. C. W. Cole's detailed examination of the arch-mercantilist, Colbert; P. J. Thomas's monograph, *Mercantilism and the East India Trade*; the series of articles embracing an argument, started by Wilson and Heckscher and continued by others, on the balance of trade and the international payments mechanism. These are but a few, and a select list is given in the bibliography at the end of this volume.

The purpose of the present selection is threefold. First, to illustrate some differing treatments of an historical concept. Second, to indicate some of the problems, and the stimuli to thought, raised specifically by Heckscher's treatment of the concept. Third, to show the current trend in the debate. Throughout, the emphasis is primarily, though not solely, on mercantilism in action rather than mercantilist thinking as part of the history of economic analysis.

I

The contrast between English and German approaches to the subject is very evident. Despite the disagreements between Bog and van Klaveren, both employ a series of categories, beyond mere mercantilism: imperial mercantilism, pseudo-mercantilism, anti-mercantilism, fiscalism, semi-fiscalism. For Bog, drawing upon the view of Anton Tautscher, mercantilist economic policy has 'a rigorously logical structure'[1]; mercantilism and cameralism are one and the same; and with the practical awareness of the problems of reconstruction in the states of the Holy Roman Empire after the disasters of the Thirty Years War, 'the spirit of the mercantilist age was born'.[2] This is all a long way indeed from Judges' plea that we should:

> consider ourselves absolved from the necessity of having to reconcile the conclusions derived from detailed researches into the antecedents and effects of edicts, statutes and

[1] Below, p. 166.   [2] Below, p. 175.

municipal by-laws, spread over the whole European and
colonial field within a period of more than three centuries,
with the canons of an imaginary system conceived by
economists for purposes of theoretical exposition and mishandled by historians in the service of their political ideals.[1]

Van Klaveren's refusal to see mercantilism as something informed by a consistent body of theory brings him nearer to the
viewpoints expressed by some English writers; his concern
with the fiscal problems of governments and the role of corruption, even if presented somewhat obsessively, raises practical
matters of great importance. But one cannot help wondering
whether his 'fiscalism' and 'semi-fiscalism' – as things in themselves, counter-concepts to mercantilism – are any more readily
capable of isolation than mercantilism itself. Bog attributes to
me the contention that economic policy at this period was so
dominated by political purposes, by power politics, that there
was no room for anything that could properly be called economic policy. 'In other words, absolutism devours mercantilism.'[2] I certainly did not say this,[3] as reference to my own article
reprinted below will make clear. But the doubt about a defin-
able mercantilist policy remains. It is maybe one which we
should preserve in the cause of scholarly inquiry rather than
seek to dispel by magical incantation. Can we be sure of
distinguishing something called economic policy in an age
which had no corpus of systematic economics? 'In a real
sense,' as A. W. Coats observed in his reply to my own
criticism of Heckscher,[4] 'there is no such thing as *economic*
policy.' If this is true today, when economists abound, within
governments and without, how much more so is it true of
seventeenth-century Europe? Let us readily concede that
much contemporary thinking about economic matters was
influenced by a concern for the balance of trade; and that
state measures to encourage the export and discourage the

[1] Below, pp. 58–9.   [2] Below, p. 165, also p. 180.
[3] The erroneous impression may perhaps have arisen from Bog's having
apparently derived his knowledge of my expressed views from an article in
Dutch by J. G. van Dillen (see below p. 213) which purported to summarize
them, at least in part.
[4] A. W. Coats, 'In Defence of Heckscher and the Idea of Mercantilism',
Scandinavian Economic History Review, V, No. 2 (1957).

import of manufactured goods were widespread. Go further and accept van Klaveren's criterion of mercantilist economic policy: 'the objective is always the development, from an agrarian base, of an industrial, commercial and maritime superstructure coupled with an attempt to secure a bigger share in the profits of international commerce for one's own citizens'. Regard may thus be paid to two pervasive mercantilist themes: the belief in a fixed cake of commerce so that one nation's gain therein must be at the expense of another's loss; and the concern with the fostering of activities other than agriculture. Yet even when all this is granted we are still far from a body of systematic, logically constructed knowledge which can be called mercantilist economic theory. And it is surely an historical absurdity to see this as enduring, developing, and being consistently put into operation, state by state, problem by problem, over three centuries and all Europe.

The detection of underlying causes, the evocation of a set of principles, the discovery of rules, the ability to predict from the explanation of reality: these are essential to the economist who seeks, though he may not always obtain, scientific accuracy. So Adam Smith, as the father of modern economics, could hardly have dealt with what he saw, rightly or wrongly, as the follies of the existing ways of thought and behaviour, in any other way than he did. Without systematization, no destruction; without destruction of the old, no formulation of the new. Yet we make an invalid methodological step if we take the results of his act of systematization and seek to use them as a sufficient explanation for the policies of governments. Smith took the views of Mun and other writers; he dissected Acts of Parliament; and he assumed that the latter were necessarily the product of the ideas contained in the former, assisted, of course, by the sinister pressures of merchants and manufacturers. He did not ask why governments should behave as they did in specific circumstances, for once he had abstracted the mercantile system from the totality of experience, it became an explanatory device. Of the vast apparatus of customs duties which the English government erected from about 1688 onwards, and which so enraged Smith in 1776, it has recently been written:

Examination of the legislation itself brings out an unfamiliar picture of government motives: one revealing the
influence neither of economists' theories nor ministers' long-
term commercial policies, but simply of urgent fiscal needs.
The strongest influence on the creation of a new tariff structure at the end of the seventeenth century was the need of
government for money to pay for costly wars; tariffs were
the response to these needs, rather than the implementation
of a policy derived from economic theories of that or any
other day.[1]

But to Adam Smith, the heavy duties would never have been
imposed, 'had not the mercantile system taught us, in many
cases, to employ taxation as an instrument, not of revenue, but
of monopoly'.[2] Here is the essence of his approach. The
mercantile system has moved imperceptibly from an analysis of
aggregate trends to the cause of specific actions. And emotive
power is added by the use of the word 'monopoly'. This Smith
uses unfailingly in his enduring suspicion of traders and producers alike. Did France show the same distressing mercantilist
symptoms? Then this was due mainly to –

the policy of Mr Colbert, who, notwithstanding his great
abilities, seems in this case to have been imposed upon by
the sophistry of merchants and manufacturers, who are
always demanding a monopoly against their countrymen.[3]

It is one of the nicer ironies that a man who mistrusted business-
men should have become the founder of the economic liberalism which offered them maximum freedom of action.

The Smithian origin of the concept has left its mark on all
subsequent development and use. Conceived in pejorative
terms, it had, almost inevitably, to achieve approval when the
dominance of economic liberalism was first seriously chal-
lenged. But when it was given its wider meaning and habili-
tated – not *re*-habilitated because it had never existed as a
named and recognized object of conscious approval – the pro-

[1] Ralph Davis, 'The Rise of Protection in England, 1689–1786', *Economic
History Review*, 2nd series, XIX, No. 2 (August 1966), p. 306.
[2] *Wealth of Nations* (Modern Library Edition, ed. Edwin Cannan, New York,
1937), p. 833.   [3] Ibid., p. 434.

cedure was carried out by those interested in the historical process of national unification. As both Judges and Viner make clear in their articles, the pioneers of this approach were German, and their emphasis lay heavily upon the contributions to political power allegedly made by ideas and enactments of the sort about which Smith had been so scornful. Schmoller's presentation marked a high point in a sequence of writings elaborating stages of economic development and which begin with Friedrich List, whose most celebrated work, *Das Nationale System der politischen Ökonomie* appeared in 1841.[1] The emphasis of the German historical school upon state-building, upon political and economic unification, meant a concomitant emphasis upon the totality of the environment in which ideas and actions took place. This was an essential element in the sundry stages of growth which members of the school detected in history; and, of course, it was in direct contrast to Smith's abstraction from totality, his attempt to isolate economic variables and economic policy. *Mutatis mutandis*, this holds good also for two important variants of the German historical approach to economic developments, those of Werner Sombart and of Karl Marx. The concept of mercantilism does not much figure in the Marxist treatment of history. It has been called 'the ideology of the monopoly trading companies',[2] and, by Maurice Dobb, 'a system of State-regulated exploitation through trade . . . essentially the economic policy of an age of primitive accumulation'.[3] Dobb seems also to have doubts about the reality of the 'system', for he notes elsewhere that the doctrines of mercantilist writers were far less homogeneous than classical economists represented them. Yet he sees their views on trade as acquiring meaning if they are applied 'to the exploitation of a dependent colonial system', and if the writers are regarded as 'spokesmen of industrial rather than merchant capital (or perhaps one should say of merchant capital that was already acquiring a direct interest in production)'.[4]

[1] See on this Bert F. Hoselitz (ed.), *Theories of Economic Growth* (New York and London, 1960), especially the chapter by the editor called 'Theories of Stages of Economic Growth'.

[2] Quoted Judges, below p. 59n.

[3] Maurice Dobb, *Studies in the Development of Capitalism* (1946), p. 209.

[4] Ibid., p. 204.

So we now have the happy situation that across the 170 years between 1776 and 1946 the voices of classical and Marxist economics join in sonorous agreement about the machinations of monopoly-seeking merchants – even if they disagree about their significance. They may well be right, but unfortunately neither provides evidence of the sort which historical scholarship demands.

Here, indeed, is the rub. Evidence is what historians need; theories are what economists make. Classical economists, the German historical school, to a much lesser extent the Marxists: all offer origins, definitions, and varying significance for a set of views expressed by a miscellaneous collection of writers, officials, pamphleteers, merchants, and statesmen. And then, contemplating the edicts, proclamations, and statutes which sometimes seem to embody some of these views, they move in to fashion that causative link which best suits their model of change. Jacob Viner's article demonstrates the falsity of the interpretation, much favoured by the German school, of mercantilism as a system predominantly seeking power. His article is specifically concerned with mercantilist doctrine. But it contains a salutary observation about the importance of that doctrine which anyone on the brink of using 'mercantilist' as a quick short cut to explanation of policy should have engraved in some suitably prominent place:

> In human affairs ... there is always room for divergence between dogma and practice, between principles and the actual behaviour of those who profess them. It is doctrine, and not practice, which is the main concern here. The task of ascertaining how much or how little they corresponded in the age of mercantilism, and what were the forces which caused them to deviate, is the difficult duty of the historian, in whose hands I gladly leave it.[1]

II

Despite the scale, the learning, and the outstanding intellectual qualities, Heckscher's *Mercantilism* does not really perform this

[1] Below, p. 81.

'difficult duty of the historian' to which Viner refers. A major work of synthesis, it is eclectic in its inspiration in so far as it examines the idea of the mercantile system as developed both by the classical economists and by the German historicists. The notion is analysed in relation to national unification, state power, protection, monetary arrangements, and as a conception of society. In assessing what he sees as the achievements of mercantilist policy, Heckscher judges it through the eyes of the classical tradition of liberal economics; he looks unfavourably upon its theoretical content; he regards its approach to society as amoral. Though mercantilism is said to be only an 'instrumental concept', that concept is consistently treated and referred to as a system: a system of power, a system of national unification, a monetary system. The 'system' is unquestionably seen as the informing light of European economic policy over three centuries. For good or for evil, successfully or unsuccessfully, with or without logical consistency according to the tenets of classical or neo-classical economics: these are criteria of Heckscher's judgement. But this does not fill the gap between ideas and actions, between doctrine and practice. Looking at the final act of policy, Heckscher rarely examines the diversity of influences which led to the acts of state.

No doubt Heckscher accurately described his work as a 'contribution to the history of economic policy as a common European problem'. But three points need to be made about this. First, the common element in formulating policy is always assumed to be the common 'system' of thought called mercantilism; what is specifically ruled out is that the policy may have been the outcome, even in part, of the existence of common elements in the economic situation, in the circumstances of economic life. Second, the assessment of the policy in terms of its success or consistency or morality seems to preclude assessment of the contribution of mercantilist ideas in relation to other contributions. Third, the emphasis upon a 'common European problem', in combination with the classical economists' approach, i.e. isolating economic variables from others, means that inadequate regard is paid to the elements which are not common, in space or in time: variations by country or region, variations according to secular or short-term movements in the economic situation.

All these are areas of inquiry opened up as a result of Heckscher's comprehensive and ingenious theoretical synthesis. And there is some indication that the debate is moving gradually away from the continued pursuit of mercantilism as a thing in itself towards examination of specific acts, periods, phases, or areas of government policy in relation to both economic and social matters. Here we can consider only a few examples, some illustrated in the articles reprinted, some not.

III

The fiscal needs of the state provide an obvious area of government action and a potent influence upon policy. Heckscher's comparative neglect of this 'contribution to economic policy' was pointed out by Herbert Heaton in 1937.[1] In quite different ways the articles by Jacob van Klaveren and by Martin Wolfe, reprinted below, underline the relevance to mercantilist ideas and actions of the state's revenue needs. The historian has not only to examine the varying sorts of tax arrangements which states instituted but also to scrutinize most carefully any act of state so as to distinguish between professed objectives and real intentions. Already, as debate proceeds along these particular lines, one can see some of the extreme swings of opinions engendered by the expanded version of mercantilism. To Wolfe mercantilism is 'a programme to improve the treasury through the economy'.[2] This relates specifically to the France of Louis XIV and to Colbert's economic policy. But in Gabriel Ardant's *Théorie sociologique de l'impôt* the fiscal origins of mercantilism have been so generalized that:

> Sans les nécessités fiscales ressenties en Europe aux XVIe et XVIIe siècles avec la constitution des 'Etats modernes', l'évolution économique n'aurait pas subi l'impulsion qui lui fut donnée par des souverains et des ministres qui, à tort ou

---

[1] H. Heaton, 'Heckscher on Mercantilism', *Journal of Political Economy*, XLV, No. 3 (1937).

[2] Below, p. 203.

à raison, ne croyaient pas à un progrès spontané de l'industrie et du commerce suffisant pour les besoins de l'état.[1]

In short, it was the pursuit of the second of Adam Smith's objectives for political economy, 'to supply the state or commonwealth with a revenue sufficient for the public services',[2] that created mercantilist policies. Again, we must beware: Ardant's evidence is drawn virtually entirely from late-seventeenth-century France; and the author concedes that ' "Colbertisme" ait paru le prototype du mercantilisme'.[3] Mercantilism without Colbert has some affinity to *Hamlet* without the Prince of Denmark.

In van Klaveren's treatment of the financial problems of the state as contributory elements in the formation of economic policy the concepts of fiscalism, pseudo-mercantilism, and corruption appear as distorting agents, twisting mercantilist notions from their original intent. The very invention of such terms may seem a tribute to the need to climb down from the generality which 'mercantilism' has acquired into the sordid area of practice. But again we must note the specific context, this time of both van Klaveren's and Bog's concern: the problems of the German states, *circa* 1650–1800. Of course, these had economic elements in common with, say, England or Holland or France, just as there were common features of ideas as between German cameralism and English mercantilism. But was it not the specific problems – as seen and interpreted by contemporaries – of specific economies which provided the distinctive characteristics of thought and action? The political, dynastic, religious, economic, social, and financial conditions of the congerie of states which made up the Empire in 1700 were, in truth, so drastically different from those of, say, England or Holland, as to overshadow the similarities. All were 'pre-industrialized' economies, certainly, but within that general category the states of the Empire were industrially and commercially still more 'underdeveloped' or 'backward'. Though ultimate aims were similar, immediate problems were different. The remedies applied, though owing much to the

[1] G. Ardant, *Théorie sociologique de l'Impôt* (2 vols., Paris, 1965), Vol. I, p. 706.
[2] *Wealth of Nations*, p. 397.
[3] Ardant, op. cit., II, p. 708.

general ideas called mercantilist and to the specific example of Colbert, did not produce a pattern of economic policy which can be readily subsumed under the same rubric as that which might be used to describe the Statute of Artificers of 1563 or the Navigation Act of 1651 without a grotesque wrench of the meaning of a word. Only in Germany, as Bog points out, was cameralism systematically studied, even to the extent of establishing university chairs in the subject; England had no counterpart to the Commercial Colleges; the bitter clash between fiscal exigencies and expansionist hopes was not echoed to anything like the same extent in England's booming mercantile economy; the population situation was different, and so, totally, was the political structure. Despite the influence of English *ideas* upon such German cameralists as Becher and von Schröder, as indicated in Charles Wilson's article, the ultimate patterns of policy were the products of very divergent influences and situations.

Examples of these variations between countries and of differing notions hiding under the same name could be multiplied for sundry aspects of mercantilist ideas and actions. The coverage of Heckscher's book, despite its comprehensiveness, is not in reality Europe-wide. Holland, for instance, is treated cursorily and patchily; in particular, he does not bring out the extreme contrast between a high degree of regulation and state intervention in some spheres, notably industry and fishing, and a comparative absence of such measures in others, notably commerce and finance. By the very nature of his preconceptions, Heckscher ignores the extent to which the force of economic circumstances frequently dictated the shape of policy enactments.[1] A quite different sort of example is provided by the divergent interpretations of mercantilist notions to be found in W. D. Grampp[2] and Lionel Rothkrug.[3] The former, dealing specifically with English writers (mainly late seventeenth-century) and with doctrine rather than practice, finds numerous

[1] W. D. Voorthuisen, *De republiek der verenigde nederlanden en het mercantilisme* (The Hague, 1965, English summary).

[2] 'The Liberal Elements in English Mercantilism', *Quarterly Journal of Economics*, LXVI, No. 4 (1952), and *Economic Liberalism* (2 vols., New York, 1965).

[3] *Opposition to Louis XIV: The Political and Social Origins of the French Enlightenment* (Princeton, 1965).

anticipations of economic liberalism in their attitudes, e.g. towards the role of the price-mechanism, in a utilitarian conception of self-interest, and in their approval of competition. Ridiculing the notion that they confused money and wealth, and quite unconcerned with the fiscal question, Grampp contends that the major objective of mercantilist *policy* was full employment; with this assumption their policy measures can be explained far better than by 'supposing some other purpose directed their ideas'.[1] In Rothkrug's book, on the other hand, mercantilism comprises 'traditional principles of political economy'[2] which were laid down, in France, by such sixteenth-century writers as de Seyssel and Bodin, later expanded by Laffémas and Montchrétien, and put into operation by Richelieu, Mazarin, and Colbert. The principles are exhibited as possessing a 'mercantilist ethic', as having marked affinities with the sentiments of Machiavelli, as being cynical and immoral, and as running counter to religious ideals and Christian humanism. An 'anti-mercantilist camp' is seen as forming part of the opposition to Louis XIV's policies.

Despite these diversities wrought by the 'instrumental concept', mercantilism remains a convenient shorthand for a set of ideas. Possessed of certain common elements, they nevertheless varied a good deal, by time and by country. Their logical structure and their relationship to preceding and succeeding ideas are matters of study for the historian of economic thought. The historian who is concerned with the doings of governments, however, needs to use the concept with a care amounting to suspicion, lest he is entrapped into explaining them as mercantilist simply by reference to ideas already called mercantilist.

Future research, stimulated by this debate, might well proceed along two main paths.

First, there needs to be more inquiry into the structure of, and relationships between, the pre-industrialized economies of the time, with a view to securing a better understanding of why contemporaries should have held the common opinions which they did. In pursuing this inquiry we need to jettison the pejora-

---

[1] Grampp, *Economic Liberalism*, Vol. I, p. 55.
[2] Rothkrug, op. cit., p. 87.

tive attitudes of the classical and neo-classical economists from whom we have inherited the very name of the mercantile system. This is not a version of *tout comprendre, c'est tout pardonner*, nor does it imply a simple economic determinism. It is to suggest that we do what all inquirers into the past have always done and cannot help doing: use the tools at our disposal. If we construct and test hypotheses about the economic working of such economies, we may obtain a better insight into contemporary policy *recommendations* – which are not the same as enactments – than if we start, as did Adam Smith, by condemning the policies for the purpose of substituting our own recommendations.

Take, for example, the market situation for manufactured goods. In very rough terms the position was as follows. Production was highly labour-intensive; technological change, though existent, was slow; therefore productivity-increasing, cost-reducing innovations were infrequent, and such lowering of real costs as was achieved came either through reduction of wages (possibly by gratuitous population increase and a worsening of already endemic under-employment) or through slow changes in patterns of organization, e.g. the evolution of putting-out methods. Consequently, in any existing market price-competition as a consequence of the ability to lower costs was rare (it might occur, in the short-run, through monetary changes, e.g. devaluation or depreciation of currencies; or, in the longer-run, through technological or organizational changes operating to lower either transport costs or production costs). On the demand side, most people were too poor to have a surplus income to spend on other than the basic necessities of life. Therefore the value of purchases by the mass of the people probably formed a small proportion of the total sales of goods sold on commercially organized national or international markets. (Their needs were met, to some unknown and changing extent, by local markets or in subsistence sectors of regional economies.) Consequently, and in view of the supply conditions which made price-reduction difficult, increases in aggregate sales of manufactured goods on such markets were likely, in the main, to be achieved through either (*a*) increases in consumers' incomes or (*b*) the finding of new markets. Within (*a*) the increases could occur, more probably but on only a limited scale, among existing buyers or (*b*), less probably, among the 'poor', i.e. outside the existing buyers. Faced with this situation, any individual seller or individual government wishing to promote aggregate exports saw at least two possible courses as obvious. One was the capture of existing markets, served by other sellers or other nations, by means of commercial treaties, negotiated concessions, diplomatic action for or against mercantile groups, or ultimately, war. The other was the discovery of new markets, through colonization or settlement, again aided if necessary by the power of the state.

An understanding of the contemporary economic situation may be a better guide to contemporary recommendations than a criticism of policy. How otherwise should we approach the seventeenth-century concern to find new markets? Recommendations to deal with the observed situation were, of course, not uniform. Some contemporaries, such as Defoe, advocated higher wages; others, such as Mandeville, praised extravagance: both sought to increase consumption. But all were aware of, not to say obsessed with, the extreme difficulty of aggregate expansion in consumption. And they were right to be. Whether in Colbert's celebrated memoir of 1669[1] or in a less well-known one from Davenant, the message is clear.

> ... for there is a limited stock of our own product to carry out, beyond which there is no passing: as for example, there is such a quantity of woollen manufactures, lead, tin, etc. which, over and above our own consumption, we can export abroad, and our soil as it is now peopled, will not yield much more; and there is likewise a limited quantity of these goods which foreign consumption will not exceed.[2]

From these positions, Colbert's 'trade causes perpetual strife' (un combat perpétuel)[3] or Child's 'all trade [is] a kind of war-

[1] P. Clément, *Lettres, instructions et mémoires de Colbert* (Paris, 1869), Vol. VI, pp. 264–9.
[2] C. Davenant, *Discourses on the Public Revenues and the Trade of England: III. On the Plantation Trade*, in *Works* (ed. Whitworth, 5 vols., 1771).
[3] Clément, op. cit., p. 269.

fare'[1] are logical consequences. But the warfare takes its particular form, though not its general existence, from the particular economic circumstances. To describe the present-day 'warfare' as 'neo-mercantilism'[2] is, from an historian's viewpoint, simply to misunderstand the nature of the earlier situation, whatever the validity of the criticism of current policies.

This is only a crude sketch of an approach to one aspect of mercantilism. More refined analysis of many more aspects is needed. But in the process we must be careful not to assume that ideas and actions are mere 'reflections' of the economic situation. So the second path of inquiry which might fruitfully be trodden leads to analyses of the totality of influences bearing upon state policy. This follows from the questioning of the existence of 'economic policy' as an isolatable entity. The economist, for his purposes, may try to isolate economic forces and make policy recommendations; but the historian, if he is to do his job properly, must take cognizance of the total situation in which the forces are at work. The study of government economic policy in this period demands, for example, adequate awareness of contemporary social structure and *mores*. These were communities in which the great mass of the ordinary people, 'the poor', were, as Sir Thomas Smith said of sixteenth-century England, those who –

> ... have no voice nor authority in our commonwealth and no account is made of them, but only to be ruled.[3]

Economic recommendations were made and economic policy carried out in societies in which such sentiments were commonplace. Problems of public order loomed large in economies suffering from an endemic shortage of foodstuffs. How far at any particular time were policies related to movements in overseas trade, foodstuff prices, or population? We have to take heed of such influences, as we must also of the location of political power, the strength of urban gilds, or the role of

[1] Josiah Child, quoted W. Letwin, *The Origins of Scientific Economics* (1964), p. 44.

[2] Joan Robinson, *The New Mercantilism* (Cambridge, 1966).

[3] Sir Thomas Smith, *De Republica Anglorum: a Discourse on the Commonwealth of England*, ed. L. Alston (Cambridge, 1906), p. 46.

overseas trade in a country's economy. The great importance of fiscal questions needs no further emphasis. Suffice to stress the interdependence between such questions and other elements in the total situation. Inelasticities of revenue, for instance, were themselves induced partly by the inelasticity of aggregate demand and partly by political and social pressures which, variously in different countries, exempted from taxation the wealth of certain classes or failed to tap the sectors of most rapid accumulation.

If research is to proceed along these lines it must examine the actions of particular national governments in particular sets of situations. If such studies can be comparative so much the better. But, above all, let them try to place the ideas called mercantilist into the context of the groups of men we call governments, open to sundry pressures and various influences, grappling with specific problems. By all means let us heed Keynes's often-quoted remark:

> . . . the ideas of economists and political philosophers, both when they are right and when they are wrong, are more powerful than is commonly understood. Indeed the world is ruled by little else. Practical men, who believe themselves to be quite exempt from any intellectual influences, are usually the slaves of some defunct economist. Madmen in authority, who hear voices in the air, are distilling the frenzy of some academic scribbler of a few years back.[1]

But if we should try to take it from the 1930s and apply it to the 1630s, then we should at least remember that the world over which the madmen then exercised their authority was, in many significant ways, dissimilar to ours; that the practicality of practical men sprang from different experiences; and that neither the voices in the air nor the frenzy of academic scribblers belonged to economists, defunct or otherwise – for the good reason that they, like mercantilism, had yet to be invented.

D. C. COLEMAN

[1] John Maynard Keynes, *The General Theory of Employment Interest and Money* (1936), p. 383.

18 *Revisions in Mercantilism*

NOTE. I would like to record my gratitude to George Hammersley for his translations of articles 6 and 7 and for his further assistance and co-operation when I came to make a number of editorial amendments to his texts.

D.C.C.

1 Mercantilism

ELI F. HECKSCHER

[This article was first published as No. V in the series 'Revisions in Economic History' in the *Economic History Review*, Vol. VII, No. 1, 1936–7.]

The Editor of the *Economic History Review* has asked me to write a short article on Mercantilism in the series 'Revisions in Economic History'. This has proved a more difficult task than I had anticipated, first because it presupposes in the writer a definite conception of what the accepted doctrine is; and that is not at all clear to me. Secondly, the vastness of the subject makes it literally impossible even to mention, in the small space available to me, the many instances where I find a different relationship between different parts of the subject than that usually described; or, generally, a new point of view. And even with regard to the somewhat arbitrarily selected points raised here it is impossible to give chapter and verse for my conclusions.[1]

The general weakness characteristic of the earlier treatment of mercantilism was the same as that prevailing in other fields of economic history, namely, the exclusively national outlook of scholars and their lack of theoretical analysis. The first defect places an undue emphasis upon dissimilarities between

---

[1] I must, therefore, confine myself to a general reference to my book *Mercantilism* (George Allen & Unwin, Ltd., London, 1935; two vols.). The – outspoken or implied – egotism of the present article is a matter of sincere regret to me; but what has now been said explains it to some extent. Fortunately, I am at the same time able to embrace the occasion of noticing some constructive criticisms of the book in question. Besides those mentioned below I should like to call attention to an article upon the German edition of my book, 'Le mercantilisme: un état d'esprit', by Professor Marc Bloch, in the *Annales d'histoire économique et sociale*, Vol. VI (1934), pp. 160–3, and to the very valuable Introduction to the *Nuova Collana di Economisti*, Vol. III, 'Storia Economica' (Torino, 1936), by the editor, Professor Gino Luzzatto. – For a summary, I may refer to the article on 'Mercantilism' in the *Encyclopædia of the Social Sciences*, Vol. X (1933), pp. 333–9, though it contains some minor errors.

countries and even gives the impression that purely national factors were much more influential than they really were; the second is, in my opinion, even more damaging, as it frequently prevents scholars from seeing what the problems are and how they should be solved. When all is said, economic developments have followed similar lines all over the western world; and all economic developments, in whatever civilization they are found, must raise problems akin to those of present-day economic life, though they give the historian the important advantage that he is able to see their outcome – which is far from being the case with contemporary conditions and occurrences.

As to the international aspect, I think that Sombart stands on a pinnacle of his own, but also Unwin (in his most important book) draws very instructive comparisons between England and France. With regard to a theoretical background to the treatment of mercantilism, I hardly know of any author since Adam Smith who possesses it, with the exception of Professor Viner. In addition to these two defects there is a third, i.e. the merging of the subject of mercantilism into that unwholesome Irish stew called 'modern capitalism'. If those two words have a distinct meaning it ought to be connected with what is called in economic science 'capital'; and in that case mercantilism, though, of course, related to it, is to a great extent outside the subject. If, on the other hand, 'modern capitalism' is an expression intended to cover everything in economic life that paved the way to modern conditions, it is simply a misleading name for the economic history of Europe since the end of the Middle Ages.

The different treatment accorded to mercantilism by, say, Adam Smith, Schmoller, and Cunningham is principally rooted in insufficient attention to the difference between ends and means. The ends of statesmen in the economic field between, say, the beginning of the sixteenth and the middle of the eighteenth centuries were, of course, diversified; but I think it may be said that at least two tendencies played a very great part, i.e. that towards the unification of the territory of the state economically and the use of the resources of their countries in the interests of the political power of the state – more of this below. But important as this was in itself, it does *not* constitute the most characteristic contrast to what came later. An illustration may be found in the fact that the foremost, and by far the most intelligent, among German mercantilists, Johann Joachim Becher, gave his principal work a title which differed only very slightly from that of the *Wealth of Nations*. Consequently, the most important difference did not lie in the choice of ends but in opinions as to the best way of achieving those ends, i.e. in the choice of means. Through this, mercantilism became not only a specific type of economic policy but, even more, a characteristic body of economic ideas; for the views as to what constituted the best means were rooted in conscious or unconscious interpretations of the tendencies of economic life. Through this, mercantilism came to mean a discussion of the relations between causes and effects of economic factors; it paved the way to a theory of economics, in spite of having started from purely practical considerations. It is not, in this case, a question of a choice between theory and practice but of practice leading unintentionally to theory. I do not think any student with a theoretical insight can fail to see, especially when studying the writers of the seventeenth century, how they came more and more, and almost in spite of themselves, to work out theories of the relation between causes and effects in the economic field

Returning now to the ends pursued by mercantilist statesmen, opposite views have recently been expressed. A German scholar, Dr Hugo Rachel, in a review in the *Forschungen zur Brandenburgischen und Preussischen Geschichte* (Vol. XLV, pp. 180 f.), has said – in strong opposition to his own teacher, Schmoller – that the important point of view of mercantilist statesmen was not the idea of economic unity but that of economic power. Though some of the facts adduced for this contention do not appear to me at all convincing, I think there is something to be said for this criticism of my previous treatment of the subject.[1] It is not only that the attempts at unity were, with few exceptions, failures – such was the result of the

---

[1] For a strongly worded criticism of some of the utterances in this review see that by Professor Carl Brinkmann in the *Historische Zeitschrift*, CXLIX, 1933, p. 123.

majority of mercantilist measures; even these attempts them-selves were to a great extent half-hearted. It is difficult to find more than two bold attempts in this direction in the leading countries. One is the Statute of Artificers of 1563 in England, the other Colbert's tariff of 1664. Besides these two, the unify-ing measures in customs administration in Sweden in the seven-teenth century were to a very great degree successful; but Sweden, like England, was a country where disintegration had been avoided in the earlier period, and consequently in Sweden the problem of unification was little more than a question of merging new territories into the body of the old. And that was effected without great difficulty.

This consideration gives rise to a suspicion that mercantilist statesmen did not take their unifying work seriously. They were, however, unable to shirk altogether the task of adapting the medieval framework of European society to new economic and social conditions. This task I have also interpreted, per-haps incorrectly, as part of the unifying work of mercantilism. It fell into two rather distinct categories. The one was con-cerned with 'feudalism', i.e. the disintegration caused by more or less anarchical measures undertaken by the lawless or self-willed territorial lords and provincial nobles in their own interests. Briefly stated, there was little need for any activity against this tendency in England and Sweden. In Germany, on the other hand, the need for it was greater than almost anywhere else; but the efforts to overcome this anarchy came to very little. The country where both the need was great and something was done to satisfy it was France; the French monarchy was able to achieve some remarkable results in this field, though much of the old disorder was allowed to survive until the great revolution.

Even more important than 'feudalism' was that particular type of disintegration which resulted from the independence of the towns; and in spite of some dissimilarities, most European countries presented the same fundamental features in this respect. The author who has done most to elucidate this part of the subject is Georg von Below; and though his studies were almost entirely confined to Germany, and therefore left aside the most important countries in the mercantilist era, his conclusions appear to me to be generally unassailable, even when extended to other continental countries. The medieval towns had created the most consistent, vigorous, and long-lived system of economic policy that has ever existed, the most important parts of which were the gild system and the internal regulation of industry in general, and the organization of foreign trade and commerce. The fight against medieval municipal policy was most successful in the country in which it was least constructive – that is, England. There, after an attempt at a really constructive policy under the earlier Stuarts, the gild system was allowed to fall to pieces under the impact of new economic forces. When Cunningham gave the name of 'Parliamentary Colbertism' to the policy pursued in the period after 1689 he should have added that it was Colbertism not only without Colbert but also, which is even more important, without the vast administrative machinery created by Colbert – that it was, in fact, a system almost without any administrative machinery at all. On this point I think the views of Unwin were almost entirely correct. How far this explains the fact that what is usually called the Industrial Revolution came to England first, instead of beginning in continental countries – which were probably less backward than England before that time – is, of course, impossible to decide with certainty.[1] Many other factors made their contribution, and I can only record my personal impression that the absence of administrative control was one of the most important. The exigencies of space prevent me from going into the causes of the peculiar character of this disintegration of the old order of administration in England; but further researches have in my opinion decidedly strengthened the view put forward by Professor Tawney that the most potent force was the attitude of the Common Law courts.[2]

[1] It may be noticed in passing that the interesting article by Mr J. U. Nef, 'The Progress of Technology and the Growth of Large Scale Industry in Great Britain', in the *Economic History Review*, V (1934), ought – if at all possible – to be supplemented by a comparison between the *extent* of innovations at different periods of time; for that a new process, or the erection of an extensive establishment, takes place does not give a measure of the actual importance of the new factor. See also 'Early Capitalism and Invention', by G. N. Clark, ibid., VI (1936).

[2] See also the article by Mr Donald O. Wagner, 'Coke and the Rise of Economic Liberalism', ibid., VI (1935).

B

In this respect France was the opposite of England; and continental developments were mostly of the French type, though much less advanced. French policy, like that of the rest of the continental countries, consisted in a sustained and very painstaking attempt at regulation; but it resulted in upholding, and greatly enlarging the sphere of, medieval methods, not in adapting them to a changing world. The great administrative power of the French monarchy enabled it to perpetuate the gild system and to spread it over a far greater area than it had regulated during the Middle Ages. Throughout the Continent the result was the same. Mercantilism made itself responsible for what bears the imprint of the Middle Ages, and carried the medieval system, especially in Germany, far down into the nineteenth century. Even the enlargement of the local organizations into national units – an important part of the policy of unification – remained for the most part on paper.

This policy was not altogether ineffective; and least of all in France. If European industry had continued on the lines of its earlier development, catering for the needs of the upper classes or the Church, France would have remained the leading industrial country in Europe. When, on the contrary, industry came to mean mass production for mass consumption the old system of regulation had to disappear. It is therefore difficult to assign any important positive influence to mercantilism, as it worked out in practice, in the creation of modern industry, as contrasted to industry on the old lines. In foreign trade and business organization the influence of mercantilism was much more complicated. The Dutch and English method of equipping trading companies with powerful privileges, not to say sovereign powers, certainly gave a great impetus to their development and was a characteristic example of western mercantilism. The initiative in these cases, however, was almost entirely private, and it is hard to say how far this policy, as embodied, e.g., in the British Bubble Act of 1719, retarded the spread of new forms of business organization to wider circles. But this exceptionally interesting and important subject must now with reluctance be left aside.

Summing up the results of mercantilism as a unifying system, there cannot be the slightest doubt that what it left unfulfilled was enormous when compared with its positive results. The real executor of mercantilism was *laissez-faire*, which did almost without effort what mercantilism had set out but failed to achieve. The most spectacular change in this respect was effected by the French *Constituante* in 1789-91; but English results were perhaps in the long run even more important, and in this case very little of what disappeared has so far come to life again.

The second of the aims of mercantilist policy emphasized by Cunningham – that of power – has met with a great deal of criticism from reviewers of my book, foremost among them Professor Viner (*Economic History Review*, VI, 1935, pp. 100 f.). I agree with my critics on that point to the extent of admitting that both 'power' and 'opulence' – to make use of the terms employed by Adam Smith – have been, and must be, of importance to economic policy of every description. But I do not think there can be any doubt that these two aims changed places in the transition from mercantilism to *laissez-faire*. All countries in the nineteenth century made the creation of wealth their lode-star, with small regard to its effects upon the power of the state, while the opposite had been the case previously. I think Cunningham was right in stressing the famous saying of Bacon about Henry VII: 'bowing the ancient policy of this Estate from consideration of plenty to consideration of power'.

The most important consequence of the dominating interest in power, combined with the static view of economic life as a whole, was the incessant commercial rivalries of the seventeenth and eighteenth centuries, which degenerated easily into military conflict. One of the most serious mistakes of Sombart in his treatment of mercantilism has been his iterated statements of the 'dynamic' character of mercantilism, as contrasted with the 'static' one of *laissez-faire*. It is true that mercantilists believed in their almost unlimited ability to develop the economic resources of their own country (a belief that was even more strongly held by nineteenth-century writers and politicians), but they only hoped to do so at the expense of their neighbours. That the wealth of the world as a whole could increase was an idea wholly alien to them, and in this they were 'static' to a degree. The commercial wars were the natural outcome of this combination; they could not have played the same part either in the Middle Ages, when economic bias was truly 'static', or in the nineteenth century, when it was 'dynamic' throughout.[1]

But all that has now been said of the aims of mercantilist policy is less significant to economists than the mercantilist attitude to *means*. It must also, I think, be admitted that mercantilism was more original in this latter field than in the field of economic unity and economic power. This aspect of mercantilism reveals itself most clearly in its relation to two distinct though closely allied objects, commodities and money. It goes almost without saying that the need for a theoretical treatment is particularly great in this part of the subject.

With regard to commodities, it is necessary to stress the fact that they can be, and actually have been, viewed from at least three mutually exclusive angles. In the eyes of the merchant goods are neither welcome nor unwelcome; they form the basis of his transactions, to be both bought and sold; he does not want to exclude them, but neither does he want to keep them. The consumer, however, is a partisan of 'plenty'; he is bent upon ensuring a large supply, while sales interest him much less. Lastly, to the producer under a system of exchange sales are everything; in his eyes an over-supply is the ever-present danger, while he sees nothing objectionable in keeping the market understocked. It might, no doubt, have been expected that these three aspects of commodities should have existed side by side, either blended judiciously in the minds of ordinary sane people or represented by different social groups. To some extent this was so; but much less so than might have been expected.

The merchant's point of view can never have prevailed throughout, for the number of merchants must always have been small in comparison with the whole population. Still, it played a very important part, especially in medieval and six-

---

[1] The terms 'static' and 'dynamic' are used in a rather different connotation in present-day theoretical economic discussion; and their ambiguity would make it desirable to give them up in the social sciences altogether.

teenth-century towns like Hamburg, Antwerp, Amsterdam, etc., which were made 'staple towns' for different commodities; and that type of policy may therefore properly be labelled 'staple' policy. The citizens were afraid of their city being depleted of necessities by unlimited exports on the part of the merchants.

The dominating feeling throughout the Middle Ages, mostly in towns, which were almost the only repositories of medieval economic policy, was the one natural to consumers; they wanted to hamper or prevent exports, but favoured imports; their tendency was a 'love of goods'; their policy may be called one of provision. It is easy to show, even statistically, how measures directed against exports were predominant throughout the Middle Ages, and how difficult this tendency was to overcome, especially with regard to foodstuffs. But however long-lived the medieval view was, it did not prevent an opposite tendency from gaining ground, a 'fear of goods', a policy directed against imports instead of exports – in one word: protection. This became the mercantilist policy when concerned with commodities as distinct from money; and I do not think there can be any doubt that it constituted the most original contribution of mercantilism to the development of economic policy. It became more and more all-pervading, carrying at last also the citadel of the 'policy of provision', the encouragement of a great supply of foodstuffs; introducing in its stead import prohibitions or import duties on foodstuffs, as well as bounties on exports of food.

It is important not to overlook the fact that protection here does not mean simply interference with foreign trade. All the three policies now under consideration were in agreement about interference; none of them was anything approaching *laissez-faire*. The characteristic feature of mercantilism in this respect went much farther than that; it meant a particular attitude to commodities. The protectionist attitude may even be said to be natural to the man in the street in a money economy, where the connection between purchases and sales disappears, being concealed by the cloak of money. If so, the gradual advance of money economy during the later Middle Ages explains the likewise progressive spread of protection from the more to the less advanced countries.

It is well known from later discussions on commercial policy that one of the greatest difficulties of protection, from a political point of view, consists in the fact that the protection of one branch of production means an increased burden upon those branches which make use of its products. In other words, the question arises how the factors of production should be treated. This difficulty is insoluble in principle, but various practical solutions are always attempted. What is interesting from the present point of view is the solution found by mercantilism on two points which appear in modern eyes to be perhaps the most important of all, those of foodstuffs and labour. With regard to agriculture, the European continent long continued to regard it simply as a prerequisite of industry and therefore to keep down the prices of its products; but the opposite tendency, that represented by England, triumphed in the nineteenth century in almost every country. With regard to labour the early attitude retained its influence; for labour was not at all 'produced', and therefore the quantity of it could be kept down without any disadvantage to 'production'. The outcome was the 'economy of low wages', which had a host of advocates among mercantilists and dominated actual policy almost throughout; this aspect of the subject has been studied (from a standpoint different from mine) by Edgar Furniss in his far too little-known but really brilliant treatise, *The Position of the Laborer in a System of Nationalism*. It should be added, however, that this view was not quite universal among mercantilist writers, because it clashed with some other tenets of their mercantilism; and especially noticeable is an utterance by Daniel Defoe, who is otherwise the reverse of profound; almost alone among mercantilist writers, he stressed the view that it is meaningless to be able to sell goods if this means impoverishing those who are producing them. This paved the way for the position taken up by Adam Smith.

We have now to consider the mercantilist attitude to money. Everybody knows the old definition of mercantilism, which identified wealth with money. Though there are many expressions in mercantilist literature which make this evident, it is necessary to interpret them in the light of their contexts and to give them the benefit of every doubt, for the writers were mostly practical people, unversed in difficult theoretical problems and often unused to putting their ideas on paper. It is easy to see the close relation between an eagerness for an excess of imports of precious metals and a policy favouring exports and hampering imports of commodities; for the excess value of exports must be paid for by bullion or money. It is, however, a fact that mercantilism did not break new ground in wanting to increase the stock of money within a country. That was common before its time; it existed during the Middle Ages, side by side and inconsistently with an eagerness to retain commodities other than precious metals at the same time. What mercantilism meant, so far, was the reconciliation of the commodity aspect and the money aspect of the problem by a new policy with regard to commodities. It is clear that in this consists its most fundamental innovation.

But, on the other hand, mercantilism as a system of money led to a more profound discussion of economic 'theory' than can be found in any other part of its intellectual activity. The general result of an analysis of its teaching is that very few of its tenets can be explained by particular external conditions existing at the time, but that, on the other hand, most of its conclusions follow more or less naturally from quite plausible suppositions. It was therefore only to be expected that this first attempt to grapple with these difficult problems should result in the treatment they received at the hands of these early writers. I am afraid that what can be said within a short space on this part of the subject will appear even more dogmatic than the rest of this article; but it is impossible to leave aside what to economists is perhaps the most interesting side of mercantilism; and an attempt to explain these views must therefore be made. Mr J. M. Keynes, in his recent book, *The General Theory of Employment, Interest and Money*, has based a considerable part of one chapter (Chap. XXIII) upon my treatment of some of these ideas, concluding that they were much more in accordance with a correct theory of economics than has been thought during the last century and a half and than I have been led to think myself. It could be wished that the discussion to which this book of Mr Keynes, like all its predecessors, has given rise should be made to embrace the views of mercantilists; but here I must confine myself to an explanation of how they arrived at their conclusions without examining the correctness of their views.

It is difficult to understand, or at least to explain, the monetary views of mercantilists without distinguishing between their opinion of money or precious metals outside and inside the mechanism of exchange. Outside that mechanism there arose the view that money was more or less identical with capital. John Locke, the philosopher, is perhaps the best exponent of these ideas, as he is able to express himself with much greater clearness than most of the writers, without differing in substance from them. He explicitly said that money has a double function. First, it yields an income by giving interest and is of the same nature as land, which gives rent; here money is considered as a factor of production, as interest-bearing capital. When it was believed that money yields an annual income like that of land nothing was more natural than that it should be coveted to an unlimited extent. That the inflow of precious metals was considered to be of utmost importance likewise followed from theoretical considerations, which are easy to explain without the assistance of a supposition that they had in actual fact some (unknown) specific purpose to fulfil. For, as is still often the case in popular discussion, consumption was considered to be of no value in itself, and a surplus over consumption was considered equivalent to an increase in wealth. This increase was naturally believed to consist in an addition to the stock of money available within the country; and as money, in a country without gold and silver mines and making no use of paper money, could only come from outside, the conclusion necessarily followed that only by an excess of exports of commodities over imports and a consequent influx of money could a country grow rich.

Considered inside the mechanism of exchange, i.e. as means of exchange, money had the all-important function of increasing circulation, from which followed innumerable benefits. In the eyes of many mercantilist writers, one of these was rising prices; Samuel Fortrey gave a succinct expression of this view when saying that 'it might be wished, nothing were cheap amongst us but only money'. It is easy to understand that the gospel of high prices went well together with that of scarcity of goods, or with fighting the danger of 'a dead stock, called plenty'. Besides, it was believed that a country which had low prices as compared with neighbouring countries would 'sell cheap and buy dear', i.e. that the prices prevailing in the respective countries of production would determine those at which the commodities would be sold abroad – without considering that if, e.g., English goods sold in France more cheaply than the French goods themselves they would be in great demand and thereby be raised in price. The easily explicable eagerness for an ever-increasing circulation at last gave rise to a particularly interesting variant of the theory, namely, paper-money mercantilism, represented in the first place by the famous John Law. It is easy to see that this tenet would do away with a great deal of the usual theory of mercantilism; for the need for precious metals, and consequently for an excess of exports, would disappear. But before our own times paper money was normally regarded with great suspicion, so that the old type of theory generally prevailed.

Lastly, mercantilism had a side which has until now been mostly overlooked. That may be called its general conception of society. The remarkable feature of this conception was its fundamental concord with that of *laissez-faire*; so that, while mercantilism and *laissez-faire* were each other's opposites in practical application and economic theory proper, they were largely based upon a common conception of society. No less remarkable is the character of this common conception, which is one that has usually been considered typical of *laissez-faire* and appears to be almost the opposite of mercantilism, as usually understood. Especially noticeable is the likeness between writers like Sir William Petty and Thomas Hobbes, on the one hand, and the leaders of English utilitarianism, such as Bentham, Austin, and James Mill, on the other.

From other points of view the existence of ideas common to mercantilism and its successor ought to be less surprising, for they were in harmony with the general trend of thought dominating Europe since the Renaissance. Philosophically, their basis was the concept of natural law, and connected with that was a belief in unalterable laws governing social life in general, a growing tendency to stress social causality, and consequently to deprecate interference directed against effects instead of causes. On principle, mercantilist authors and statesmen not only believed in but actually harped upon 'freedom', especially 'freedom of trade'; the expression, *la liberté est l'âme du commerce* occurs hundreds of times in the correspondence of Colbert. To some extent this was doubtless due to the influence of the merchant class, though that influence was much weaker in a country like France than in England and Holland; and the fundamental identity of outlook between these three countries shows the existence of other factors besides. The most important of these undoubtedly was the influence of what may be called, by a somewhat hackneyed word, emancipation – emancipation from belief in traditional political and social institutions, and the contrary belief in social change. Closely allied to this was the emancipation from religious and ethical ideas in the social field, a secularization and an amoralization. Mercantilists came more and more to recommend amoral means to amoral ends; their most typical exponent in that respect was the Dutch–English physician Mandeville, but Sir William Petty belonged to the same category; both, it should be noted, were entirely unconnected with the merchant class. Non-religious and amoral views came to light in every direction, in the treatment of interest-taking, in the recommendation of luxury, in the tolerance of heretics and Jews as favourable to trade, in opposition to celibacy, alms-giving, etc.

As I said just now, the remarkable thing is not the existence of these views but the fact that while they were common to both mercantilism and *laissez-faire*, mercantilist and *laissez-faire* policies were poles asunder. I think the explanation of this apparent antinomy is to be found in one fundamental difference, namely, in the mercantilists' disbelief and the liberals' belief in the existence of a pre-established harmony. In the eyes of mercantilists the desired results were to be effected 'by the dextrous management of a skilful politician'; they were *not* expected to follow from the untrammelled forces of economic life. And the result was remarkable. If I may be allowed to quote a previous conclusion of my own: it was precisely this general mercantilist conception of society which led statesmen to even greater ruthlessness than would have been possible without the help of such a conception; for though they had rationalized away the whole social heritage, they had not arrived at a belief in an immanent social rationality. Thus they believed themselves justified in their interference and, in addition, believed in its necessity, without being held back by a respect for such irrational forces as tradition, ethics, and religion. The humanitarian outlook was entirely alien to them, and in this they differed fundamentally from writers and politicians like Adam Smith, Malthus, Bentham, Romilly, and Wilberforce. Lastly, the influence of their social philosophy upon their actions was weaker than that of their other conceptions.

There remains the question, whether it is admissible to speak of mercantilism as a policy and as a theory governed by an inner harmony; this has often been denied in later years, and quite recently by Mr T. H. Marshall in a review in the *Economic Journal* (Vol. XLV, 1935, p. 719). As to those parts called, in my sketch of mercantilism, a system of protection, money, and society, it appears to me beyond doubt that such a harmony existed. This does not, of course, mean that all statesmen and all writers were in complete agreement in their arguments, and even less that they all advocated the same measures. In the choice of practical issues they were greatly influenced by personal and class interests; but what shows the fundamental unity of their underlying principles is that opposite measures were advocated on the basis of a common body of doctrine. Also the fact that writers outside the clash of commercial interests, such as Petty and Locke, argued on exactly the same lines as the protagonists as well as the opponents of powerful commercial interests like those of the East India Company seems to prove it.

Needless to say, the relation between opinions on economic means and those on economic ends – the latter identical with commercial and monetary policy as applied to a unifying system and a system of power – was less intimate. However, the connection with the power of the state was quite clear to numerous statesmen and pamphleteers when they advocated protection and an increase in the supply of money; colonial policy is particularly enlightening in this respect, as can be seen, e.g., from the books by G. L. Beer. On the other hand, with regard to mercantilism as a unifying system, there is the difficulty that in England, where ideas on protection and money supply were for the most part elaborated, the unifying side of mercantilism was of small importance. On the Continent, however, Colbert presents a clear-cut expression of *all* sides of mercantilism as here understood; and he is not only the one great statesman who completely adopted mercantilism but he was also given to working out on paper the principles underlying his actions to an extent uncommon among practical politicians. I therefore think it admissible to consider all aspects of mercantilism, as defined here, as interconnected, while admitting that the unifying aspect was more independent of the rest than the others were among themselves. This, of course, does not mean that what has here been called mercantilism belonged in all its ingredients exclusively to the period between the end of the Middle Ages and the nineteenth century. Like all other historical realities, it drew largely upon ideas and external realities surviving from previous ages, and in its turn influenced later developments. Mercantilism is simply a convenient term for summarizing a phase of economic policy and economic ideas.

2 The Idea of a Mercantile State

A. V. JUDGES

[This article was first published in the *Transactions of the Royal Historical Society*, fourth series, Vol. XXI, 1939.]

The chief purpose of this paper is to formulate a question. What, to put the matter briefly, have we in mind when we talk of the mercantile state; and what functional value is possessed by our ideas about it when we are engaged in the processes of reconstructing the political and economic life of the centuries in which it is commonly believed to have flourished? Various meanings have been given to the words *mercantile system* and also to the more austere *mercantilism* which German scholarship has coined for us to use when we wish to attempt a distillation of the policies attributed to practitioners of that system. Most of us would doubtless be ready to admit that these terms of art of the economist have been useful in bringing large groups of facts and theories into focus; and therein lies their justification. But the concepts which they awkwardly try to express have had a steadily diminishing utility in recent years as our knowledge has advanced, and (like other premature generalizations in the history of ideas) it would seem that they are being perpetuated because we shrink from generalizing anew.

One of the first things we require of a system is that it should be capable of systematic demonstration; while an 'ism' to be worthy of serious consideration must offer a coherent doctrine, or at least a handful of settled principles. In what measure can the mercantile system and mercantilism bear scrutiny when we approach them in this fashion?

The truth seems to be that there was never a living doctrine at all, nothing that can be compared with vital philosophies of action like physiocracy or liberalism or Marxism. Mercantilism never had a creed; nor was there a priesthood dedicated to its service. While some of the beliefs which its supposed philosophy is said to have subsumed were still widely and indeed vigorously upheld when the subject was first discovered to have independent reality, no one appears to have offered to defend its essentials or come forward to die fighting for the altar of the faith. The altar was really an affair of archaeological reconstruction. First erected by men who fortified their attachments to their own faith by abusing the discredited and superstitious antics of their ancestors, it was later refashioned with many curious devices by the pious hands of those who wished to persuade themselves that current ideals could be sanctioned by the genius and wisdom of the past.

The discovery of the existence of a body of mercantile beliefs was made in the eighteenth century by men who found security for their own faith in a system of natural law. The bond of mutual sympathy among these observers was created far less by any similarity in their practical recommendations than by their common distrust of the current expedients of statecraft in Western Europe; expedients which seemed designed with an almost cunning premeditation to hinder the maximization of both happiness and productive capacity by setting up barriers to the economic self-expression of the individual citizen. Quesnay and his disciples the *économistes* in France and Smith in Britain were themselves creators of politico-economic theories claiming universal validity. It was perhaps only natural that they should seek to strengthen the outlines of their own proposals by systematizing the theories which they discerned lurking behind the institutions that came under their fire. The dummy dragon they set up, articulated and endowed with organic functions by its indignant creators, had the fire of life breathed into it by the avenging angels themselves.

Of course, economic liberalism already had an interesting history before the American revolt and the birth of the *tableau économique*. But the critics of state interference had not hitherto stood sufficiently aloof from the regulative attitude of mind to see it as something essentially alien to their ideas. Non-interventionist policies had made their appearance in the works of pamphleteers from the early seventeenth century onwards. And one group of English writers, North, Child, Davenant, and Barbon, supported by an indistinct fringe of even less consistent skirmishers, have been elevated to the position of a Tory school of free traders.[1] Pioneers they unquestionably were, and at times convincing free traders in their enunciation of principle. But Davenant and his fellows could be restrictionists of the extremest kind when it came to discussing specific proposals.[2] Gournay and Hume were both moderate protectionists, and if the former has been endowed by his admirer Turgot[3] with a creed of non-interventionism not improperly recognized by the traditional attribution to him of the incantation *Laissez-faire, laissez-passer*, the latter had an authoritarian bias, and was content to chastise, certainly with unsurpassed brilliance, a number of current 'fallacies' and 'species of ill-founded jealousy ... prevalent among commercial nations'. Dean Tucker, also, although one of the most devastating critics of unreason in an age dedicated to its converse, has one foot in an older camp. He says: 'Abolish every tax and remove all impediments whatever which might prevent Self-Love – the Grand Mover – from operating for the public good'; but he would tax the Grand Mover where it threatens to 'decline from the great road of private virtue and public happiness'.[4] His gospel of freedom is qualified by numerous cautionary provisos, and, indeed, he does not rank himself among the evangelists.

Our earliest introduction to the operative words is in 1763, in the *Philosophie Rurale* of Victor Riquetti, Marquis de Mirabeau, Quesnay's most excitable follower. 'Absurd inconsistency of the mercantile system' (*système mercantile*), he writes in a marginal note.[5] The passage is an attack on the idea that a nation profits from the importation of money; and on the same page he ridicules the approximation of the commercial policy of great empires to the standards of a counting-house in

---

[1] W. J. Ashley, 'The Tory Origin of Free Trade Policy', *Q.J.E.*, July 1897, reprinted in *Surveys Historic and Economic* (1900), pp. 268 ff.

[2] 'For one moment they reach an elevation from which they can contemplate the planet as a whole, and at the next moment their vision is confined to the horizon visible from an English shop window' (Leslie Stephen, *Engl. Thought in the Eighteenth Century* (1902 edn.), Vol. II, p. 297).

[3] 'Eloge de Gournay' in *Œuvres de Turgot*, 1844, Vol. I, pp. 262–91.

[4] Josiah Tucker, *Elements of Commerce and Theory of Taxes* (Bristol, 1755), pp. 169–70.

[5] *Phil. Rurale, ou Écon. générale et politique de l'Agric.* (Amsterdam, 1763), p. 329.

words that sound strikingly like a prophetic echo of Adam Smith's well-known invective upon 'the sneaking arts of underling tradesmen'.[1] Smith was admittedly not unfamiliar with the *Philosophie Rurale*.[2] Is this where he found the mercantile system patterned in the fashion he himself was to adopt?

Smith and the later Physiocrats took up their position outside the habit of mind which they stigmatized as mercantile. For the latter, whose beliefs were based on the conviction that the real income of society was derived from the fields and quarries, the commercial, or regulative, or mercantile system was a sterile compost of the obsessions of merchants and industrialists. They summed it up as a preoccupation with national profit margins in the balance of trade.

For Smith the corpus of physiocratic doctrine was also an artificial system, only less objectionable than the mercantile system of the tradesmen because less in conflict with natural order. For every nostrum that strives by encouragements and restraints to force men in one occupation to employ at the expense of others a greater store of the capital of society than they would otherwise be entitled to, 'retards instead of accelerating the progress of society towards real wealth and greatness'.[3] His natural bias in favour of agriculture led him to treat the landowners' system of the physiocrats with a tempered sympathy and to curtail his criticism of their proposals. Did he not assert that the interests of the landowners were 'strictly and inseparably connected with the general interests of society'?[4] But if English political economy had come to regard commerce between nations as something which in the final analysis could be profitable to only one party the French had proceeded to the discovery that it contributed to the wealth of neither. To Smith's mind it was evident that both must profit. The reason for his decision to devote the longest section of the *Wealth of Nations* to an examination of the mercantile system was that he saw it as a system in being – a reality of the contemporary world – which could be documented and assailed by reference to legislation and practice.

When the attack is opened at the beginning of Book IV, the

[1] *Wealth of Nations*, ed. Cannan (1904), I, p. 457.   [2] Ibid., II, p. 177.
[3] Ibid., II, p. 184.   [4] Ibid., I, p. 248.

mercantile system seems to have for Smith a fundamental unity of principle. What was this principle? It was not, to be sure, that wealth consists solely in money, or in gold and silver, although this is 'a popular notion' introduced to us in the first paragraph, a catch-phrase which even the best English writers had carelessly slipped into accepting in the course of debate.[1] Much of the subsequent discussion has unfortunately been led up a false path by the failure of commentators to observe that the appearance of the mercantile system is delayed until the sixth paragraph of the chapter in question.[2] Here it is announced as the reasoning of the merchants who in the seventeenth century rebelled against the attempts of governments to prohibit the international traffic in bullion. Their libertarian arguments brought conviction to the authorities, at least in some countries, and the consequence was a lifting of restraints laid upon the export of gold and silver. To create conviction it was, however, necessary to appeal to current prejudices. Thomas Mun and the other tractarians of the commercial school accordingly justified their plea for the extension of foreign trade (for which they had their proper motives) by showing that, suitably managed, commerce with other nations enriched the country. The scientific study of the bases of national prosperity was not, of course, a matter upon which they had a specialist's claim to offer opinions, but, as they were in possession of the platform, it was not unnatural that merchants should claim that they were the principal benefactors. *England*'s *Treasure by Forraign Trade*, the title of Mun's second and posthumous contribution to political economy, published in 1664, could be accepted as the slogan of this school of commercial expansion. Out of this literature arose the calculus of the balance of trade,[3] a touchstone of principle which was to determine what forms of exchange might be encouraged as tending to yield a net balance in treasure and what forms should be discouraged on account of the drain of precious metal they set in motion.

[1] Ibid., I, pp. 396, 416.

[2] Cf. Edwin Cannan, *Review of Econ. Theory*, pp. 12–13, where the necessity for this qualification is brought out.

[3] Actually this theorem of the general balance was already hoary with age. We meet it in English tracts and official memoranda at least a century earlier.

Smith was not greatly concerned, I believe, to discover whether or not the equation *money equals wealth* – the popular maxim to which most of his predecessors had paid occasional lip-service – was a vital ingredient in the 'system'. It is rather the consequences of the deplorable behaviour of legislators clumsily trying to execute the injunctions of the balance theorists by means of tariffs, prohibitions, drawbacks, bounties, and commercial monopolies that provokes him to the fullest use of his analytical skill and deflating satire. Except in his reflections on the marketing of corn, he is careful to exclude by implication a large range of internal restrictions from the operations of mercantile statecraft. But in almost every field he saw very clearly that public interference was wasteful and corrupt, prodigal above all of administrative effort.[1] This helps to explain his exaggeration of the malignancy and power of gild control[2] in the corporate towns and his distrust of joint-stock enterprise with its tradition of privilege and licensed incompetence. The conclusions which he had previously reached in his Edinburgh lectures by a process of *a priori* reasoning starting from the principle of Natural Liberty, he now re-established with a great wealth of inductive argument supported by wide historical reading and empirical experience of the problems of administration.[3] The effect was overwhelming.

As with the economic writings of Bentham,[4] we are left with a picture of the waste and inefficiency of most forms of public interference as then practised, but not with the sense that the State direction of human affairs is by definition nugatory. Indeed, whoever attempts the instructive task of culling from the works of Adam Smith a list of what Bentham would call the proper *agenda* of public authority must be surprised by the amplitude of his reservations to any thorough-going notion

[1] Cf. E. Halévy, *Growth of Philosophical Radicalism*, p. 104, etc.

[2] Arnold Toynbee supposed that Smith was influenced by the gild restriction-ism of Glasgow, where James Watt tried to set up as a craftsman (*Lectures on the Ind. Revolution of the 18th Century* (1925 impr.), p. 52). The picturesque legend of Watt's persecution by the hammermen seems now to have received its death-blow (H. W. Dickinson, *James Watt, Craftsman and Engineer* (1937), pp. 25–6).

[3] Cf. W. R. Scott, *Adam Smith as Student and Philosopher*, pp. 124–5.

[4] *Manual of Pol. Econ.*, Chap. 3; *Observations on the Restrictive and Prohibitory Commercial System* (first printed 1821), section 2; John Bowring, *Works of Jeremy Bentham* (1843), Vol. III.

of a *laissez-faire* policy, even within the field of overseas trade.

For many years the study of economic thought as an historical phenomenon was allowed to drop. Further investigations on the lines of those conducted by Dr Redford and his group of Manchester workers on the activities of the organizations of the commercial and industrial interests may show that the more thoughtful of the manufacturers who led the campaign for a more open trade and helped to promote the Eden Treaty of 1786 had some breadth of vision on economic policy as a whole. But their liberalism seems at best half-hearted. They could oppose a revenue excise on pig iron, plead for fewer restrictions on trade with the Continent, while using all their lobbying resources to wreck a commercial treaty with Ireland. And like the first movement for political reform, the early free-trade campaign was stifled in the dark days of the Revolutionary Wars. The two movements, moreover, came to be inextricably mixed, for the revised corn laws now occupied the foremost place in the schedule of interference measures; and the support of the landlords was still essential to politicians.

Nevertheless, when the smoke begins to clear away the initiative in liberal reform seems to be with the statesmen, supported with no great enthusiasm by city merchants and bankers, and with the group of active intellectuals who are to become known to us as the Classical Economists. According to Newmarch, the year 1820 which witnessed the presentation by Alexander Baring of the Merchants' Petition in the Commons also saw 'the system of prohibition, protection and fiscal confusion at its height'.[1]

At about this point the tide turns. In reality, of system there was none. As we watch reformers at work and listen to the arguments offered by those who defend restrictive laws it becomes evident that the policies now standing their trial are but little concerned with the retention of a favourable balance of trade or any group of related propositions. They are concerned almost entirely with the protection of sheltered trades, the defence of shipping monopolies, and the profits of agriculture – a fine miscellany of vested interests.

[1] Tooke and Newmarch, *Hist. of Prices* (1857), Vol. V, p. 400.

The administrative chaos in which creative architects like Huskisson and Senior, using simple mechanical formulae, tried to build, or at least remodel, was a combination of survivals inherited from different strata of time and temperament. Some things, like the Navigation Laws and the rules of the Statute of Artificers, were heritages of policy. Others, perhaps the more formidable obstacles, were heritages of expediency, and consisted for the most part of customs schedules and fiscal regulations originally devised by eighteenth-century legislators for nothing more socially significant than security for public loans. Huskisson and Peel and Gladstone liquidated a commercial system which may be described far less correctly as a protectionist order than as a latter-day revision of a revenue system of unfathomable complexity balanced on the inadequate foundation of a tonnage and poundage law which had been devised for the traffic conditions of the fifteenth century. It was, in fact, a piecemeal system of which many parts had ceased to pay even for their keep.

The exponents of economic liberalism felt called upon to destroy an economic regime; but it was a regime lacking order and a coherent philosophy. In its place they offered a plan of an ordered society, a *Planwirtschaft*, which must surely possess more of the attributes of an economic and social 'system' than we can discern in the policy fashioned by their predecessors. Far from being satisfied with expedients, they allowed their ideas to play upon a projected social structure exhibited in complete diagrammatic form. The proposed functions of their state fell into an orderly pattern, a scheme of property, inheritance, contractual relationships, and regulated currency, so devised that sellers of goods and services might find unhindered self-expression; they made provision for a rigidly fenced enclosure within which business men, workpeople, and the investing public could play at being free.

The notion presupposed an organized institutional policy and a political programme: the rule of non-intervention must be established by the creation of a new set of institutions, of which the simplified working model in the mind of Ricardo was the conventional framework of the market in which he gained his experience of man's behaviour, namely the London

Stock Exchange. The function of the state was to keep the ring so that production and exchange might operate freely on principles of their own through the instrumentality of human beings whose individual power and influence upon the market were infinitesimally small. Monopolistic and privileged forces should be excluded by public action. The liberal reform movement was this action. The utilitarian wing were convinced that social efficiency under the new dispensation demanded incursions into living conditions, and even called for mediatized institutions to bring influence to bear upon conditions of employment; and it has been well observed that 'no sooner had the Benthamites given a man freedom to choose his own church and his own market than they took away his freedom to dispose of his own sewage'.[1]

To discover another such rule of principle and rules for its adoption we must go back to the school of Aquinas and the canonist lawyers. The stretch of time between these reigns of coherent social policy seems like a vast interim full of uncoordinated specifics. Professor Heckscher has recently drawn attention in convincing fashion to the agreement between *laissez-faire* theories and the notions of the pre-classical age, inasmuch as they were at one in accepting the postulate that individual self-interest supplied the motive power which drove production and exchange. To that extent both were mechanistic: superhuman agencies were repudiated. If anything, it may be suggested that the 'mercantilist' outlook on the economic scene was metaphysical to an even less degree than the later one. The Heaven-ordained laws of Supply and Demand hardly appeared as the outcome of a special creation until the evangelical movement had given full thought to social questions. Had the earlier economists conceived of an Invisible Hand lightly playing over the operations of the free exchange of goods and services they would certainly have questioned its benevolent intentions. 'Trade indeed will find its own Channels,' wrote Sir Francis Brewster in 1702, deploring the luxury traffic's superior attractions for capital as compared with the fisheries, 'but it will be to the ruin of our Nation, if not Regulated.'[2]

[1] D. C. Somervell, *The Victorian Age*, p. 24.   [2] *New Essays on Trade*, p. 61.

In the works of the masters of the classical period there is little evidence of acquaintance with the principles which might be said to underlie a regulated or mercantile economy. Some of them were too busy focusing attention upon the lack of reason and goodwill displayed by sectional interests and groups – the landed interest which 'dominated the unreformed Parliament, restricted the mobility of labour by parish settlement and the Speenhamland system, and maintained the Corn Laws for the protection of corn prices and land-rents';[1] and the unproductive habits of all those who spent but did not produce.

Detached arguments in support of state restrictionism, of course, received much attention and criticism. The doctrine of comparative costs, if it was not at this time a complete novelty in economic literature,[2] was more strictly formulated to give theoretical justification to the attack on tariffs and prohibitions. It could offer another way of looking at gains and losses. The old balance-of-trade theories received attention in so far as they impeded appreciation of revised ideas on monetary distribution and international prices. And although money moved in the forefront of discussion, its relevance to the fundamental relationships between productive factors (now the main consideration in the theory of wealth creation) became entirely subsidiary. This may be seen most clearly in the attacks launched on the seventeenth- and eighteenth-century arguments which linked up the rate of interest with the supply of money for investment. And it is symptomatic of present-day tendencies that the watchword of Mr Maynard Keynes's latest contribution to the theories of money and employment is Back to the Mercantilists, by way of reaction to Ricardo and his English successors.[3] In combating the notion that money was

[1] M. Dobb, *Pol. Econ. and Capitalism*, p. 50.

[2] As J. Viner points out (*Studies in the Theory of International Trade*, p. 440), the anonymous author of the very remarkable *Considerations on the E. India Trade* (1701), states what is essentially the doctrine in rather different terms from those employed by Ricardo.

[3] Believing that statesmen aimed at a high equilibrium level of investment and employment, 'there was wisdom,' Mr Keynes holds, 'in their intense preoccupation with keeping down the rate of interest by means of usury laws . . ., by maintaining the domestic stock of money and by discouraging rises in the wage-unit; and in their readiness in the last resort to restore the stock of money by devaluation, if it had become plainly deficient through an unavoidable foreign

wealth this group of writers is usually content to explain that the heresy must have arisen as a result of the necessity of evaluating commodity relationships in terms of cash. As J. B. Say put it,

> They have taken the means for the end. The money which they receive only for the purpose of spending is confounded with the product they propose to consume; as might happen if men, seeing that it was necessary to go through a door to enter a house, and failing to bother at all about the desirability of the house such as other men experience, proceeded to tell one: have doors, and you will always have houses.[1]

Malthus, Ricardo, James Mill, and Torrens have no constructive analysis to offer of pre-Smithian thought and policy. But Nassau Senior, in his Oxford lectures in 1827, devoted part of his time to an examination of the mercantile system, 'which at present clogs all our actions and disturbs all our reasonings'. He discussed its monetary aspects at some length in tones of shocked disapproval, summed up the commercial restrictions as having been contrived to produce individual gain at the cost of the common loss, remarking that public opinion noticed only the concentration of gain and seemed unaware of the diffusion of the loss. Unless I am mistaken, this was the first broadside assault on the 'system' since the *Wealth of Nations*, and it is important for our purpose because Senior passed from the balance-of-trade policies to some reflections on national jealousies and the manifest aim of mercantile policy to be independent of foreign commodities. This leads to the destruction of the mutual security of nations, to say nothing of privation at home. 'The half-naked subjects of Caractacus were doubtless independent of foreign supplies, and so is the semi-

---

drain, a rise in the wage-unit, or any other cause' (*General Theory of Employment, Interest and Money*, Chap. 23). Without finding myself in a position to endorse much of Mr Keynes's interpretation of English economic theory of the seventeenth and eighteenth centuries, I do think he succeeds, in passages similar in perspicacity to the quotation above, in illuminating some of the *ends* of monetary policy in those times, ends which have been persistently misunderstood by critics who found altogether too facile an aid to destructive analysis in J. S. Mill's exposition of the theory of international trade.

[1] J. B. Say, *Cours Complet d'Écon. Politique* (1852 edn.), Vol. II, pp. 205–6.

barbarian who burrows in the ruins of Persepolis, and gathers his dates among the ruins of palaces.'[1]

Autarky, or self-sufficiency for purposes of defence, had now been brought in to widen the supposed objects of mercantile policy.

John Stuart Mill, who constituted himself the *rapporteur* of the deliberations of the English classical economists, was more strictly in the orthodox Adam Smith tradition. But he displayed no historical understanding. The mercantile system, with its obsessions about the precious metals, 'looks like one of the crude fancies of childhood. . . . Once questioned indeed, it was doomed.' Yet the reasoning was not unnatural among minds which 'had not yet become familiar with certain modes of stating and of contemplating economical phenomena'. He marvelled that in Australia 'the exploded fallacies of the mercantile system are revived with a simple ignorance of all that has been written and proved against them'.[2]

Cairnes somewhat later distinguished the system of protection from the system of the balance of trade, the former taking the place of the latter in historical sequence, 'to underpin the tottering edifice'. In this process native industry was substituted for the precious metals as the cause of riches; but these were different aspects of the same system, and commercial problems were still viewed in the same way.[3]

The dissemination of thought about the system was largely, however, the work of the camp-followers and vulgarizers among the economists. J. R. McCulloch appears to have been the writer principally responsible for the spreading of the crude notion that the essential doctrine of the mercantile system was the identification of money with wealth.[4] An omnivorous but careless student of early economic works, he declared this to be

[1] Nassau Senior, *Three Lectures on the Transmission of the Precious Metals* (2nd edn.), pp. 39, 45–51, 95.

[2] J. S. Mill, *Principles*, Preliminary Remarks; *Letters*, ed. H. S. R. Elliott, Vol. II, pp. 154–5.

[3] J. E. Cairnes, *Some Leading Principles of Pol. Econ. newly expounded* (1874), p. 450.

[4] 'The supporters of the mercantile system like their predecessors held that gold and silver alone constituted wealth' (*Principles* (4th edn., 1849), p. 30); cf. also *Literature of Pol. Econ.*, *passim*, and Introductory Discourse prefacing McCulloch's editions of *Wealth of Nations*.

the core of the old policy of restriction; but it was not all, for the mercantile writers actually secured the ascendancy of their commercial policy by a system of industrial regulation inherited from the medieval towns. This was a point which may have been suggested to him by a discourse by Francesco Mengotti called *Il Colbertismo*, published in Florence in 1792. In McCulloch's hands the theory had become narrower, the scope of its application somewhat wider.[1] McCulloch edited, and provided an historical introduction for, the most popular edition of the *Wealth of Nations* that circulated in early Victorian England. Buckle, Macaulay, Lecky, and a not inconsiderable number of less influential writers took their history of political economy from him. Any residual qualifications to a very bald and unhistorical interpretation fell to the ground in the process of transference.

Only one other name in the purely English tradition calls for special mention. Leslie Stephen, whose *English Thought in the Eighteenth Century* was published in 1876, knew his literature as few others had done; but on its economic side his reading was not wide. Even so, he was one of the first to realize that after the Restoration the discussion of money balances was giving place to considerations of stored-up labour, and that the main preoccupation of publicists from the English Revolution onwards was with employment and poor-law problems, not with the manipulation of specie payments. But this is anticipating a later trend of observation; and it is time to go back to a very different method of approach, which may be described as the *generalized* view of the mercantile system in distinction from the *restricted* view of the English classical school.

The English economists, who never went far beyond the conception for which Adam Smith takes credit as chief inventor, viewed the mercantile system as an agglomeration of commercial interferences fortified by a monetary fallacy which was itself based upon a misunderstanding of the real nature of international exchange. The approach was highly unsympa-

---

[1] Mengotti's Colbertism is divisible into two parts, the first the system of the balance of trade, the second the regulation of industry. See Custodi, *Scrittori Classici Italiani di Economia Politica* (1804), Parte Moderna, tomo XXXVI, pp. 251 ff.

thetic, the treatment limited as to period and range. It was not until Bagehot and Cliffe Leslie protested against the claims of universality which had been advanced for the abstract political economy of a highly capitalized and competitive society that English thought became infected with the idea that 'unorthodox' policies might have been living necessities for economic communities in their backward days. Cliffe Leslie even suggested that the classical definitions of wealth – mere abstractions as they looked to him – originated in opposition to the doctrines 'erroneously imputed to the mercantile School', and were no more than negative statements.[1]

Germany was the proper nursery of the generalized view of the mercantile state; but the birth appears to have been foreshadowed, if it did not actually occur, in the theatre of the newly founded King's College in the Strand in 1833, when Richard Jones launched the study of political economy there in an inaugural lecture. Jones developed his ideas about the relative nature of economic doctrines elsewhere. On this occasion[2] he was content to describe the inception and practice of bullionist restrictions in their fourteenth-century historical setting and later, and to suggest that monetary policy had proceeded by stages. Beginning with the balance-of-bargain system – the expression was Jones's invention – which demanded that imports and exports should be forced to balance in the transactions of individual merchants, and necessitated staples, statutes of employment, and royal exchangers to secure enforcement, policy underwent a change within the expansive years 1558–1660. Legislators then revised their notions of policy and went over to the balance-of-trade system, which sought only a general balance on the aggregate trade of the country.[3]

---

[1] Cliffe Leslie, *Essays in Pol. and Moral Phil.* (1879), pp. 219–20, etc.; W. Bagehot, *Econ. Studies* (1880), pp. 16–20.

[2] 'Primitive Pol. Econ. in England', *Edin. Rev.*, April 1847, pp. 426 ff., reprinted in R. Jones's *Lit. Remains*, ed. Whewell (1859), pp. 293 ff.

[3] Travers Twiss devoted his admirable course of Oxford lectures in 1846–7 (*View of Progress of Pol. Econ.* (1847)) to the early development of economic ideas, and accepted the generally held view that the mercantile system came in with Mun. Twiss seems not to have been influenced at all by Jones, but he makes acknowledgement to Adolphe Blanqui's important *Hist. de l'Écon. Politique* (first published 1838), though disagreeing with him on certain matters, e.g. the

Relativity and evolutionary stages were part of the methodological equipment of *Historismus*. This is not a proper place
to discuss the general philosophical position of the German
historical school. But we may remind ourselves that the school
assumed its relativist character by transferring to the economic
sphere the arguments relating to the history of legal institutions which had been used by Savigny, coloured as they were
by the stress he put upon national idiosyncrasies; that it
inherited some of the traditions of political and academic
cameralism with its faith in the conditioning functions of the
state in economic life; and that it was strongly influenced by
recent German idealist philosophy. It is also important to
remember that the nexus between money and the production of
wealth had been given an insignificant place in the economic
literature of central Europe. Oncken has stated that he met the
statement 'Money is Wealth' only once in his wide acquaintance
with German economic writings.[1]

Fichte, the spiritual father of the modern totalitarian state,
had reacted against the internationalism of Smith, and desired
to safeguard the rule of natural law within a fenced-in territorial
enclosure closed against the marauding incursions of flag-
waving bagmen. But the full revolt against Manchester
liberalism was delayed until List had made out his – journalistic-
ally effective – case for the tariff protection of industrial
economies in an immature stage of development, and until
Roscher and Knies had demonstrated the necessity for studying
economic concepts and rules of action as products of the time
and circumstances wherein they arose. Economics in the hands
of their followers was no abstract science, but the study of the
laws of evolution stage by stage as exhibited in the life of
nations. It has sometimes been said that members of the school
were not economists at all, but historians or sociologists; and
there is just enough truth in this to explain Menger's complaint
that 'the historians have stepped upon the territory of our
science like foreign conquerors, in order to force upon us their

claims of Mun's contemporary Antonio Serra to be considered a liberal thinker.
On the comparative importance as pioneers of Mun and Serra see Marx at his
most playfully sarcastic in Chapter 10 contributed to Part II of Engels' *Anti-
Dühring*.
[1] Palgrave, *Dict. of Pol. Econ.* (1919), Vol. II, p. 198 n.

language and their customs, their terminology and their methods'.[1] Intolerance, not to say malignity, was displayed on both sides when the great struggle opened in the seventies between the respective supporters of the inductive and deductive methods. The younger historical school was forced into an untenable position. Little of what it endeavoured to contribute to economic theory has stood the test of time; but its services to history have had more enduring value, if only for its examination of the springs of political action.

The mercantile state naturally received close attention. In this atmosphere the proper course was not to explode its reputed fallacies but to explain its reality as a stage in the growth of society. Features of bygone economic policy which would have been dismissed elsewhere as irrelevant to the discussion were investigated with loving care as examples of paternalist mercantile strategy. For Roscher a system which had lasted for centuries could not be wholly erroneous, and was worthy of examination. It struck him, for example, that an immensely significant feature of benevolent despotism, and of early economic discussion generally, was the insistence, whether for agricultural, industrial, or military reasons, on adequate measures for encouraging population growth. Hildebrand and Bücher developed, though in different fashion, the idea of stages in economic progress from the primitive to the complex. In the latter's judgement the state was compelled by historical necessity to employ measures of guidance in nursing the community through the critical transition from town economy to national economy, until liberalism could at length be given rein for *its* formative career. Not infrequently the state, in the drive towards the goal, manipulated its material into forms unduly artificial. But 'the theory of the balance of trade became a necessity when the transition [towards a commercial economy] indispensably postulated the increase of the monetary medium of circulation'.[2] Professor Sombart has more recently followed up this idea, using a different framework of

[1] *Die Irrthümer des Historismus*, preface, quoted J. N. Keynes, *Scope and Method* (1891), p. 306.
[2] Karl Bücher, *Die Entstehung des Volkswirtschaft* (first published 1893, Engl. transl., 1901), pp. 136 ff.

stages, in his treatment of mercantilism as the political economy of early capitalism.

It was left for Gustav Schmoller to create a synthetic picture of mercantilism in rounding off the work of his predecessors. This he accomplished using a remarkably deep intuition of the forces underlying public policy in combination with a strong sense of the transcendence of the human will in a world where systematic laws of economic life were only valid on a superficial reckoning. It is hardly an exaggeration to say that he formed his notion of mercantile policy on the study of the struggle for unification and national self-expression guided by the electors and kings of Prussia. As a process of state-building it was concerned as much to provide for the fluidity of resources and products within the country, by the removal of tolls,[1] local privileges, and currency defects, as to compel the respect of the country's neighbours by a spirited economic policy along and beyond the frontiers. It advocated free-trade or prohibition principles according to the circumstances of the case; and not only according to concrete conditions but according to the goal towards which the country was striving. The state was a formative agent; it gave existence to organized society; and both political and economic life were forces to be regulated by the government. 'The mercantilist ideal was not only the legitimate ideal for those centuries but the only proper end. And the ends aimed at have not yet completely lost their legitimacy,' he wrote in 1900.[2] Only a firm and enlightened central authority could co-ordinate the necessary measures for the creation of a national economy (*Volkswirtschaft*) out of anarchy. Such a conviction led him to the somewhat startling conclusion that the economic decline of the Netherlands was caused by the exclusion from public life of the House of Orange in the Stadtholderless period, 1650–72.[3]

---

[1] The careful investigation since made by E. Rachel in the *Acta Borussica* shows, however, that in the case of Germany, where Schmoller's *liberating* mercantile policy is supposed to find its clearest expression, the unification of the tolls was the last thing the territorial princes were able to secure. See Heckscher (*Mercantilism*, Vol. I, pp. 56 ff.) for a shattering treatment of the myth.

[2] *Grundriss der Allgemeinen Volkswirtschaftslehre* (Vol. I, 1900), p. 86.

[3] 'Studien über die Wirtschaftliche Politik Fr. des Grossen und Preussens', in 7 parts in *Jahrbuch für Gesetzgebung, usw.*, 1884. Transl. in part as *The Mercantile System and its Historical Significance* (N.Y., 1931), p. 53.

Much proceeds from Schmoller's prime assumption that state agencies were more effective in pushing trade and capturing fields of enterprise than the unhampered activity of private traders could have been. But it is idle to seek to discover from the wealth of apparently conflicting examples offered in his writings whether mercantilism favoured the use of economic means to serve the ends of national greatness or the use of political means to achieve successes in the industrial and commercial spheres. There is no fundamental distinction to be drawn between the kinds of means employed by the purposeful and ruthless state authority. The Western powers traded with their rivals while at war with them, and fought them with prohibitions and Navigation Acts while nominally at peace.

> The heroic struggle of the Dutch for religious freedom . . . displays itself . . . as a century-long war for the conquest of the East Indian colonies, and the equally long privateering assault on the silver fleets of Spain and the Spanish-American colonial trade. . . . Even the expedition of Gustavus Adolphus to Germany was a move in the game which was being played for the trade of the Baltic.[1]

Schmoller's range of illustration seems to permit no aspect of state activity within a span of centuries to escape the comprehensiveness of his definition. Even the balance-of-trade policies have their place, although 'the whole idea and doctrine of the balance of trade . . . was only the secondary consequence of a conception of economic processes which grouped them according to States'.[2]

In 1868, at the age of nineteen, William Cunningham went to continue his university studies in Germany. That he chose to go to Tübingen, Schmoller's old university, is no more than a coincidence. That he came home profoundly influenced by German conceptions of the state and German notions of order and discipline is a fact which has a bearing on his intellectual progress.[3] Fourteen years later *The Growth of English Industry and Commerce* made its first and, one might say,

---

[1] Ibid., pp. 64–5.   [2] Ibid., p. 61.
[3] W. R. Scott, *William Cunningham*, 1849–1919, British Academy *Proceedings*, Vol. IX; p. 3 of reprint.

embryonic appearance, in a single volume. The progress of this remarkable book through its successive editions is in a very real sense a measure of the advance of economic history in England in Cunningham's working lifetime. It was obvious from the beginning that the title was a misnomer. The book was a study of the rise of authoritarianism and its decline, and 'the fruitfulness . . . of this field of study . . . had to be demonstrated', as Professor Scott has pointed out, 'in the face of the traditions of the Classical School'.[1] When the 1892 edition appeared it was made the object of a vigorous attack by W. A. S. Hewins, who was in a few years to become the first Director of the London School of Economics. Hewins was shocked by Cunningham's indiscriminate praise for regulative measures. To call the Corn Bounty Act of 1689 'a masterly stroke of policy' which proved itself to be the corner-stone of English prosperity in the eighteenth century was, he thought, not so much excessive as wrong-headed. For Cunningham, he suggested, the *pursuit of national power* performed the same functions as prime mover in the seventeenth century as *desire of wealth* did in the nineteenth. He paraphrased Cunningham unkindly but not untruly in a *pastiche* which must have stung his victim:

> The mercantile system is concerned with man solely as a being who pursues national power, and who is capable of judging of the comparative efficacy of means to that end. It makes entire abstraction of every other human passion or motive, except those which may be regarded as perpetually antagonizing principles to the pursuit of national power – viz., neglect of shipping and aversion to a fish diet.[2]

Cunningham's rejoinder was not very effective; but he stuck to his belief in the Corn Bounty Act and the fish diet.[3] Already he was interested in projects for the reconstruction of commercial policy.[4] The South African War and Chamberlain's

[1] Ibid., p. 5.

[2] *Economic Journal*, 1892, Vol. II, pp. 694 ff.

[3] *Economic Journal*, 1894, Vol. IV, pp. 512 ff.; and cf. *Richard Cobden and Adam Smith* (publ. by Tariff Reform League, 1904), pp. 29–30.

[4] *Modern Civilization in its Econ. Aspects* (1896).

Tariff Reform proposals swept him on to the public platform, as they swept Hewins himself into the Tariff Commission, as an advocate of imperial preference.[1] The third edition of the *Modern Times* section of the History appeared in 1903 with a startling epilogue. *Laissez-faire* had been a manifest failure. How could a directed national policy repair the damage? The postscript was in reality a protectionist tract, tricked out with historical parallels. Bismarck's socialism from above, for instance, is seen to bear a curious resemblance to the work of the early Stuart Council.[2] The tone of this polemic was modified in subsequent editions; but Cunningham's affection for the alleged mercantilist policy of Burleigh – who 'was wonderfully successful in reducing the waste which had come to be so generally current in the fifteenth century'[3] – his belief that the essential policy of common or 'general interest' in the old Colonial System was right, even his suspicion that the genuine spirit of regulative control had been thwarted by the growth of democratic institutions during the period which he oddly described as the era of Parliamentary Colbertism – these convictions remained until the end.

Cunningham had indeed developed the generalized view of mercantilism in a more convincing fashion than had any other writer or teacher. His was perhaps a more satisfying exposition than the German attempts, because it was inspired in the main by the institutional life-story of a single well-knit community. English examples of the operation of the unifying principles came too early, or were too limited, to distract attention seriously from the great topics of naval efficiency and imperial solidarity which run as coloured threads through his examination of the growth of national policy; yet industrial and social control receive adequate attention as expressions of mercantile trends.

The influence of this great teacher has been such that students of history have experienced no little difficulty in preserving appreciation for whatever may be the merits of the restricted view. Sir William Ashley was more cautious than

---

[1] W. A. S. Hewins, *The Apologia of an Imperialist*, Vol. I, Chaps. 2 and 3.
[2] *Growth of Engl. Industry and Commerce in Mod. Times* (1903), p. 879.
[3] *Progress of Capitalism in England* (1916), p. 83.

Cunningham, but he was under the spell of *Historismus*, with its
love of stages and time sequences. Even the title of his most
important historical work, *An Introduction to English Economic
History and Theory*, displays a challenge. George Unwin, who
took a different side in the South African War controversy,
brought a mind of tougher fibre than Cunningham's to bear on
the history of paternalist regulation, and found it wanting in
sincerity and effectiveness. He emphasized 'the tendency to
over-estimate the active part which wise forethought and the
deliberate pursuit of clear ideas has played in the economic
history of nations', at the same time admitting that positive
interference measures had shaped the course of events in a
very definite and sometimes disastrous fashion. 'It is an un-
doubted fact, says Voltaire somewhere, that spells and incanta-
tions are capable of destroying whole flocks of sheep, if ac-
companied by sufficient quantities of arsenic.' This saying had
always appeared to Unwin 'to afford a suggestive introduction
to the study of the influence of ideas, of theory, upon economic
development'.[1] We may approve or disapprove of his scepticism; we may hold that he even exaggerated the influence of
thought upon policy; it can hardly be conceded that he gave
sharper definition to the idea of the mercantile state.

The responsibility for questioning the propriety of the
generalized description has been lightly assumed by one or two
economists in this country and America; but our monographs
and textbooks in economic history are still vaguely comprehensive in their use of terms; and it may be that the reluctance
of writers to overhaul their terminological equipment has been
to some extent justified by certain considerations arising out of
the fuller examination of pre-Smithian economic writings
which has been in progress during the last few years. Professor
Heckscher of Stockholm, in what will doubtless establish itself
as the classic exposition of the thought and policy of the period
of early capitalism in Europe, has produced an eclectic survey
of the manifold tendencies of that age.[2] His masterly analysis of

[1] *Studies in Econ. Hist.*, p. 158.
[2] *Mercantilism*; first published in Swedish in 1931; the English version, with
author's revisions, in 1935. Professor Heckscher has summarized his views in an
article of the same title in the *Economic History Review*, November 1936, pp. 44 ff.

C

conflicting trends brings out certain common assumptions which may have caused statesmen to close their eyes to the often fundamental divergence of interest existing among consumers, producers, and distributing agencies, so that they allowed themselves to be dominated now by 'love of goods', now by 'fear of goods'; now by the glamour of bullion, now by the magical appeal of paper-money inflation. But when all has been said I think the highest common factor in the harvest of notions and policies brought to the surface by Professor Heckscher's efficient trawl can be no more than this: a belief in official intervention as a corrective to evils which must arise from the neglect of public interest in the actions of individuals and of institutions subordinate to the political authority. And the political authority wanted unity and wanted power; not, surely, exceptional ends in the history of human programmes!

It is proper, however, to insist on the book's positive contributions to the study of the subject. Only one can be mentioned here. In demonstrating that the theory of money looked upon currency from two points of view, Professor Heckscher has cleared the field for a more systematic approach. It was no longer necessary to elevate bullion to a special position as a store of value, and to some extent as a factor of production, when credit instruments and bank money began to show their ability to function in place of gold and silver. The balance-of-trade concepts of Misselden and Serra were no longer deadly instruments in eighteenth-century controversy. But the consideration of circulating money, money as a means of exchange and as a price-determinant, whatever might be its material composition, was almost as lively an issue as it came to be later on in the bullion debates. The control of the rate of interest and the lowering of the price of labour were now the practical questions. Such things did prompt theoretical analysis. On the one hand, rising prices signified the ability to clear stocks, increase sales, raise rents; on the other, the reduction of the cost of productive agents, especially labour, would allow the country to force manufactured goods on its neighbours. Under suitable control conditions a favourable trading balance was ardently to be desired because it might be held to indicate the sending out of embodied labour effort – an artificial and, so to speak, gratuitous product – in exchange for the indestructible material on which the circulating media could be still further expanded – or often just for the satisfaction of keeping people at work. The full employment of labour was desired for many reasons. It is worth recalling, for example, that from the end of Elizabeth's reign the cost of poor relief in this country fell on the ratepayers. And a careful examination of the arguments relating to production for export used in Great Britain from the Restoration onwards has suggested to more than one investigator – I have in mind Professor Viner of Chicago and Dr E. A. J. Johnson of Cornell in particular[1] – a new variant of the restricted view of mercantilism; the balance of trade being conceived in terms not of gold and silver but of the number of labourers, or units of labour, applied to the commodities exchanged in international trade. The policy, of course, aimed at an *excess* of such exports of realized labour.

So we have to add to our accumulated stock a fresh body of interpretation – an important and acceptable increment, it is true; but is the subject of our discussion not becoming somewhat embarrassingly miscellaneous? Are we prepared to allow that every act of authority involving interference displayed some element of the true tradition of the mercantilist spirit? There are indications that at any moment we may be confronted with an attempt to resurrect and pin down in a display cabinet the mercantilist theory of the disposition of capital resources at home and abroad. How, if I may pose one conundrum, ought one to regard the Bubble Act of 1720? Was this a mercantilist measure? It threatened with all the penalties of praemunire the promoters of any association of investors which had shares offered for public subscription, unless, that is, a charter could be produced. It was restrictive, certainly; paternalist in its intention to protect the ignorant investor; and it may be held to have interfered seriously with the free employment of the accumulated capital of several generations. But might it not be treated as an anti-mercantilist gesture? It foreshadowed the ultimate doom of the great licensed mono-

[1] J. Viner, *Studies in the Theory of International Trade*, pp. 51–7; E. A. J. Johnson, *Predecessors of Adam Smith*, Pt. III; cf. also E. S. Furniss, *Position of the Laborer in a System of Nationalism*.

polies. Was it not, moreover, a vindication of the principle of private enterprise? 'Trade seldom requires the aid of such combinations,' roundly asserted the Attorney-General in 1761, 'but thrives better when left open to the free speculations of private men.'[1] How does the Act work into Adam Smith's treatment of corporations? What would Schmoller have made of it? Finally, what do its consequences mean when treated as far as possible on their own merits – divorced from early Stuart patent procedure, on the one hand, and the principles of nineteenth-century company law, on the other?

Any programme of limited investigation into the phenomena of policy must proceed by employing the well-known methods of inductive inquiry until the material is isolated and built into some sort of pattern. At every stage the testing and application of general ideas must, of course, go on, whether the interpretation deals with the monetary, or the labour, or the capital, or the land, or the governmental, or any other aspect of policy. Must the idea, or rather complex of ideas, of the mercantile state necessarily be forced into the process until it dominates the whole structure of the finished work? In this respect, at least, the critics among the economists of current historical method seem to be mistaken. We ought, perhaps, to set out with a better equipment of theoretical concepts; but there is one little group of postulates we could well dispense with.

The plea I wish to advance is that we should now consider ourselves absolved from the necessity of having to reconcile the conclusions derived from detailed researches into the antecedents and effects of edicts, statutes, and municipal by-laws, spread over the whole European and colonial field within a period of more than three centuries,[2] with the canons of an

---

[1] B. C. Hunt, *Development of Business Corporations*, p. 11.

[2] When did mercantilism flourish? Most, though not all, of our authorities allow it an exclusively post-medieval career. It is commonly believed that it passed through several stages, among which 'bullionism' sometimes appears as a sort of curtain-raiser to the 'general-balance' act. Arnold Toynbee (op. cit., p. 56) taught that the mercantile system came to an end at the point in time at which Adam Smith seems to have made it begin. Luigi Cossa, a representative stratifier, distinguished three phases; (*a*) specie regulation and exchange control; (*b*) originating 'in the last centuries of the Middle Ages', a 'balance-of-bargains'

imaginary system conceived by economists for purposes of theoretical exposition and mishandled by historians in the service of their political ideals. If I have interpreted aright the doctrinal syntheses to which numberless historians have tried to accommodate themselves, it is clear that many of the rationalized ambitions and fears and jealousies which are their subject matter have been active throughout the world, as perhaps never before, since the economic crisis of 1931. It might be argued to the disadvantage of the present day that what we have gained in logical precision we have lost in sincerity; for it has never been suggested that the restrictionists of the old school claimed for the measures they proposed in their own country's favour that they brought great benefits to other communities.[1]

In the history of nations the brief episode of economic individualism, reflecting, as Continental observers have never tired of reminding us, the special conditions and requirements of this country, may prove to have been a unique experience. The word *neo-mercantilism* is already appearing with ominous frequency in serious discussions. Are we threatened with a further extension of the old aspects and stages? There appears to be much to be said for overhauling our armoury of classes and categories in order that we may avail ourselves of instruments of greater precision. It would be false to the spirit of a paper which has been almost entirely destructive in intention to suggest even a provisional inventory of more suitable equipment. Moreover, 'finding flaws in labels is much easier than finding patently superior substitutes'.

I can only suggest that such simple expressions as *national*

---

calculus; (*c*) tne era of the balance-of-trade proper (*Introd. to the Study of Pol. Economy* (Engl. transl., 1893), Historical Part, Chap. 4). Sir William Holdsworth (*Hist. of Engl. Law*, XI, p. 380) restricts the period to the eighteenth century. The notions of the Whigs, triumphing over the commercial liberalism of the Tory peace of Utrecht, 'gave rise to the economic system which is generally known as the mercantile system'. The latest work of neo-Marxist interpretation published by I. S. Plotkinov treats mercantilism as 'the ideology of the monopoly trading companies'. Beginning in the age of colonial expansion, it used state power for the protection of trade, controlling trade in the interest of the state. The plunder of colonies served as the main source of primary accumulation of capital. In the next stage of economic development 'the rise of industrial capitalism destroyed mercantilism', according to Mr Christopher Hill in his summary of Plotkinov's views (*Economic History Review*, May 1938, p. 167).
[1] Cf. L. Robbins, *Econ. Planning and International Order*, p. 16.

policy would have more meaning if they could be applied without inward misgivings to all and every chapter in the history of
a nation; for even a *laissez-faire* state has an economic policy,
and may be striving for greatness.[1] And if a community believes
in restrictions and public controls, let us analyse their intentions
and consequences with the help of appropriate tools of restricted capacity, borrowing either from the vocabulary of the
period studied or from the current terminology of the political
and economic sciences. As for the peculiar ethos which some
people believe to have brooded for ten or fifteen generations
over the European peoples – if it can be designated at all with
verbal exactitude, it seems to demand at least something more
convincing than the barbarous expressions I have inflicted on
you so many times this evening.

[1] L. Brentano, *Der Wirtschaftende Mensch in der Geschichte*, s. 29.

3 Power versus Plenty as Objectives of Foreign Policy in the Seventeenth and Eighteenth Centuries

JACOB VINER

[This article was first published in *World Politics*, Vol. 1,1948.]

In the seventeenth and eighteenth centuries economic thought and practice were predominantly carried on within the framework of that body of ideas which was later to be called 'mercantilism'. Although there has been almost no systematic investigation of the relationship in mercantilist thought between economic and political objectives or ends in the field of foreign policy, certain stereotypes have become so prevalent that few scholars have seriously questioned or examined their validity. One of these stereotypes is that mercantilism was a 'system of power', that is, that 'power' was for mercantilists the sole or overwhelmingly preponderant end of foreign policy, and that wealth, or 'plenty', was valued solely or mainly as a necessary means to attaining or retaining or exercising power. It is the purpose of this paper to examine in the light of the available evidence the validity of this interpretation of mercantilist thought and practice. Tracing the history of ideas, however, always runs to many words, and limitations of space force me to confine myself, even with respect to bibliographical references, to samples of the various types of relevant evidence. That the samples are fair ones I can only attest by my readiness in most cases to expand them indefinitely.

The pioneer historians of mercantilism were nineteenth-century German scholars, predominantly Prussians sympathetic to its economic and political philosophy, and especially to its emphasis on state interests as opposed to the private interests of citizens. The interpretation of mercantilism by Schmoller as primarily a system of state-building is familiar, and commonly accepted by economic historians.[1] A similar stress on the political aspects of mercantilist commercial policy is common in the German writings. The proposition that the mercantilists sought a favourable balance of trade, wealth, and the indefinite accumulation of the precious metals solely as means to power seems first to have been launched by Baron von Heyking, who indeed claims priority for his interpretation.[2] Schmoller similarly interpreted the uncorrupted mercantilism of Prussia and of the non-maritime countries in general, but he maintained that the 'imperialism' of the maritime powers was a debased mercantilism, characterized by an unscrupulous use of military power to promote ultimate commercial ends, and half-condemned it on that ground.[3]

This distinction between 'pure' mercantilism, a 'Staatsmerkantilismus', which can obtain its full development only in an absolute monarchy, and the mercantilism of countries where the commercial classes are influential and the state has to serve and to reconcile private economic interests, is also made much of by a later German writer, Georg Herzog zu Mecklenburg Graf von Carlow. For 'pure' mercantilism, the ruling principle

[1] I suspect, nevertheless, that it is highly questionable. The economic unification of the nation-state appears mostly to have occurred before the advent of mercantilism, as in England, or after its decay, as in France, Spain, Russia, Switzerland, Italy, the United States, or the British Dominions, if the national unification of tariffs or other significant criteria are applied. Even Colbert promoted regional as well as national self-sufficiency. As Moritz Bonn has commented (*Journal of Political Economy*, LIV (1946), 474), 'A parochialist like Gustav Schmoller naturally deduced his impressions of mercantilism from the policies of primitive Prussia.'

[2] *Zur Geschichte der Handelsbilanztheorie*, Berlin, 1880, Chap. 2, 'Die Beziehungen der Theorie der Handelsbilanz zur Theorie des politischen Gleichgewichtes'. The claim for priority is on p. 43. This chapter is a pioneer and valid demonstration of the existence of a close relationship between mercantilist balance-of-trade and balance-of-power theorizing and policy, but there is not a trace of valid demonstration in it that wealth considerations were made wholly subservient to power considerations.

[3] See his *Umrisse und Untersuchungen* (Leipzig, 1898), especially Chap. I, 'Das Merkantilsystem in seiner historischen Bedeutung', pp. 42–60; see also 'Die englische Handelspolitik des 17. und 18. Jahrhunderts', in *Jahrbuch für Gesetzgebrung, Verwaltung, und Volkswirtschaft*, XX (1899), 1211–41. F. Brie, *Imperialistische Strömungen in der Englischen Literatur*, 2nd edn. (Halle, 1928), p. 68, characterizes English mercantilism of the eighteenth century, along Schmollerian lines, as 'kaufmännisch gefärbte Imperialismus'.

is not economic but the promotion of the power of the state.[1]
In general, however, the historians have not distinguished
between the mercantilism of the absolute and the constitutional
states, and where they have dealt at all with the questions of the
ultimate aims of mercantilism they have almost invariably
asserted that these were solely or preponderantly political,
although only too often with ambiguity or even outright self-
contradiction, and almost invariably without presentation of
substantial evidence.

A case in point is William Cunningham, the English economic
historian. His predominant interpretation of English mercantilism was that it sought power rather than or much more than
plenty, and that it valued plenty solely or mainly as an instrument or support of power, although he easily slipped, in this as
in other analytical issues, into ambiguity if not hopeless contradiction.[2] An English economic historian sympathetic to mercantilism, W. A. S. Hewins, regarded this interpretation as
unfair to the mercantilists, and offered the following rendition
of Cunningham's position to indicate its inacceptability:

   . . . one might almost imagine him [i.e. Cunningham] saying:
   'The mercantile system is concerned with man solely as a
   being who pursues national power, and who is capable of

[1] *Richelieu als merkantilistischer Wirtschaftspolitiker und der Begriff des Staatsmerkantilismus* (Jena, 1929), pp. 198 ff.

[2] Cf. for contradiction with the view that power was the predominant objective, *The Growth of English Industry and Commerce in Modern Times,* Vol. II, *In
Modern Times, Part I* (Cambridge, 1903), p. 459: 'From the Revolution till the
revolt of the colonies, the regulation of commerce was considered, not so much
with reference to other elements of national power, or even in its bearing on
revenue, but chiefly with a view to the promotion of industry.' Cf. also, *The
Wisdom of the Wise* (Cambridge, 1906): 'In the pre-scientific days the end which
men of affairs kept in view, when debating economic affairs, was clearly understood; the political power of the realm was the object they put before them, . . .'
(p. 21). 'We recognize [today] that the defence of the realm is essential to welfare,
but we are no longer so much concerned about building up the power of the
country, or so ready to engage in aggressive wars *for the sake of commercial
advantages,* as Englishmen were in the eighteenth century' (p. 22) (the italics are
mine). The contradiction the italicized words seem to indicate may not be real,
since Cunningham may have had in mind that the 'commercial advantages' were
sought for the sake of the contribution to British power, but such exposition,
ambiguous, if not contradictory, is so common in the literature that it provides of
itself a justification for an article such as the present one.

judging the comparative efficacy of means to that end. It
makes entire abstraction of every other human passion or
motive, except those which may be regarded as perpetually
antagonizing principles to the pursuit of national power –
viz., neglect of shipping and aversion to a fish diet. The
mercantile system considers mankind as occupied solely in
pursuing and acquiring national power.'[1]

All the German and English economic historians who found
in mercantilism the complete subordination of economic to
political considerations seem to have been themselves sympathetic to the subordination of the individual to the state and to
the exaltation of vigorous nationalism characteristic of mercantilism, and to have been hostile to nineteenth-century liberalism
and its revolt against the residues of mercantilist legislation.
Where this was combined, as in Schmoller and Cunningham,
with a dislike of the rise of the bourgeois and his values to dominance over politics, to attribute to the mercantilists the conception of power as the sole or preponderant end of national policy
was to praise rather than to blame them.

Eli Heckscher, the great Swedish economic historian and the
outstanding authority on mercantilism today, follows the standard interpretation of the mercantilist objectives, but clearly to
add to their shame rather than to praise them. Heckscher is an
outstanding liberal, an individualist, a free-trader, and clearly
anti-chauvinist. When to the section of his great work dealing
with the foreign policy of the mercantilists he gives the heading
'Mercantilism as a System of Power',[2] and applies it to mercantilism in general and not only to the mercantilism of the absolute monarchies or of the non-maritime countries, he is reinforcing the indictment of it which he makes on other grounds,
for to him 'power' is clearly an ugly name for an ugly fact.
More systematically, more learnedly, and more competently

[1] In a review of Cunningham's *Growth of English Industry and Commerce* in the
Economic Journal, II (1892), 696. Cunningham, in a reply to Hewins and other
reviewers, ibid., IV (1894), 508–16, permitted this interpretation of his position
to pass without comment, although it must have been obvious to him that
Hewins regarded it as a *reductio ad absurdum*.

[2] *Mercantilism*, translated by Mendel Shapiro, 2 vols. (London, 1935), II,
13–52.

than anyone else, he supports his thesis that the mercantilists subordinated plenty to power. His argument calls therefore for detailed examination if this proposition is to be questioned.

Heckscher really presents an assortment of theses, ranging from the proposition: (1) that for mercantilists – whether for most, or many, or only some, not being made very clear – power was the *sole* ultimate end of state policy, with wealth merely one of the means to the attainment of power through the 'eclectic' thesis; (2) that power and plenty were parallel ends for the mercantilists, but with much greater emphasis placed on power than was common before or later, to the concession; (3) that mercantilists occasionally reversed the usual position and regarded power as a means for securing plenty and treated purely commercial considerations as more important than considerations of power. His central position, however, and to this he returns again and again, is that the mercantilists expounded a doctrine under which all considerations were subordinated to considerations of power as an end in itself, and that in doing so they were logically and in their distribution of emphasis unlike their predecessors and unlike the economists of the nineteenth century.

It is difficult to support this account of Heckscher's position by direct quotation from his text, since he presents it more by implication and inference from mercantilist statements than by clear-cut and explicit formulation in his own words. That mercantilists according to Heckscher tended to regard power as the *sole* end is to be inferred by the contrasts he draws between the position he attributes to Adam Smith – wrongly, I am sure – that 'power was certainly only a means to the end . . . of opulence', and the 'reverse' position of the mercantilists,[1] the 'reverse', I take it, being the proposition that wealth was only a means to power. That there is something special and peculiar to mercantilism in conceiving power as an end in itself underlies all of Heckscher's exposition, but the following passages come nearest to being explicit. 'The most vital aspect of the problem is whether power is conceived as an end in itself, or only as a means for gaining something else, such as the well-being of the nation in this world or its everlasting salvation in

[1] *Mercantilism* II.

the next.'[1] This leaves out of account, as an alternative, Heckscher's 'eclectic' version, where both power and plenty are ends in themselves. On John Locke's emphasis on the significance for power of monetary policy, Heckscher comments, with the clear implication that the injection into economic analysis of considerations of power is not 'rational', that it is 'interesting as a proof of how important considerations of power in money policy appeared even to so advanced a rationalist as Locke'.[2]

Heckscher later restated his position in response to criticisms, but it seems to me that he made no important concession and indeed ended up with a more extreme position than at times he had taken in his original exposition.

> The second of the aims of mercantilist policy . . . – that of power – has met with a great deal of criticism from reviewers of my book . . . I agree with my critics on that point to the extent of admitting that both 'power' and 'opulence' . . . have been, and must be, of importance to economic policy of every description. But I do not think there can be any doubt that these two aims changed places in the transition from mercantilism to *laissez-faire*. All countries in the nineteenth century made the creation of their wealth their lode-star, with small regard to its effects upon the power of the state, while the opposite had been the case previously.[3]

The evidence which Heckscher presents that the mercantilists considered power as an end in itself, and as an important end, and that they considered wealth to be a means of power need not be examined here, since there is no ground for disputing these propositions and, as far as I know, no one has ever disputed them. That the mercantilists overemphasized these propositions I would also not question. Nor will I enter here into extended discussion of the rationality of these concepts beyond stating a few points. In the seventeenth and eighteenth

---

[1] *Mercantilism*, II, 16.   [2] Ibid., II, 47.

[3] 'Revisions in Economic History, V, Mercantilism', *Economic History Review*, VII (1936), 48. The foreign policy implications of the nineteenth-century economics, I believe, need investigation as much as do the aims of mercantilism. Until such investigation is systematically made, comparisons with mercantilism are liable to be misleading with respect to the true position of both bodies of doctrine.

centuries colonial and other overseas markets, the fisheries, the carrying trade, the slave trade, and open trade routes over the high seas were all regarded, and rightly, as important sources of national wealth, but were available, or at least assuredly available, only to countries with the ability to acquire or retain them by means of the possession and readiness to use military strength.

In the seventeenth and eighteenth centuries also, 'power' meant not only power to conquer and attack, and the prestige and influence which its possession gave, but also power to maintain national security against external attack. 'Power as an end in itself' must therefore be interpreted to include considerations of national security against external aggression on the nation's territory and its political and religious freedom. Given the nature of human nature, recognition of power as an end in itself was therefore then neither peculiar nor obviously irrational unless there is rational ground for holding that the promotion of economic welfare is the sole sensible objective of national policy to which every other consideration must be completely subordinated.

There remains, therefore, to be examined only whether Heckscher has demonstrated that mercantilists *ever* regarded power as the *sole* end of foreign policy, or ever held that considerations of plenty were *wholly* to be subordinated to considerations of power, or even whether they ever held that a choice has to be made in long-run national policy between power and plenty.

Despite his wide knowledge of the mercantilist literature, Heckscher fails to cite a single passage in which it is asserted that power is or should be the *sole* end of national policy, or that wealth matters *only* as it serves power. I doubt whether any such passage can be cited or that anyone ever held such views. The nearest thing to such statements which Heckscher does cite are statements maintaining that wealth is a means of power and is important as such, unaccompanied by express acknowledgement that wealth is also important for its own sake. In almost every case he cites it is possible to cite from the same writer passages which show that wealth was regarded as valuable also for its own sake. The passage of this type which Heckscher most emphasizes is a 'passing remark' of Colbert in a letter:

'Trade is the source of finance and finance is the vital nerve of war.' Heckscher comments that Colbert here 'indicates clearly the relationship between means and ends'.[1] But argument from silence is notoriously precarious, and if it were to be pressed would work more against than for Heckscher's thesis, since there is a great mass of mercantilist literature in which there is no mention whatsoever, and no overt implication, of considerations of power. Colbert does not here indicate that the relationship was a one-way one. To make a significant point Heckscher would have to show that Colbert would not also have subscribed to the obverse proposition that strength is the vital nerve of trade and trade the source of finance.

Of all the mercantilists Colbert is the most vulnerable, since he carried all the major errors of economic analysis of which they were guilty to their most absurd extremes both in verbal exposition and in practical execution, and since, either as expressing his own sentiments or catering to those of his master, Louis XIV, he developed more elaborately than any other author the serviceability to power of economic warfare, the possibilities of using military power to achieve immediate economic ends, and the possibilities of substituting economic warfare for military warfare to attain national ends. Even in his case, however, it is not possible to demonstrate that he ever rejected or regarded as unimportant the desirability for its own sake of a prosperous French people or the desirability of guiding French foreign policy, military and economic, so as to augment this prosperity. In many of his official papers he is obviously catering to Louis XIV's obsession with power and prestige, or perhaps to a conventional fashion of *pretending* that a great monarch would be so obsessed,[2] so that there is no

[1] *Mercantilism*, II, 16.

[2] Cf. the following passage in his famous 'Mémoire au Roi sur les Finances' of 1670: 'Il est certain, Sire, que Vostre Majesté ... a dans son esprit et dans toute sa nature la guerre par préférence à toute autre chose ... Vostre Majesté pense plus dix foix à la guerre qu'elle ne pense à ses finances' (*Lettres, Instructions et Mémoires de Colbert*, P. Clément, ed. (Paris, 1870), VII, 252). This long memoir is a plea to the king to look to his economic policy, including economic warfare, as an essential instrument for attaining his ends. Even in the case of Louis XIV himself, it is easy to show from his writings that the prosperity of his people, while no doubt inexcusably underemphasized, was a matter of some concern to him for its own sake.

reason to reject as unrepresentative of his genuinely held views such passages as the following:

> ... comme toutes les alliances entre les grands rois ont toujours deux fins principales, l'une leur gloire particulière et quelquefois la jonction de leurs intérests, soit pour conserver soit pour acquérir ... et l'autre les avantages de leurs sujets, ... Et quoyque dans l'ordre de le division, celuy de l'avantage de leurs sujets soit le dernier, il est néanmoins toujours le premier dans les esprits de bons princes ...
>
> Les avantages de leurs sujets consistent à les maintenir en repos au dedans et à leur procurer par le moyen du commerce, soit plus de facilités de vivre aux nécessiteux, soit plus d'abondance aux riches.[1]

Certain peculiar features of mercantilist economic analysis - features incidentally which modern apologists for mercantilist economics, such as Lipson, seem strangely to avoid discussing – do seem to imply a disregard on the part of mercantilists for economic welfare.[2] What was apparently a phase of scholastic economics, that what is one man's gain is necessarily another man's loss, was taken over by the mercantilists and applied to countries as a whole. They incorporated this with their tendency to identify wealth with money, and with their doctrine that, as far as money was concerned, what mattered was not the absolute quantity but the relative quantity as compared with other countries. Since the quantity of money in the world could be taken as constant, the quantity of wealth in the world was also a constant, and a country could gain only at the expense of other countries. By sheer analogy with the logic of military power, which is in truth a relative matter, and with the aid of the assumption of a close relationship between 'balance of power' and 'balance of trade,' which, however, they failed

---

[1] 'Dissertation sur la question quelle des deux alliances de France ou de Hollande peut estre plus avantageuse à l'Angleterre', March 1669. *Lettres*, VI, 261. A letter of Colbert to Louis XIV in 1681 contains the following passage: 'Ce qu'il y a de plus important, et sur quoi il y a plus de réflexions à faire, c'est la misére très-grande des peuples' (C. Dareste de la Chavanne, *Histoire de l'Administration en France* (Paris, 1848), II, 258).

[2] See Ephraim Lipson, *The Economic History of England*, Vols. II–III, 'The Age of Mercantilism', 3rd edn. (London, 1943).

intelligently to analyse, the mercantilists were easily led to the conclusion that wealth, like power, also was only a relative matter, a matter of proportions between countries, so that a loss inflicted on a rival country was as good as an absolute gain for one's own country. At least one mercantilist carried this doctrine to its logical conclusion that plague, war, famine, harvest failure, in a neighbouring country was of economic advantage to your own country.[1] On such doctrine, Adam Smith's trenchant comment is deserved, although he exaggerates its role in mercantilist thought and practice:

> By such maxims as these, however, nations have been taught that their interest consisted in beggaring all their neighbours. Each nation has been made to look with an invidious eye upon the prosperity of all the nations with which it trades, and to consider their gain as its own loss. Commerce, which ought naturally to be, among nations, as among individuals, a bond of union and friendship, has become the most fertile source of discord and animosity. The capricious ambition of kings and ministers has not, during the present and the preceding century, been more fatal to the repose of Europe, than the impertinent jealousy of merchants and manufacturers. The violence and injustice of the rulers of mankind is an ancient evil, for which, I am afraid, the nature of human affairs can scarce admit of a remedy. But the mean rapacity, the monopolizing spirit of merchants and manufacturers, who neither are, nor ought to be, the rulers of mankind, though it cannot perhaps be corrected, may very easily be prevented from disturbing the tranquillity of any body but themselves.[2]

Heckscher cites mercantilist doctrine such as Adam Smith here criticizes as evidence that the mercantilists were not interested in economic welfare for its own sake, but subordinated it to considerations of power. Adam Smith's assumption that the exposition of such doctrine was confined to merchants rather

---

[1] Theodor Ludwig Lau, *Aufrichtiger Vorschlag*, 1719, as reported in Walther Focke, *Die Lehrmeinungen der Kameralisten über den Handel* (Erlangen dissertation, 1926), p. 59.

[2] *Wealth of Nations*, Cannan, ed., I, 457–8.

than statesmen (or philosophers) is invalid. But in so far as it was expounded by merchants, it is scarcely conceivable that these were so different from merchants at other times that they were governed more by chauvinist patriotism than by rapacity. The significance of such doctrine is not that those who adhered to it placed power before plenty, but that they grossly misunderstood the true means to and nature of plenty. What they were lacking in was not economic motivation but economic understanding.

What, then, is the correct interpretation of mercantilist doctrine and practice with respect to the roles of power and plenty as ends of national policy? I believe that practically all mercantilists, whatever the period, country, or status of the particular individual, would have subscribed to all of the following propositions: (1) wealth is an absolutely essential means to power, whether for security or for aggression; (2) power is essential or valuable as a means to the acquisition or retention of wealth; (3) wealth and power are each proper ultimate ends of national policy; (4) there is long-run harmony between these ends, although in particular circumstances it may be necessary for a time to make economic sacrifices in the interest of military security and therefore also of long-run prosperity.

The omission of any one of these four propositions results in an incorrect interpretation of mercantilist thought, while additions of other propositions would probably involve internal dispute among mercantilists. It is to be noted that no proposition is included as to the relative weight which the mercantilists attached to power and to plenty, respectively. Given the general acceptance of the existence of harmony and mutual support between the pursuit of power and the pursuit of plenty, there appears to have been little interest in what must have appeared to them to be an unreal issue. When apparent conflict between these ends did arise, however, differences in attitudes, as between persons and countries, did arise and something will be said on this matter later.

That plenty and power were universally regarded as each valuable for its own sake there is overwhelming evidence, in the contemporary writings of all kinds, and what follows is more or less a random sampling of the available evidence. In the text accompanying and interpreting the Frontispiece of Michael Drayton's poem, *Polyolbion*, 1622, there is the following passage:

> Through a Triumphant Arch see Albion plac'd,
> In Happy site, in Neptune's arms embrac'd,
> In Power and Plenty, on her Cleevy Throne

In Barbier d'Aucour's *Au Roy sur le Commerce, Ode*, 1665,[1] an early French equivalent of *Rule Britannia*, appear the following lines:

> Vos vaisseaux fendant tous les airs,
> Et cinglant sur toutes les Mers,
> Y porteront vostre puissance;
> Et ce Commerce plein d'honneur,
> Fera naistre dans vostre France,
> Un flus et reflus de bon-heur.

Montchrétien opens his book with this passage: 'Ceux qui sont appellez au gouvernement des Estats doyvent en avoir la gloire, l'augmentation et l'enrichissement pour leur principal but.'[2] Another Frenchman, writing in 1650 says:

> Deux choses sont principalement necessaires pour rendre un Estat florissant; c'est assavoir le Gouvernement, & le Commerce; & comme sans celuy-là il est impossible qu'il puisse longtemps subsister; de mesme sans celuy-cy on le voit manquer de mille sortes de choses importantes à la vie, & il est impossible que les peuples acquierent de grandes richesses.[3]

John Graunt, in 1662, states that 'the art of governing, and the true politiques, is how to preserve the subject in peace, and

---

[1] The citation from D'Aucour in the text is made from a reprint extracted from J. Carnandet, *Le Trésor des Pièces Rares ... de la Champagne* (Paris, 1863–6). D'Aucour was a tutor of Colbert's son. F. C. Palm, *The Economic Policies of Richelieu* (Urbana, 1920), pp. 178–9, quotes from an earlier *Ode à ... Richelieu*, in much the same vein by Jean de Chapelain (1595–1624), which similarly stresses power and plenty.

[2] *Traicté de l'œconomie politique* [1615], Th. Funck-Brentano ed. (Paris, 1889), p. 11.

[3] Cited from Ch. Vialart dit St Paul, *Histoire du Ministère d'Armand ... Duc de Richelieu* (Paris, 1650), I, 332.

plenty'.[1] An anonymous English writer, in 1677, declares that:
'The four main interests of a nation are, religion, reputation,
peace, and trade . . .'[2] William III, in his declaration of war
against France in 1689, gives as one of the reasons that Louis
XIV's 'forbidding the importation of a great part of the
product and manufactures of our Kingdom, and imposing
exorbitant customs upon the rest, are sufficient evidence of his
design to destroy the trade on which the wealth and safety of
this nation so much depends'.[3] In the preamble of 3 and 4
Anne, cap. 10, are the following words: 'The Royal Navy, and
the navigation of England, wherein, under God, the wealth,
safety, and strength of this Kingdom is so much concerned,
depends on the due supply of stores for the same.'[4] An English
pamphlet of 1716 on the relations with Russia, after describing
the Tsar as 'a great and enterprising spirit, and of a genius
thoroughly politic' attributes to him and his people 'an insati-
able desire of opulency, and a boundless thirst for dominion'.[5]
William Wood, a noted mercantilist writer, refers to the English
as 'a people . . . who seek no other advantages than such only
as may enlarge and secure that, whereby their strength, power,
riches and reputation, equally encrease and are preserved . . .'[6]
Bernard Mandeville discusses how 'politicians can make a
people potent, renown'd and flourishing'.[7] An anonymous
English writer states in 1771 that: 'Nature, reason and observation all plainly point out to us our true object of national
policy, which is commerce; the inexhaustible source of wealth
and power to a people.'[8] In an undated memoir of Maurepas to

[1] *Natural and Political Observations made upon the Bills of Mortality* [London,
1662], (John Hopkins University Reprint, Baltimore, 1939), p. 78.
[2] *The Present State of Christendom, and the Interest of England, with a Regard to
France* [1677], in *The Harleian Miscellany* (London, 1808), I, 249.
[3] As cited in *Mercator, or Commerce Retrieved*, No. 1, London, 26 May, 1713.
[4] Cited in G. S. Graham, *Sea Power and British North America* 1783–1820
(Cambridge, Mass., 1941), p. 143.
[5] *The Northern Crisis; or Impartial Reflections on the Policies of the Czar* [London,
1716], as reprinted in Karl Marx, *Secret Diplomatic History of the Eighteenth Century*
(London, 1899), p. 32.
[6] *Survey of Trade*, 2nd edn. (London, 1719) Dedication, pp. iv–v.
[7] *The Fable of the Bees* [6th edn., 1732], F. B. Kaye ed. (Oxford, 1924), I, 185.
[8] *Considerations on the Policy, Commerce and Circumstances of the Kingdom* [London,
1771], as quoted in the preface to G. S. Graham, *British Policy and Canada*, 1774–
1791 (London, 1930).

Louis XVI, on the commerce of France, occur the following passages: 'Le commerce est la source de la félicité, de la force et de la richesse d'un état . . . La richesse et la puissance sont les vrais intérêts d'une nation, et il n'y a que le commerce qui puisse procurer l'une et l'autre.'[1]

Such evidence as the foregoing that in the age of mercantilism wealth and power were both sought for their own sakes could easily be multiplied many fold. In English literature of the period of all kinds, from poetry to official documents, the phrases 'power and plenty', 'wealth and strength', 'profit and power', 'profit and security', 'peace and plenty', or their equivalents, recur as a constant refrain. Nor is there any obvious reason, given the economic and political conditions and views of the seventeenth and eighteenth centuries, why power *and* plenty should not have been the joint objectives of the patriotic citizen of the time, even if he had freed himself from the mercantilist philosophy. Adam Smith, though not a mercantilist, was speaking for mercantilists as well as for himself when he said that 'the great object of the political economy of every country, is to increase the riches and power of that country'.[2]

In all the literature I have examined I have found only one passage which is seriously embarrassing for my thesis, not because it subordinates in extreme fashion economic to political considerations but for the reverse reason. The passage, in an anonymous and obscure pamphlet of 1754, whose authorship I have been unable to determine, is as follows:

You want not, Gentlemen to be informed by me, that commerce is the nearest and dearest concern of your country. It is what should be the great object of public attention in all national movements, and in every negotiation we enter into with foreign powers. Our neighbours on the Continent may, perhaps, wisely scheme or quarrel for an augmentation of dominions; but *Great Britain, of herself, has nothing to fight for, nothing to support, nothing to augment but her commerce.* On our foreign trade, not only our wealth but our mercantile

---

[1] *Mémoires du Comte de Maurepas* (Paris, 1792), III, 195.
[2] *Wealth of Nations*, Cannan ed., I, 351.

navigation must depend; on that navigation our naval strength, the glory and security of our country.'[1]

It is much easier indeed to show that power was not the sole objective of national policy in mercantilist thought than to explain how historians ever came to assert that it was. The evidence they cite in support of this proposition is not only extremely scanty but is generally ambiguous if not wholly irrelevant to their thesis. It would be extremely difficult, I am sure, for them to cite even a single passage which unmistakably rejects wealth as a national objective worth pursuing for its own sake or unconditionally subordinates it to power as an ultimate end. It is only too probable that there has been operating here that intellectual 'principle of parsimony' in the identification of causes which, whatever its serviceability in the natural sciences, has in the history of social thought worked only for ill.

Cunningham and Heckscher[2] make much of a passage of Francis Bacon's made famous by modern scholars in which he speaks of King Henry VII 'bowing the ancient policy of this estate from consideration of plenty to consideration of power' when in the interests of the navy he ordered that wines from Gascony should be imported only in English bottoms. As a fifteenth-century measure, this falls outside the period of present interest, but Bacon, no doubt, put much of his own ideas, perhaps more than of Henry VII's, in his *History of the Reign of King Henry the Seventh*. It is relevant, therefore, that Bacon speaks of Henry VII as conducting war for profit, and attributes to him even over-developed economic objectives. In 1493 Henry VII had declared an embargo on all trade with the Flemish provinces because the pretender, Perkin Warbeck, was being harboured there. The embargo after a time 'began to pinch the merchants of both nations very sore, which moved

---

[1] *Mercator's Letters on Portugal and its Commerce* (London, 1754), p. 5. The italics are not in the original text.

[2] Heckscher refers to this as 'a very characteristic passage' (*Mercantilism*, II, 16), but I find it difficult to cite a duplicate whether from Bacon's writings or in the period generally. See also Heckscher, 'Revisions in Economic History, V, Mercantilism', *Economic History Review*, VII (1936), 48: 'I think Cunningham was right in stressing the famous saying of Bacon about Henry VII: "bowing the ancient policy of this Estate from consideration of plenty to consideration of power".'

them by all means they could devise to affect and dispose their
sovereigns respectively to open the intercourse again'. Henry
VII, no longer apprehensive about Warbeck, was receptive.
'But that that moved him most was, that being a King that
loved wealth and treasure, he could not endure to have trade
sick, nor any obstruction to continue in the gate-vein, which
disperseth that blood', and by the *intercursus magnus* of 1495-6
with the Archduke of Austria he negotiated the end of the
trade war.[1]

Not so frequently stated as that power and plenty are properly
joint objectives of national policy but undoubtedly a pervasive
element in the thought of the period is the proposition that they
are also harmonious ends, each reinforcing and promoting the
other. The idea is expressed in the maxim attributed to Hobbes:
'Wealth is power and power is wealth.'[2] There follow some
passages in which the idea is spelled out somewhat more fully:

Foreign trade produces riches, riches power, power
preserves our trade and religion.[3]

It is evident that this kingdom is wonderfully fitted by the
bounty of God almighty, for a great progression in wealth
and power; and that the only means to arrive at both, or
either of them, is to improve and advance trade . . .[4]

For as the honesty of all governments is, so shall be their
riches; and as their honour, honesty, and riches are, so will
be their strength; and as their honour, honesty, riches, and
strength are, so will be their trade. These are five sisters that
go hand in hand, and must not be parted.[5]

[1] See *The Works of Francis Bacon*, James Spedding, ed. (London, 1858), VI,
95-6; 172-3. Cf. also *Considerations touching a War with Spain* [1624], in *The Works
of Francis Bacon* (Philadelphia, 1852), II, 214, where he says that: 'whereas wars
are generally causes of poverty or consumption . . . this war with Spain, if it be
made by sea, is like to be a lucrative and restorative war. So that, if we go roundly
on at the first, the war in continuance will find itself.' On the other hand, in his
Essays or Counsels [2nd edn., 1625], *Works* (London, 1858), VI, 450-1, he makes
what appears to be a clear-cut statement that the prestige of power ('grandeur')
is more important than plenty.
[2] J. E. Barker, *Rise and Decline of the Netherlands* (London, 1906), p. 194.
[3] Josiah Child, *A Treatise concerning the East India Trade* (London, 1681), p. 29.
[4] Idem, *A New Discourse of Trade*, 4th edn. (*ca.* 1690), Preface, p. xliii.
[5] Andrew Yarranton, *England's Improvement by Sea and Land* (London, 1677),
p. 6.

Your fleet, and your trade, have so near a relation, and such mutual influence upon each other, they cannot well be separated; your trade is the mother and nurse of your seamen; your seamen are the life of your fleet, and your fleet is the security and protection of your trade, and both together are the wealth, strength, security, and glory of Britain.[1]

By trade and commerce we grow a rich and powerful nation, and by their decay we are growing poor and impotent. As trade and commerce enrich, so they fortify, our country.

The wealth of the nation he [the 'Patriot King'] will most justly esteem to be his wealth, the power his power, the security and the honour, his security and honour; and by the very means by which he promotes the two first, he will wisely preserve the two last.[2]

De la marine dépendent les colonies, des colonies le commerce, du commerce la faculté pour l'État d'entretenir de nombreuses armées, d'augmenter la population et de fournir aux entreprises les plus glorieuses et les plus utiles.[3]

George L. Beer has commented, with particular reference to the statement from Lord Haversham quoted above, that 'The men of the day argued in a circle of sea power, commerce and colonies. Sea power enabled England to expand and to protect her foreign trade, while this increased commerce, in turn, aug-

---

[1] Lord Haversham in the House of Lords, 6 November, 1707, *Parliamentary History of England*, VI, 598. Cf. also James Whiston, *A Discourse of the Decay of Trade* (London, 1693), p. 3:

For, since the introduction of the new artillery of powder guns, &c., and the discovery of the wealth of the Indies, &c. war is become rather an expense of money than men, and success attends those that can most and longest spend money: whence it is that prince's armies in Europe are become more proportionable to their purses than to the number of their people; so that it uncontrollably follows that a foreign trade managed to the best advantage, will make our nation so strong and rich, that we may command the trade of the world, the riches of it, and consequently the world itself. . . . Neither will the pursuing these proposals, augment the nation's wealth and power only, but that wealth and power will also preserve our trade and religion, they mutually working for the preservation of each other . . .

[2] Lord Bolingbroke, 'The Idea of a Patriot King', in *Letters on the Spirit of Patriotism* (London, 1752), pp. 204, 211.

[3] Petit, a colleague of the French Foreign Minister, Choiseul, in 1762, as cited by E. Daubigny, *Choiseul et la France d'Outre-Mer après le Traité de Paris* (Paris, 1892), p. 176.

mented her naval strength.'[1] Circular reasoning this may have been, but it was not, logically at least, a 'vicious circle', since under the circumstances of the time it was perfectly reasonable to maintain that wealth and power mutually supported each other, that they were, or could be made, each a means to the augmentation of the other.[2]

In contending that for the mercantilists power and plenty were regarded as coexisting ends of national policy which were fundamentally harmonious, I do not mean that they were unaware that in specific instances economic sacrifices might have to be made in order to assume national security or victory in an aggressive war. But as a rule, if not invariably, when making this point they showed their belief that such economic sacrifices in the short run would bring economic as well as political gains in the long run. The selfishness from a patriotic point of view of tax-payers resisting war-time impositions for armament or for war was always a problem for statesmen in the age of mercantilism, and sometimes the parsimony of monarchs was also a problem. It was also necessary at times for statesmen to resist the pressure from merchants to pursue petty commercial ends which promised immediate economic gain but at the possible cost of long-run military security and therefore also of long-run national prosperity. The mercantilist, no doubt, would not have denied that if necessity should arise for choosing, all other things would have to give way to considerations of the national safety; but his practice might not rise to the

---

[1] *The Old Colonial System, 1600–1754* (New York, 1912), I, 16.
[2] Edmond Silberner, *La Guerre dans la Pensée Économique du XVIᵉ au XVIIIᵉ Siècle* (Paris, 1939), concentrates on the search for attitudes towards war, idealizing or pacific, rather than on the motivations of foreign policy, but it presents a rich collection of extracts from the contemporary literature which in so far as it is pertinent to the present issue is, I believe, wholly confirmatory of my thesis. Cf. also, by the same author, *The Problem of War in Nineteenth Century Economic Thought* (Princeton, 1946), p. 286: 'In the protectionist view, there is a reciprocal action between the economic and war: industrialization facilitates the conduct of war, and military victories increase the possibilities of industrialization and of economic prosperity. This point of view recalls that of the mercantilists: wealth increases power, and power augments wealth.' The thesis presented in the text above is also supported not only by the title but by the contents, if I understand his Italian aright, of Jacopo Mazzei's article, 'Potenza Mezzo di Ricchezza e Ricchezza Mezzo di Potenza nel Pensiero dei Mercantilisti', *Rivista Internazionale di Scienze Sociali*, XLI (1933), 3–18.

level of his principles, and his doctrine would not lead him to recognize that such choice was likely to face him frequently. It is not without significance that it was an anti-mercantilist economist, Adam Smith, and not the mercantilists, who laid down the maxim that 'defence is more important than opulence'. A typical mercantilist might well have replied that ordinarily defence is necessary to opulence and opulence to effective defence, even if momentarily the two ends might appear to be in conflict.

Queen Elizabeth was notoriously parsimonious, and one of her diplomatic agents, Buckhurst, in reasoning with her in 1587 when the safety of England against the menace from Spain appeared to call for rearmament, anticipated Adam Smith's maxim:

> And alwaies when kinges and kingdoms do stand in dout of daunger, their safetie is a thing so far above all price of treasure, as there shold be no sparing to bring them even into certainty of assurans.

He accordingly advised Elizabeth to

> unlock all your cofers and convert your treasure for the advauncing of worthy men and for the arming of ships and men of war, that may defend you, sith princes' treasures serve only to that end and lie they never so fast nor so full in their chests, can no waies so defend them.[1]

Statesmen frequently found it necessary to warn against endangering political ends by unwise pursuit of temporary or petty commercial gains in response to pressure from business interests. This was especially true in connection with the relations between England and France during the Seven Years' War, which to many contemporaries seemed to be conducted with too much attention to economic considerations of minor importance. Just before the outbreak of the conflict, when it was still being debated whether the issue between the two countries should be settled by economic or military means,

---

[1] 'Correspondentie van Robert Dudley Graaf van Leycester', Part II, *Werken uitgiven door het Historisch Genootschap*, Utrecht, 3rd Series, No. 57 (1931), pp. 239, 240.

Lord Granville was reported as 'absolutely against meddling with trade – he called it, vexing your neighbours for a little muck'.[1] And in the face of the struggle itself, Mirepoix, the French Ambassador to England, is said to have commented 'that it was a great pity to cut off so many heads for the sake of a few hats'.[2] In the course of controversy over the Newfoundland fisheries after the ending of hostilities, in 1763, Choiseul appealed to Halifax: 'mais pour l'amour de Dieu, ne laissons pas des querrelles de pêcheurs dégénérer en querelles de nations'.[3]

To some extent this point of view may have been a reflection of a certain disdain for trade in general which was beginning to affect the aristocratic class who conducted the foreign relations of the time. It would be a mistake, however, to explain it in terms of basic disregard for economic considerations, rather than as belief that the pursuit of temporary and minor economic benefits should not be permitted to dominate foreign policy. Such is the position of John Mitchell, who makes clear elsewhere that 'power and prosperity' are the proper ends of policy:

> It is well known, that our colonies in America are rather more under the tuition and influence of the merchants in Britain, than the government perhaps, and that all public measures relating to them are very much influenced by the opinions of our merchants about them. But the only things that they seem to attend to are the profits of trade . . . This, it is true, is necessary to be considered likewise, but it is not the only thing to be attended to. The great thing to be considered by all states is power and dominion, as well as trade. Without that to support and protect our trade, it must soon be at an end.[4]

---

[1] *The Diary of the Late George Bubb Dodington*, new edn. (London, 1784), pp. 344–5.

[2] [William Knox], *Helps to a Right Decision* (London, 1787), p. 35; cf. also a slightly different version in *Letters Military and Political from the Italian of Count A. Algorotti* (Dublin, 1784), p. 129. The hats were involved, of course, because beaver skins were the main prize of the American fur trade, and the hair from these skins was the basic raw material for the men's hats of the time.

[3] Cited in *Mélanges d'histoire offerts à M. Charles Bémont* (Paris, 1913), p. 655.

[4] *The Contest in America between Great Britain and France* (London, 1757),

While mercantilist doctrine, moreover, put great stress on
the importance of national economic interests, it put equally
great stress on the possibility of lack of harmony between the
special economic interests of the individual merchants or
particular business groups or economic classes, on the one
hand, and the economic interest of the commonwealth as a
whole, on the other. Refusal to give weight to *particular*
economic interests, therefore, must never be identified with
disregard for the national economic interest as they conceived
it, in interpreting the thought of the mercantilists. In human
affairs, moreover, there is always room for divergence between
dogma and practice, between principles and the actual behaviour of those who profess them. It is doctrine, and not practice,
which is the main concern here. The task of ascertaining how
much or how little they corresponded in the age of mercantilism, and what were the forces which caused them to deviate, is
the difficult duty of the historian, in whose hands I gladly leave
it.

It was the common belief in France, however, that commercial objectives and particular commercial interests played a
much greater role in the formulation and administration of
British than of French foreign policy, and some Englishmen
would have agreed. There was universal agreement, also, that
in 'Holland' (i.e. the 'United Provinces'), where the merchants
to a large extent shared directly in government, major political
considerations, including the very safety of the country or its
success in wars in which it was actually participating, had
repeatedly to give way to the cupidity of the merchants and

Introduction, p. xvii. Cf. also *A Letter to a certain Foreign Minister, in which the
grounds of the present war are truly stated* (London, 1745), p. 6: 'That we receive great
benefits from trade, that trade is a national concern, and that we ought to resent
any attempt made to lessen or to injure it, are truths well known and out of
dispute, yet sure the British people are not to be treated like a company of merchants, or rather pedlars, who, if they are permitted to sell their goods, are to
think themselves well off, whatever treatment they may receive in any other
respect. No, surely, the British nation has other great concerns besides their
trade, and as she will never sacrifice it, so she will never endure any insult in
respect to them, without resenting it as becomes a people jealous of their honour,
and punctual in the performance of their engagements.'

The occasion for this outburst was a Prussian 'rescript' insisting that Britain
should not intervene in quarrels between German states, since they had nothing
to do with British commerce.

their reluctance to contribute adequately to military finance. Whether in the main the influence of the commercial classes, where they had strength, worked more for peace or for war seems to be an open question, but there appears little ground for doubt that with the merchants, whether they pressed for war or for peace, the major consideration was economic gain, either their private gain, or that of their country, or both.

The material available which touches on these strands of thought is boundless, and there can here be cited only a few passages which give the flavour of contemporary discussion. We will begin with material relating to the influence of the merchant and of commercial considerations on British policy.

Sir Francis Bacon, in reporting a discussion in Parliament, in the fifth year of James I's reign, of the petition of the merchants with regard to their grievances against Spain, makes one of the speakers say that: 'although he granted that the wealth and welfare of the merchant was not without a sympathy with the general stock and state ['estate?'] of a nation, especially an island; yet, nevertheless, it was a thing too familiar with the merchant, to make the case of his particular profit, the public case of the kingdom.' The troubles of the merchants were partly their own fault: they so mismanaged their affairs abroad that 'except lieger ambassadors, which are the eyes of kings in foreign parts, should leave their sentinel and become merchants' factors, and solicitors, their causes can hardly prosper'. Wars were not to be fought on such minor issues. Another speaker was more sympathetic to the merchants, who were 'the convoy of our supplies, the vents of our abundance, Neptune's almsmen, and fortune's adventurers'. Nevertheless, the question of war should be dealt with by the King and not by Parliament, presumably because the merchants wielded too much influence there. Members of Parliament were local representatives with local interests; if they took a broader view it was accidental.[1]

Allies or potential allies of England sometimes were troubled by England's supposed obsession with commercial objectives as making her an unreliable ally where other interests were involved. In September 1704 a minister of the Duke of Savoy issued a memorial which the English representative at that court

[1] *The Works of Sir Francis Bacon* (Philadelphia, 1852), II, 193–9.

reported as holding that England and Holland, 'the maritime
powers, (an injurious term, I think, which goes into fashion,)
were so attentive to their interests of trade and commerce, that,
perhaps, they would . . . abandon the common interests of
Europe' in the defeat of France in the war then under way.[1]
When Pitt declared to Catherine the Great of Russia that no
Russian conquest could give offence to England, she was
sceptical, and replied: 'The acquisition of a foot of territory on
the Black Sea will at once excite the jealousy of the English,
whose whole attention is given to petty interests and who are
first and always traders.'[2]

Montesquieu and Quesnay both thought that in England,
unlike France and other countries, the interests of commerce
predominated over other interests:

> D'autres nations font céder des intérêts de commerce à des
> intérêts politiques; celle ci [i.e. England] a toujours fait céder
> ses intérêts politiques aux intérêts de son commerce.[3]
>
> en Angleterre . . . où les lois du commerce maritime ne se
> prêtent point aux lois de la politique; où les intérêts de la
> glèbe et de l'État sont subordonnés aux intérêts des négoci-
> ants; où le commerce des productions de l'agriculture, la
> propriété du territoire et l'État meme ne sont regardés que
> comme des accessoires de la métropole, et la métropole
> comme formée de négociants.[4]

The history of British policy and practice with respect to
enemy and trade with the enemy during war provides abundant
and occasionally startling evidence that considerations of plenty

[1] *The Diplomatic Correspondence of the Right Hon. Richard Hill* (London, 1845), I,
479; see also II, 751.
[2] Cited by Edward Crankshaw, *Russia and Britain*, New York, no date (*ca.*
1943), pp. 45–6.
[3] Montesquieu, *De l'Esprit des Lois*, Book XX, Chap. 7.
[4] *Œuvres Économiques et Philosophiques de F. Quesnay*, Auguste Oncken, ed.
(Paris, 1888), p. 429. Quesnay is referring here specially to Britain's policy with
respect to the trade of the colonies. Adam Smith's comment on the monopolistic
aspects of this policy was more acid: 'To found a great empire for the sole purpose of raising up a people of customers, may at first sight appear a project fit
only for a nation of shopkeepers. It is, however, a project altogether unfit for a
nation of shopkeepers; but extremely fit for a nation whose government is
influenced by shopkeepers' (*Wealth of Nations*, Cannan, ed., II, 114).

did not always automatically give way to considerations of power. There is much in British history, as in the history of Holland, of France, and of Spain, to support the statement of Carl Brinkmann that: 'The history of war trade and trade war is a rich mine of interest to the economic and social historian just for the peculiar ways in which the autonomy of business connections and traditions is seen cutting across even the sternest decrees and tendencies of political *ultima ratio.*'[1]

That in Holland commercial interests predominated was taken for granted in both France and England when foreign policy was formulated. Thurloe commented, in 1656, that all proposals of alliances of common and mutual defence, wherein provision was to be made for the good of the Protestant religion' failed 'in respect the United Provinces always found it necessary for them to mingle therewith the consideration of trade . . . The Hollanders had rather His Highness [Oliver Cromwell] be alone in it than that they should lose a tun of sack or a frail of raisins.'[2] A French naval officer, writing to Colbert with reference to the failure of the Dutch to provide the fleet which they had promised for the Levant, said that he was not at all surprised: 'les Hollandais n'agissent en cette occasion que par leur propre intérêt; et comme ils ont peu ou point de bâtiments en Levant, et qu'en leur pays ils ne regardent qu'au compte des marchands, ils n'ont garde d'envoyer et de faire la dépense d'une escadre de ce côté-là.'[3]

In the summary given in Cobbett's *Parliamentary History* of

[1] *English Historical Review*, CLIII (1924), 287. There is not space here to elaborate on this theme, but reference to one striking instance will serve to bring out the nature of the evidence available. In the 1740s, during the War of the Austrian Succession, English marine insurance companies insured French vessels against capture at sea by the British navy, and Parliament, after protracted debate, refused to make the practice illegal. Cf.: *Parliamentary History* (Cobbett, ed.), XII, 7–26 (for 1741); [Corbyn Morris], *Essay towards Illustrating the Science of Insurance, particularly whether it be Nationally Advantageous to Insure Ships of our Enemies* (London, 1747); Admiral H. W. Richmond, *The Navy in the War of* 1739–48 (Cambridge, England, 1920), III, 248–50; C. Ernest Fayle, 'The Deflection of Strategy by Commerce in the Eighteenth Century', and ibid., 'Economic Pressure in the War of 1739–48,' *Journal of the Royal United Service Institution*, LXVIII (1923), 281–94, 434–46; Charles Wright and C. Ernest Fayle, *A History of Lloyds* (London, 1928), pp. 80 ff.

[2] Cited by F. M. Powicke, 'The Economic Motive in Politics', *Economic History Review*, XVI (1946), 91.

[3] A. Jal, *Abraham Du Quesne et la Marine de son Temps* (Paris, 1883), I, 470.

the principal arguments made in Parliament in favour of moderating the peace settlement to be made with France to end the Seven Years' War, a contrast was made as to the policy proper for England and that for a country like Holland. The economic value of the British conquests of French colonies in America was great. Nevertheless it was to be remembered:

> ... that the value of our conquests thereby ought not to be estimated by the present produce, but by their probable increase. Neither ought the value of any country to be solely tried on its commercial advantages; that extent of territory and a number of subjects, are matters of as much consideration to a state attentive to the sources of real grandeur, as the mere advantages of traffic; that such ideas are rather suitable to a limited and petty commonwealth, like Holland, than to a great, powerful, and warlike nation. That on these principles, having made very large demands in North America, it was necessary to relax in other parts.[1]

There was general agreement that in France economic considerations played a lesser role in foreign policy than in England and Holland. In part, this was to be explained by the lesser importance even economically of foreign trade to France and by the lesser role of French merchants in French politics. George Lyttleton, an English observer at the Soissons Congress of 1729, where the question of the maintenance of the alliance with England was at issue, reported to his father:

> Affairs are now almost at a crisis, and there is great reason to expect they will take a happy turn. Mr Walpole has a

[1] *Parliamentary History of England*, XV (1813), 1271–2 (for 9 December, 1762). For similar views as to the propriety of a country like Holland confining her foreign policy to commercial matters and to defence, without attempting to participate otherwise in *Haute Politique*, see the instructions prepared in 1771 by the French Foreign Office for the French Ambassador to Holland, *Recueil des Instructions Données aux Ambassadeurs et Ministres de France*, XXIII (Paris, 1924), 308.

For the comments of the Anglophile Prince of Orange in the course of his attempts to keep Holland neutral during the War of the American Revolution, which proved unsuccessful because of both pressure from France and the financial ambitions of the commercial classes in Holland, see *Archives ou Correspondance Inédite de la Maison d'Orange-Nassau*, 5th Series, F. J. L. Kramer, ed. (Leyde, 1910), I, 607 ff., 618, 635 ff., 677 ff., *et passim*.

surprising influence over the cardinal [Cardinal Fleury, in charge of French foreign policy]; so that, whether peace or war ensue, we may depend upon our ally. In truth, it is the interest of the French court to be faithful to their engagements, though it may not entirely be the nation's. Emulation of trade might incline the people to wish the bond that ties them to us were broke; but the mercantile interest has at no time been much considered by this court . . . The supposition, that present advantage is the basis and end of state engagements, and that they are only to be measured by that rule, is the foundation of all our suspicions against the firmness of our French ally. But the maxim is not just. Much is given to future hopes, much obtained by future fears; and security is, upon many occasions, sought preferably to gain.[1]

Frenchmen in the period occasionally professed readiness to yield to Britain predominance in maritime trade if Britain would give France a free hand on the Continent,[2] but it would be a mistake to conclude that this reflected a readiness to concentrate on political objectives alone. Even on the Continent there were economic prizes to be won, though less glittering ones than those naval power could win overseas.

Historians, moreover, may have been too ready to find sharp differences in kind between the role of economic considerations in the making of foreign policy in England and France, respectively, in the age of mercantilism. The differences, though probably substantial, seem in the matters here relevant to have

[1] *The Works of George, Lord Lyttelton,* G. E. Ayscough, ed., 3rd edn. (London, 1776), III, 243–4.

[2] An instance in point is in a dispatch by Louis XIV to his ambassador in London, in 1668: 'Si les Anglais voulaient se contenter d'etre les plus grand marchands de l'Europe, et me laisser pour mon partage ce que je pourrais conquérir dans une juste guerre, rien ne serait si aisé que de nous accommoder ensemble.' Cited by C.-G. Picavet, *La Diplomatie Française au Temps de Louis XIV* (Paris, 1930), p. 171.

About a century later, in 1772, George III of England, alarmed by the coalition of Austria, Prussia, and Russia to partition Poland, expressed sympathy for the idea of an alliance between Britain and France despite their traditional enmity: 'Commerce the foundation of a marine can never flourish in an absolute monarchy; therefore that branch of grandeur ought to be left to England whilst the great army kept by France gives her a natural pre-eminence on the Continent' (Sir John Fortescue, ed., *The Correspondence of King George the Third* (London, 1927), II, 428–9.)

been differences in degree rather than in kind. In particular, the extent of the influence which commercial interests in France could in one way or another exercise on policy has been seriously underestimated by many historians, and both in theory and in practice absolutist government was not as absolute in power nor as non-commercial in motivation as the school text-books have taught us. French records have been misleading in this regard because the older generation of historians were not interested in economic issues and tended to leave out of their compilations of documents matter of a markedly economic character, and French historians seem for some time to have been moving towards a reconsideration of the role of economic factors in the formulation of foreign policy under the Ancien Régime.[1]

There may have been monarchs who recognized no moral obligation to serve their people's interests, and there were no doubt ministers of state who had no loyalties except to their careers and perhaps to their royal masters. Frederick the Great is said to have declared, with brutal frankness, that 'Je regarde les hommes comme une horde de cerfs dans le parc d'un grand seigneur et qui n'ont d'autre fonction que de peupler et de remplir l'enclos', and there is little in the King's voluminous writings which makes this incredible.[2] Some monarchs were,

---

[1] For representative contemporary evidence in support of these points, see: *Mémoires de Louis XIV*, Jean Longnon, ed. (Paris, 1927), p. 73; a proclamation of Louis XIV reprinted in P. M. Bondois, 'Colbert et l'industrie de la dentelle', *Mémoires et Documents pour Servir à l'Histoire du Commerce et de l'Industrie en France*, VI (1921), 263; Vauban, 'Description Géographique de l'Élection de Vézeley' [1696], in A. de Boislisle, *Mémoires des Intendants sur l'État des Généralités* (Paris, 1881), I, 738–49; G. Lacour-Goyet, *L'Éducation Politique de Louis XIV*, 2nd edn. (Paris, 1923), pp. 341 ff. For reconsiderations of the traditional views by modern historians, see A. Jal, *Abraham du Quesne et la Marine de son Temps* (Paris, 1883), II, 352–3; P. Muret (a book review), *Revue d'Histoire Moderne*, IV (1902–3), 39–43; J. Hitier, 'La Doctrine de l'Absolutisme', *Annales de l'Université de Grenoble*, XV (1903), 106–13, 121–31; Charles Normand, *La Bourgeoisie Française au XVIIe Siècle*, 1604–1661 (Paris, 1908), pp. 195, 279–87; Henri Hauser, *La Pensée et l'Action Économique du Cardinal de Richelieu* (Paris, 1944), pp. 185 ff.; Philip Dun, 'The Right of Taxation in the Political Theory of the French Religious Wars', *Journal of Modern History*, XVII (1945), 289–303.

[2] Frederick the Great did recognize, however, at least in principle and in his better moments, that the economic well-being of his people should be one of the major objectives of a monarch. See his 'Essai sur les Formes de Gouvernement et sur les Devoirs des Souverains', of which he had printed a few copies only in 1777, *Œuvres*, IX (1848), 195–210.

D

to modern taste, childish in the weight they gave to the routine symbols of prestige and protocol.[1] The personal idiosyncrasies of rulers and, above all, dynastic ambitions, exerted their influence on the course of events. Occasionally religious differences made the course of diplomacy run a little less smoothly by injecting an ideological factor into the range of matters out of which disputes could arise or by which they could be sharpened. But it seems clear that predominantly diplomacy was centred on and governed by considerations of power and plenty throughout the period and for all of Europe, and that religious considerations were more often invoked for propaganda purposes than genuinely operative in fashioning foreign policy. Even the cardinals, who in some degree monopolized the diplomatic profession on the Continent, granted that religious considerations must not be permitted to get in the way of vital national interests, and even genuine missionary enterprises could get seriously entangled with the pursuit of commercial privileges. When Louis XIII in 1626 sent an emissary to Persia with the primary purpose of promoting the Catholic religion, he instructed him at the same time to seek special privileges for French trade as compensation for the diplomatic difficulties with the English and the Dutch which would result from a French attempt to catholicize Persia. 'Sa Majesté pensait qu'on ne pouvait éviter cet inconvénient qu'en se rendant maître du commerce du pays, lequel, outre le gain des âmes, qui

---

[1] To a letter from Louis XIII in 1629 proposing closer commercial relations, Tsar Michel Federowitz of Russia replied favourably, but complained about the manner in which he had been addressed: 'Mais nous ne savons à quoi attribuer que notre nom, nos titres et nos qualités aient été oubliés a la lettre que vous nous avez écrit. Tous les potentats de la terre . . . écrivant à notre grande puissance, mettre notre nom sur les lettres et n'oublient aucun des titres et des qualités que nous possédons. Nous ne pouvons approuver votre coutume de vouloir être notre ami, et de nous dénier et ôter les titres que le Dieu tout-puissant nous a donnés et que nous possédons si justement. Que sí, à l'avenir, vous désirez vivre en bonne amitié et parfaite correspondance avec notre grande puissance, en sorte que nos royales personnes et nos empires joint ensemble donnent de la terreur à tout l'univers, il faudra que vous commandiez qu'aux lettres que vous nous récrirez à l'avenir toute la dignité de nostre grande puissance, notre nom, nos titres et nos qualités soient écrits comme elles sont en cette lettre que nous vous envoyons de notre part. Nous vous ferons le semblable en écrivant tous vos titres et toutes vos qualités dans les lettres que nous vous manderons, etant le propre des amis d'augmenter plutôt réciproquement leurs titres et qualités que de les diminuer ou retrancher.' *Recueil des Instructions*, VIII (1890), 29.

est celui que sa Majesté recherchait, offrirait encore à son royaume de notables avantages.'[1]

The role of the religious factor in Cromwell's foreign policy has been much debated. The literature of historical debate on this question is voluminous, but it is not apparent to the layman that any progress towards a definitive decision has been made, unless it is that Cromwell was a complex personality on whom economic, religious, and power considerations all had their influence, but in varying degrees and combinations at different times. George L. Beer quotes Firth as saying about Cromwell that: 'Looked at from one point of view, he seemed as practical as a commercial traveller; from another, a Puritan Don Quixote', and gives as his own verdict that 'It was "the commercial traveller" who acted, and the "Puritan Don Quixote" who dreamt and spoke'.[2] Other historians have given other interpretations.[3]

[1] G. de R. de Flassan, *Histoire Générale et Raisonnée de la Diplomatie Française*, 2nd edn. (Paris, 1811), II, 396.

In 1713 Charles XII of Sweden wrote to Queen Anne demanding that England, in conformity with her treaty obligations, give him assistance in regaining his territories in the Germanic Empire. 'It was not possible,' he said, 'that Anne could allow her mind to be influenced by the sordid interests of trade; the protectress of the Protestant religion could not fail to support the Protestant power of the north,' as against Russia. But Russia at the time was seeking admittance into the Grand Alliance against Louis XIV, and England, alarmed at the ambitions of both monarchs, made no choice. See Mrs D'Arcy Collyer, 'Notes on the Diplomatic Correspondence between England and Russia in the First Half of the Eighteenth Century', *Transactions of the Royal Historical Society*, New Series, XIV (1900), 146 ff.

[2] 'Cromwell's Policy in its Economic Aspects', *Political Science Quarterly*, XVII (1902), 46–7.

[3] Cf. John Morley, *Oliver Cromwell* (New York, 1901), p. 434; Guernsey Jones, *The Diplomatic Relations between Cromwell and Charles X. Gustavus of Sweden* (Lincoln, Neb., 1897), pp. 34–5; Frank Strong, 'The Causes of Cromwell's West Indian Expedition', *American Historical Review*, IV (1899), 245; M. P. Ashley, *Financial and Commercial Policy under the Cromwellian Republic* (Oxford, 1934); [Slingsby Bethel], *The World's Mistake in Oliver Cromwell* [1668], in *The Harleian Miscellany* (London, 1810), VII, 356–7.

I have not been able to find any systematic or comprehensive study of the role of the religious factor in power politics. The following references are a fair sample of the material bearing on this which I have come across: Leon Geley, *Fancan et la Politique de Richelieu de 1617 à 1627* (Paris, 1884), pp. 264–90; 'Discours sur ce qui peut sembler estre plus expedient, & à moyenner au sujet des guerres entre l'Empereur & le Palatin', [1621], in *Recueil de Quelques Discours Politiques* (no place given, 1632), pp. 314 ff; C. C. Eckhardt, *The Papacy and World Affairs as Reflected in the Secularization of Politics* (Chicago, 1937), p. 89; S. Rojdestvensky and Inna Lubimenko, *Contribution à l'Histoire des Relations Commerciales*

I have unfortunately not been able to find an orthodox neo-Marxian study dealing with these issues for this period. If there were one such, and if it followed the standard pattern, it would argue that 'in the last analysis' the end of foreign policy had been not power, and not power and plenty, but plenty alone, and plenty for the privileged classes only, and it would charge that members of these classes would always be there in every major diplomatic episode, pulling the strings of foreign policy-making for their own special benefit. Writing a few years ago in criticism of this theory as applied to more recent times, I ventured the following comment: 'While I suspect that Marx himself would not have hesitated to resort to the "scandal" theory of imperialism and war when convenient for propaganda purposes, I am sure that he would basically have despised it for its vulgar or unscientific character.'[1] I was 'righter' than I deserved to be.

Karl Marx studied the British diplomacy of this period, even making use of the unpublished records in the British Foreign Office, and discussed the role played by commercial objectives in British foreign policy. The ruling oligarchy needed political allies at home, and found them in some section or other of the *haute bourgeoisie*.

As to their *foreign policy*, they wanted to give it the appearance at least of being altogether regulated by the mercantile interest, an appearance the more easily to be produced, as the exclusive interest of one or the other small fraction of that class would, of course, be always identified with this or that Ministerial measure. The interested fraction then raised the commerce and navigation cry, which the nation stupidly re-echoed.

Franco-Russes au XVIIIe Siècle (Paris, 1929), p. 4; *Mémoires de Noailles* (Paris, 1777), I, 126; Cheruel, 'Le Baron Charles D'Avangour Ambassadeur de France en Suède' (1654–7), *Revue d'Histoire Diplomatique*, III (1889), 529; [Jean Rousset de Missy], *The History of Cardinal Alberoni* (London, 1719), p. 105; W. E. Lingelbach, 'The Doctrine and Practice of Intervention in Europe', *Annals of the American Academy*, XVI (1900), 17, note; 'Les Principes Généraux de la Guerre', *Œuvres de Frédéric le Grand*, XXVIII (Berlin, 1856), 50; C.-G. Picavet, *La Diplomatie Française au Temps de Louis XIV* (Paris, 1930), pp. 8, 160–6; Georges Pagès, *La Monarchie d'Ancien Régime en France* (Paris, 1928), pp. 67 ff.

[1] 'International Relations between State-Controlled National Economies', *American Economic Review Supplement*, XXXIV (1944), 324.

Eighteenth-century practice thus 'developed on the Cabinet, at least, the *onus* of inventing *mercantile pretexts*, however futile, for their measures of foreign policy'. Writing in the 1850s, Marx found that procedure had changed. Palmerston did not bother to find commercial pretexts for his foreign policy measures.

In our own epoch, British ministers have thrown this burden on foreign nations, leaving to the French, the Germans, etc., the irksome task of discovering the *secret* and *hidden* mercantile springs of their actions. Lord Palmerston, for instance, takes a step apparently the most damaging to the material interests of Great Britain. Up starts a State philosopher, on the other side of the Atlantic, or of the Channel, or in the heart of Germany, who puts his head to the rack to dig out the mysteries of the mercantile Machiavelism of 'perfide Albion', of which Palmerston is supposed the unscrupulous and unflinching executor.[1]

Marx, in rejecting the economic explanation of British friendship for Russia, fell back upon an explanation of both a sentimental pro-Russianism in high circles in Britain and an unjustified fear of Russian power. It is a paradox that the father of Marxism should have sponsored a doctrine which now sounds so non-Marxian. I cannot believe, however, that the appeals to economic considerations which played so prominent a part in eighteenth-century British discussions of Anglo-Russian relations were all pretext, and I can find little evidence which makes it credible that friendly sentiment towards foreigners played a significant role in the foreign policy of England in the eighteenth century. Leaving sentiment aside, England's foreign policy towards Russia in the eighteenth century, like English and European foreign policy in general, was governed by joint and harmonized considerations of power and economics. That the economics at least was generally misguided, and that it served to poison international relations, is another matter which, though not relevant *here*, is highly relevant now.

[1] Karl Marx, *Secret Diplomatic History of the Eighteenth Century*, Eleanor Marx Aveling, ed. (London, 1899), pp. 55–6. The italics are in the original.

4 Eli Heckscher and the Idea of Mercantilism

D. C. COLEMAN

[This article was first published in the *Scandinavian Economic History Review*, Vol. V, No. 1, 1957.]

It is more than a quarter of a century since the late Professor Eli Heckscher's *Mercantilism* first appeared, in Swedish (1931), and nearly as long since it became available in German (1932) and in English (1935). The recent publication of a revised English edition[1] offers an opportunity for a reappraisal both of the work and of the concept with which it is concerned. The latter has loomed large in the writing of economic history and in the study of economic thought. What is its value? What did it become in Heckscher's hands?

I

Adam Smith saw political economy as having two distinct objects: to provide revenue or subsistence for the people or to enable them to provide these for themselves; and to supply the state with revenue for the public services. There were two different systems by which these ends were achieved: the commercial or mercantile system and the system of agriculture. The former was 'the modern system'.[2] He spent the whole of Book IV of the *Wealth of Nations* constructing it, examining it, and denouncing it. In reality, the 'system' was the reverse of

[1] E. F. Heckscher, *Mercantilism*, Revised Edition, ed. E. F. Söderlund (London, 1955). All page references given in the present article are to this edition.

I would like to thank Professor Söderlund, as well as my colleagues Mr J. Potter and Professor F. J. Fisher for advice and assistance in connection with this article, although no responsibility attaches to them for the opinions expressed therein.

[2] Adam Smith, *An Inquiry into the Nature and Causes of the Wealth of Nations*, 1776, ed. E. Cannan. Modern Library Edition (New York, 1937), p. 397.

systematic: a jumble of devices, assembled over the course of a century or more to meet the demands of state finance, sectional interests and power politics. But there was enough theoretical similarity in its constituent parts for Smith, superb systematizer that he was, to be able to present it as a systematic absurdity.

But Smith's presentation of the mercantile system was limited in scope. It assumed, he said, that wealth consisted in gold and silver; and that, for a country not possessing gold and silver mines, the favourable balance of trade was the only way of securing this wealth. Therefore it became the object of political economy to discourage imports and encourage exports. And this was done by the following means: two sorts of restraints upon imports – high duties and prohibitions; and four sorts of encouragement for exports – bounties, drawbacks, treaties, and colonies.[1] Smith saw the system thus defined as prevailing from the end of the seventeenth century, presumably supposing that economic life was previously unencumbered by it, for he admitted that he thought it improbable that 'freedom of trade should ever be entirely *restored* in Great Britain' (my italics).[2] Though exempting from his condemnation the Navigation Act of Charles II, on the grounds of political expediency,[3] he damned this apparatus of government action comprehensively and vigorously. He damned it in order to construct, on the wreckage of its absurdities, his own theoretical structure of economic *laissez-faire*. Though he wrote the following words in particular relation to English colonial rule, they summarize adequately his particular blend of economic and moral fervour:

> To prohibit a great people . . . from making all that they can of every part of their own produce or from employing their stock and industry in the way that they judge most advantageous to themselves is a manifest violation of the most sacred rights of mankind.[4]

The Wealth of Nations preached doctrines allegedly of universal validity and in practice peculiarly apt for the expanding, industrializing Britain of the time. It became the Bible of a new politico-economic era. For nearly a century after its publication

---

[1] Smith, op. cit., pp. 418–19.   [2] Ibid., p. 437.
[3] Ibid., pp. 429–31.   [4] Ibid., p. 549.

little was heard in Britain of the outdated 'mercantile system', save for occasional shouts by some of the popularizers of classical economics, deriding the evident fatuity of its supposed principles. In the later decades of the nineteenth century, however, it reappeared on the stage, refurbished by the opponents of *laissez-faire*, and inflated by them into a gigantic theoretical balloon. Its reappearance was a reflection of the changing economic relationships of the time; the rising power and wealth of Germany was being developed with substantial government protection; and the challenge to British economic supremacy, both from Europe and from across the Atlantic, brought a challenge to the creed of *laissez-faire* – a notion taken over from a Frenchman, developed by a Scotsman, and put into practice by the English.

Although there were writers outside the German historical school who had earlier questioned the classical economists' denigration of the economics of an earlier era, Gustav Schmoller in Germany and William Cunningham in England may be taken as the outstanding actors in the revival of the idea of 'the mercantile system'.

Archdeacon Cunningham's *Growth of English Industry and Commerce* was first published in 1882. Cunningham had studied in Germany and, like certain other English historians and economists of the time, had come under the influence of German thought, which had remained unenthusiastic about the merits of Smithianism. To the volume of his work, which covered the period from the sixteenth to the eighteenth centuries, in the 1892 edition, Cunningham gave the title, 'The Mercantile System'. This he came to describe, in the 1903 edition, as 'a national system of economic policy'.[1] The pursuit of power was his *Leitmotiv*; and the apparatus of government economic action developed from Tudor to Hanoverian England was the way in which power was secured. 'The *rationale* of the whole,' he wrote, 'was the deliberate pursuit of national power; the means of attaining this end had been made the object of repeated experiment and now they were organized by statute.'[2]

[1] W. Cunningham, *The Growth of English Industry and Commerce*, 3rd edn. (Cambridge, 1903), ii, 16.
[2] Ibid., 2nd edn. (1892), II, 16.

He saw the flexibility of the Statute of Artificers as serving to maintain it as an effective system of 'industrial regulation' until the advent of machine production made it inapplicable. And the shifting, sectional conflicts of eighteenth-century English economic politics were dressed up as 'Parliamentary Colbertism'.[1]

Schmoller, concerned with the history of Brandenburg from the fifteenth to the seventeenth centuries, came to believe that 'the creation of the German territorial state was not merely a political but also an economic necessity'.[2] And in this process of state-making, the mercantile system – now blown up into *Merkantilismus* – had a vital part to play. Indeed, mercantilism *was* state-making, shaped in the conflict between the growing state policy and that of the town, the district or the various estates. It was the making of 'real political economies as unified organisms' which was at stake. And those who won were the governments which succeeded in putting political power at the service of the economic interests of the nation and state.[3] Accordingly, as he wrote in 1884:

> in its innermost kernel [mercantilism] is nothing but state-making. . .
>
> The essence of the system lies not in some doctrine of money, or of the balance of trade; not in tariff barriers, protective duties, or navigation laws; but in something far greater: namely in the total transformation of society and its organization, as well as of the state and its institutions, in the replacing of a local and territorial economic policy by that of the national state.[4]

Thus to Smith's relatively limited concept of commercial policy were added the new ingredients of national power and state-building. The notion of mercantilism was being expanded. With the growing vigour of national rivalries in the twentieth century and the abandonment, largely under economic and

---

[1] *The Growth of English Industry and Commerce*, (1892 edn.), II, 42; (1903 edn.), II, 403.

[2] G. Schmoller, *The Mercantile System and Its Historical Significance* (translated from *Studien über die wirtschaftliche Politik Friedrichs des Grossen*, 1884) (New York, 1931), p. 43.

[3] Ibid., pp. 50, 72.   [4] Ibid., pp. 50–1.

social pressures, of *laissez-faire* policies, it was not long before a
mirror was held up to the past and the increasingly important
part played by governments in economic and social matters
labelled as 'neo-mercantilistic'. Sundry books and learned
articles examined and developed the ideas and policies of the
'mercantilists'.[1] As a textbook label for three centuries of
European, or at least English, history, 'the age of Mercantilism' proved tenacious: thus did E. Lipson label the second and
third volumes of his *Economic History of England* when they were
published in 1931, treating mercantilism here as 'the pursuit of
economic power in the sense of economic self-sufficiency'.[2]
The broad synthesis of the whole notion was evidently due,
and it came in the form of Heckscher's great work.

Heckscher treated mercantilism under five main heads: as a
system of unification (covering attempts to unify tolls, weights,
and measures, and the like; various other elements in the
transference of municipal to national policies; industrial regulation; the establishment of national trading companies and
other business organizations); as a system of power; as a system
of protection; as a monetary system; and as a conception of
society. The approach was at once sceptical and humane.
Mercantilism's continuity with medieval ideas was stressed; its
alleged achievements analysed and found wanting; its theoretical content compared unfavourably with *laissez-faire*; and its
moral attitude towards humanity castigated. In this process the
notion became still bigger. This was the apogee of the idea of
mercantilism.

II

The building-up of the notion of mercantilism had not proceeded without attack. Cunningham's approach was tartly
condemned by W. A. S. Hewins in 1892, in a review of the new
edition of Cunningham's book in that year.[3] Later George
Unwin poured much cold water on the belief in the efficacy of

---

[1] For some examples, see Heckscher, *Mercantilism*, II, 262–6.
[2] E. Lipson, *The Economic History of England*, 4th edn. (London, 1947), III, 1.
[3] *Economic Journal*, II (1892), 694–700.

policy to do what it was said to do. Unwin's attitude here may
be summed up by his views on 'a tendency which is as misleading as it is all but universal – the tendency to overestimate the
active part which wise forethought and the deliberate pursuit of
clear ideas has played in the economic history of nations'.[1] This
was in 1913, though the remarks did not appear in print until
1927. Sir John Clapham played down the notion of mercantilism, and his textbook on English economic history before 1750
will have little to do with it.[2] But it was with the varied recep-
tion accorded to Heckscher's work, and especially to the
English edition, that there began to show a real reaction against
the tyranny of a long word, as well as a questioning of Heckscher's particular approach.

The questioning came predominantly from the historians
rather than from the economists. The theorists or those whose
interest lay in the history of economic thought beamed upon
this superbly systematic presentation of the idea of mercantilism. Professor A. Montgomery noted that Heckscher had
raised 'some very pertinent objections against any tendency to
overstress the reaction of economic conditions on the growth
of economic thought'.[3] Professors Jacob Viner and B. F. Haley
also picked upon this point as an especially commendable
attribute of the work. Heckscher had succeeded in 'making
mercantilism intelligible';[4] and 'by avoiding the simple explanation of economic policy in terms of the economic conditions
which called forth that policy, Heckscher had successfully
avoided the error of attempting to justify the policy on the
basis that it was the product of economic conditions'.[5] Though
Viner raised an important objection to Heckscher's treatment
of mercantilism as a system of power, for the most part criticism from economists was confined to comment on certain
limitations in the scope of the book, and these were over-

[1] G. Unwin, *Studies in Economic History* (London, 1927), p. 158.
[2] J. Clapham, *A Concise Economic History of Britain from the Earliest Times to
A.D. 1750* (Cambridge, 1949).
[3] *Vierteljahrschrift für Sozial- und Wirtschaftsgeschichte*, XXV (1932), 68.
[4] Viner in *Economic History Review*, VI, No. 1 (1935), 101.
[5] Haley in *Quarterly Journal of Economics*, L (1936), 352; cf. also S. B. Clough in
Journal of Modern History, VIII, No. 3 (1936), 357–8; and C. Brinkman in *Historische
Zeitschrift*, 149 (1934), pp. 123–4.

shadowed by the very justifiable praise for the scholarship, erudition, and skill of the work.

But if the idea of mercantilism thus remained intact for the economists it was given a nasty jolt by the historians, though they, too, expressed admiration for the obvious qualities of Heckscher's work. Marc Bloch cast a doubtful eye upon Heckscher's indiscriminate use alike of economic tracts and of legislative enactments; and on more than one count reproached him for failing to pay adequate heed to historical context, or to 'les grands phénomènes de masse de l'économie et l'influence exercée par les intérêts et les passions des groupes humains'.[1] Professor T. H. Marshall wrote of Heckscher's inability to 'establish a complete synthesis between the three elements, the situation, the ideas and the action, and demonstrate in this synthesis the presence of the unique character which he claims for his subject'. Did mercantilism have historical significance? 'In spite . . . of his enormously illuminating analysis, Professor Heckscher has not established beyond dispute the validity and utility of the term which is the title of his work.'[2] By his very expansion of the notion of mercantilism Heckscher was thus helping to create doubt as to its very existence.

Probably the most penetrating criticism was that which came from Professor Heaton in 1937.[3] Like other critics, he noted the attitude to sources, too readily drawn upon to support Heckscher's general argument, without reference to the context from which they were drawn; he took this further and emphasized the need to examine the effect, on policy and ideas, of short-term fluctuations in economic activity. He drew attention, as had Marc Bloch, to Heckscher's failure to take cognizance of particular groups or classes in society; and he further elaborated upon the absence from the work of discussion of particular governmental problems, as they affected public finance, policies of provision or protection, or the export of bullion. But he reserved his most devastating onslaught for

[1] M. Bloch, 'Le mercantilisme, un état d'ésprit', *Annales d'Histoire Économique et Sociale*, VI (1934), 162.

[2] Marshall in *Economic Journal*, XLV (1935), 718–19.

[3] H. Heaton, 'Heckscher on Mercantilism', *Journal of Political Economy*, XLV, No. 3 (1937), 370–93.

the onus which Heckscher put upon the transition from a natural economy to a money economy and for the unreality of his elaborately theoretical treatment of the desire for precious metals. Heckscher dates his 'policy of provision' from the twelfth century to the mid-fourteenth century, and sees the 'policy of protection' as beginning in the early thirteenth century in Northern Italy, spreading to the Low Countries in the fourteenth and to England in the fifteenth. So, as Heaton pointed out, there was generally only 100 years between the two policies.

Was the crucial change in that hundred years the emergence of a money economy? Was twelfth-century Italy or thirteenth-century Flanders in the grip of natural economy? Did the economies of these two countries change so markedly in such a short space of time that a fundamental change in attitude towards commodities was inevitable? Was the policy of provision as portrayed in the tenth century *Book of the Prefect* of Constantinople due to the fact that the metropolis of the Eastern Empire was operating on a natural economy? Was fourteenth-century England, which supplies Heckscher with his statistics of export control, on a natural economy?[1]

And so, of course, to the recurrent questions: What was mercantilism? Was there ever such a thing? The growth and implications of the idea were discussed at some length by Professor A. V. Judges in a paper published in 1939.[2] He examined it by reference to two main criteria: that a system must be capable of systematic demonstration; and that an '-ism' must 'offer a coherent doctrine or at least a handful of settled principles'. On these points he found the notion wanting. Pointing out that it had no living doctrine or creed, he concluded that it was an imaginary system and pleaded that we should be absolved from having to reconcile the various ideas said to be part of it.

---

[1] *Journal of Political Economy*, pp. 383–4.
[2] A. V. Judges, 'The Idea of a Mercantile State', *Transactions of the Royal Historical Society*, 4th series, XXI (1939), 41–69.

III

With the exception of Viner's point about Heckscher's treatment of the question of power,[1] this general body of criticism
is not significantly reflected in the new edition. Had serious
heed been taken of the more searching criticisms, then as
Heckscher himself wrote, in the preface to the second edition,
'this would have meant an entirely new book. . . . So basic is
this criticism that it might be said of the book as it has been said
of the Jesuits: they must be as they are or not be at all.'[2] Apart
from a number of modifications to the earlier text, particularly
to meet Viner's criticisms, the main difference between the two
editions is the presence of an additional chapter, in Vol. II, on
'Keynes and Mercantilism'. The content of this first appeared
as an article in Swedish, in 1946;[3] it does not suggest any
significant change in Heckscher's approach to the subject (see
below, pp. 103 and 105–6). What, then, of mercantilism and
Mercantilism today?

A question which readily comes to mind when examining
the idea of mercantilism is simply: Is this about economic
thought in the past or is it about economic policy?

The curiously hybrid parentage of the notion provides an
important source of this confusion. It was, as Judges put it,
'conceived by economists for purposes of theoretical exposition
and mishandled by historians in the service of their political
ideals'.[4] One might add, moreover, that it was first mishandled
by historians who were primarily *political* historians and then

---

[1] *Mercantilism* II, 13 and 359–63. This is perhaps a suitable place to point out
that, owing to a publisher's error, an important footnote has been omitted, On
p. 13 of Vol. II, there should be a footnote as follows:

The present chapter has been largely rewritten on the basis of a criticism of the
original chapter by Professor Jacob Viner in his essay 'Power versus plenty as
objectives of foreign policy in the seventeenth and eighteenth centuries'
(*World Politics*, I (1948), 1–29). This article will be discussed in detail later. See
below II, 359 ff. Addendum, para. 1.

The publishers, Messrs. Allen & Unwin, have asked me to state that an *erratum*
notice has been issued, although this will not have been inserted in the earliest
copies purchased.

[2] Ibid., I, 15.

[3] 'Något om Keynes "General Theory" ur ekonomisk-historisk synpunkt',
Ekonomisk Tidskrift, XLVIII (1946), 161–83.

[4] Judges, loc. cit., p. 68.

developed by an economist-cum-economic historian whose *economic ideals* had much in common with those of Adam Smith himself. This is one reason, perhaps, not only for the seeming unreality of the idea to the economic historian of today but also for its meaninglessness or irrelevance to the political historian. So the notion of mercantilism, as developed, is yet another of the wedges helping to keep open the gap between political and economic history. The gap is still wide today. It is not simply the product of an argument about the economic interpretation of history, though it has often been made to seem as though it were. Adam Smith had a low opinion of the wisdom of political action, but a great belief in the efficacy of certain economic principles. In speaking, for instance, about whether retaliation in a tariff dispute should be allowed, he described this as a difficult question of judgement belonging not so much to the science of the legislator, whose deliberations should be governed by general principles which remain constant, but 'to the skill of that insidious and crafty animal, vulgarly called a statesman or politician, whose councils are directed by the momentary fluctuations of affairs'.[1] Cunningham's emphasis fell upon the pre-eminence of politics; he believed in protectionism in his own time and in the merits of political action in other times: 'our national policy is *not* the direct outcome of our economic conditions . . . politics are more important than economics in English history'.[2] Schmoller's political orientation was even more striking. So engrossed was he with the idea of political achievement that he believed that the conception of national economic life, of national agriculture, industry, shipping, fisheries, of national currency and banking systems, of national division of labour and trade must have arisen before 'the need was felt of transforming old municipal and territorial institutions into national and state ones'.[3] To English history, this is largely irrelevant. Whatever its relevance elsewhere, it was in truth all part of the distasteful business by which history is pressed into the service of aggressive nationalism. His words in the 1880s found a sinister echo in the 1930s:

[1] Smith, op. cit., p. 435.
[2] Cunningham, op. cit. (1890 ed.), I, 9.
[3] Schmoller, op. cit., p. 59.

The ideals of Mercantilism . . . meant, practically, nothing
but the energetic struggle for the creation of a sound state
and a sound national economy . . . they meant the belief of
Germany in its own future, the shaking off of a commercial
dependence on foreigners which was continually becoming
more oppressive, and the education of the country in the
direction of economic autarky.[1]

Heckscher's approach resuscitated the Smithian ideas, though
without Smith's concession to political realities, but also took
over Cunningham's insistence on the secondary importance of
economic conditions and Schmoller's interest in state-building.
Consequently, mercantilism in Heckscher's hands is not, as he
claims, 'a phase in the history of economic policy'[2] but is
rather an explanatory term for the phase in economic thought
which was roughly coincident with the early growth of state
power in Europe. The price paid for the extension in range of
the term and for the brilliant explanatory synthesis achieved was
the severe damage done to its relationship with historical reality.

One of the bases of this divorce between ideas and reality
was Heckscher's use of sources. Though he spoke of policy, in
fact as already noted, he pressed into service all forms of
economic pronouncement: statutes, edicts, pamphlets, tracts
for the times. All sources thus become equal. Time and time
again, Heckscher notes the possibility that a particular piece of
economic writing may have borne some relation to the circumstances of the time, only then to insist on the relative unimportance of this factor. Although, for instance, he admits that
Thomas Mun and Sir Josiah Child had good practical reasons
as East India merchants to hold the views on money that they
expounded so skilfully, the events of the time 'played no
essential motivating part in mercantilism as a monetary system
though their influence was not altogether absent'.[3]

And this leads to the key assumption of Heckscher's whole
approach – the insistence that economic policy is not to be seen
as 'the outcome and result of the actual economic situation',[4]
but that what matters is the power and continuity of economic

---

[1] Schmoller, op. cit., p. 76.   [2] *Mercantilism*, I, 19.
[3] Ibid., II, 224.   [4] Ibid., I, 20.

ideas. This is not simply a viewpoint set out in the course of introductory remarks; it is reiterated insistently, hammered home in regard to all aspects of the subject. It will suffice to quote a few examples:[1]

> if economic realities sometimes made themselves felt, this did not divert the general tendency of economic policy. (I, 268)

> As used in this book [protectionism] does not refer to the presence or absence of governmental measures as such. . . . Protectionism is taken to be the outcome of a definite attitude towards goods. . . . (II, 58)

> Our concern here is not with economic realities but with the world of economic ideas. (II, 151)

> We need no longer suppose that some peculiar state of affairs existed, corresponding to the mercantilists' theoretical outlook. (II, 199)

This attitude secures its most extreme expression in the new chapter on 'Keynes and Mercantilism':

> There are no grounds whatsoever for supposing that the mercantilist writers constructed their system – with its frequent and marked theoretical orientation — out of any knowledge of reality however derived. (II, 347)

In practice, it was impossible for Heckscher consistently to maintain this position. Sporadically, he makes concessions to that real world in which meditation upon the complexity of economic forces is sometimes distressingly absent or often pursued in an atmosphere polluted by the baneful winds of interest and expediency. The result is a curiously capricious appeal to reality. Governmental need for revenue is the practical problem to which Heckscher is most willing to make concessions. It is hardly possible to avoid it. But Heckscher's approach means that his treatment of financial policy sits most awkwardly within the general framework which he constructed. Thus, as Heaton pointed out, he goes through forty-two pages of description and discussion of French gild monopolies before admitting

[1] See also: I, 339, 384; II, 30, 44, 54, 101-2, 121, 213, etc.

that financial needs were of paramount importance.[1] Though
Colbert's efforts to create national trading companies in France
may perhaps be made to fit into mercantilism under 'unification', the formation of similar English companies in the late
sixteenth century fits very oddly into that category; and the
rider that in fact these companies 'served as milch cows to the
government in its perpetual financial straits',[2] whatever its
degree of truth, hardly makes their situation in Heckscher's
work more convincing. And the treatment of English protectionism from the late seventeenth century onwards largely in
terms of theoretical ideas and without significant reference to
war finance and Anglo-French politico-economic relations[3]
further emphasizes the fact that this is really a work about
economic thought and not about policy.

   Again, whatever the truth of Heckscher's assertion that the
Netherlands 'did not really follow mercantilist practice' and
were 'less affected by mercantilist tendencies than most other
countries',[4] it is arbitrary largely to ignore Dutch economic
policy, save for some reference to trading companies. Heckscher indeed belittled the importance of regulation and control
in Dutch trade and industry, and ignored changes and conflicts
in Dutch policy which were clearly built not simply upon ideas
but upon the changing economic circumstances of Holland.[5]
Contemporaries had no doubts about the practical realities
which underlay Dutch policy and success. Sir William Temple
wrote of Holland in 1673:

   Thus the trade of this Country is discovered to be no effect
   of common contrivances, of natural dispositions or situations, or of trivial accidents; But of a great Concurrence of
   Circumstances, a long course of Time, force of Orders and
   Method, which never before met in the World to such a
   degree, or with so prodigious a Success and perhaps never
   will again.[6]

[1] Heaton, loc. cit., p. 377.   [2] *Mercantilism*, I, 439.
[3] Ibid., II, 112 ff.   [4] Ibid., I, 351–2.
   [5] See, e.g., C. Wilson, *Anglo-Dutch Commerce and Finance in the Eighteenth
Century* (Cambridge, 1941); also P. D. Huet. *A View of the Dutch Trade*, translated
from the French, 2nd edn. (London, 1722), Chap. III and *passim*.
   [6] W. Temple, *Observations upon the United Provinces*, 2nd edn. (London, 1673),
p. 229.

In this, was he not nearer to reality than Heckscher's appeal to 'the national characteristics of the people'?[1]

Heckscher's insistence upon the unimportance of actual circumstances in shaping policy reflected a strong distaste for anything which he regarded as smacking of economic determinism. It found him defending some indefensible positions, as in his dispute with Charles Wilson over the use of bullion in international trade in the seventeenth century.[2] Apparently what fired him to retort as vigorously as he did was that: 'Mr Wilson starts from the attitude of Lord Keynes and Professor G. N. Clark and, like them, he wants to find an explanation of mercantilist tendencies in the actual economic conditions of the times.'[3] Similarly, he attacked Bruno Suviranta's effort to show that the balance-of-trade theory had its roots in the circumstances of the time.[4] Heckscher conceded that Misselden and Mun created 'the mercantilist monetary and commercial doctrine in its narrowest sense';[5] and recent research has shown that in fact much of Mun's formulation of the balance-of-trade doctrine sprang directly from his inquiries into the depression of 1622–3.[6]

The final irony in Heckscher's determination to stand by his principles at whatever cost, is reached in his chapter on 'Keynes

[1] *Mercantilism*, I, 353.

[2] C. Wilson, 'Treasure and Trade Balances: the Mercantilist Problem', *Economic History Review*, 2nd series, II (1949); E. F. Heckscher, 'Multilateralism, Baltic Trade, and the Mercantilists', ibid., 2nd series, III (1950); C. Wilson, 'Treasure and Trade Balances: Further Evidence', ibid., 2nd series, IV (1951).

In fact not only, as Wilson demonstrated, were Englishmen and Dutchmen aware of the need for bullion in seventeenth-century Baltic trade, but so too were Frenchmen. If Colbert wanted to develop French trade with Sweden, then, as his emissary in Denmark wrote to him in 1669, it could be done, provided 'Monsieur Colbert were willing to allow a less constraint in the manner of business, and to approve, instead of that which is carried on by the exchange of goods, that which is done in cash'. Quoted, C. W. Cole, *Colbert and a Century of French Mercantilism* (New York, 1939), II, 95.

[3] *Economic History Review*, 2nd series, III (1950), 219.

[4] B. Suviranta, *The Theory of the Balance of Trade* (Helsinki, 1923); Heckscher, *Mercantilism*, II, 266. This criticism appeared in the first edition, but is repeated twice in the new edition, II, 266 and II, 354.

[5] *Mercantilism*, II, 248.

[6] B. E. Supple, 'Thomas Mun and the Commercial Crisis, 1623', *Bulletin of the Institute of Historical Research*, XXVII (1954); also R. W. K. Hinton, 'The Mercantile System in the Time of Thomas Mun', *Economic History Review*, 2nd series, VII, (1955).

and Mercantilism'. Having vigorously denounced Keynes for
supposing that the mercantilists, or indeed any other economic
writers, ever reached their conclusions by their perceptions of
actual experience, he then executed a complete volte-face in
regard to Keynes's own work. The *General Theory* 'should be
read in its historical context . . . its *specific* motivation is to be
found in the persistent unemployment in England between the
two World Wars'.[1]

Of more fundamental importance perhaps than any of these
anomalous positions into which Heckscher thus led himself by
insistence on this key assumption was that which arose from
the problem inherent in the assumption itself. If at any given
time the approach to a problem is to be assessed not in terms of
any contemporary awareness of reality but in terms of the
continuity of ideas the question immediately arises: how did
those ideas themselves arise in the first place? Did they spring
fully armed into the mind of man? Or was there some unregen-
erate past in which reality and mentality had some more positive
relationship? Heckscher votes, though hardly enthusiastically,
for the latter. The answer lies in that blurred historical distance
where life was somehow different – the Middle Ages:

> town policy was also determined by certain ethical considera-
> tions . . . [which] arose from the general social ethic of the
> Middle Ages . . . these considerations also finding some
> support in the economic circumstances of the time. (I, 129)
>   In the Middle Ages, the economic life and political out-
> look of the town had been largely a product of the conditions
> of the time. . . . (I, 135)

This enables Heckscher, in dealing with the regulation of
economic life, consistently to appeal to the 'medieval heritage'
as a determinant of action. But it raises a pretty problem in the
transition from the 'policy of provision' which he associates
peculiarly with medieval towns, to the 'policy of protection' of
the 'mercantilist' era. And here the *deus ex machina* which is
invoked to explain the change is the transition from natural to
money economy:

[1] *Mercantilism*, II, 346, 357–8.

the facts were seen much more clearly by medieval observers than by those of later times, because the conditions in precisely this connection were so much simpler.

It was the condition of *natural economy* which brought out these facts. . . . (II, 103)

The doubts which Heaton threw upon Heckscher's assumption of the prevalence of 'natural economy' in medieval Europe have been fully supported in the twenty years since Heaton wrote;[1] indeed, the twin notions of 'natural economy' and 'money economy' now seem to be of rather dubious validity and limited application. In his concern with 'natural economy', Heckscher was heavily influenced by his work on sixteenth-century Sweden'[2] and it would seem in retrospect that, valuable as that work is, it does not in all aspects provide a safe basis for generalizations about European economic life as a whole.

But if Heckscher wished to invoke this transition in order to explain one sort of change in economic policy he was unwilling to use it to explain the 'mercantilist's' desire for bullion. This led him to further contradictions of his own position. Having correlated the rise of a money economy with protectionism and dated it from thirteenth-century Italy, extending to France and England in the fifteenth century,[3] when he comes to deal with monetary questions he asserts that it was the sixteenth and seventeenth centuries which formed, 'at least in many countries . . . the period of transition from a predominantly natural to a predominantly money economy and at the same time from an insignificant to an extremely abundant silver production'.[4] It is

[1] See, for example, Marc Bloch, 'Économie-nature ou économie-argent: un pseudo-dilemme', *Annales d'Histoire Sociale*, I (1939); M. M. Postan, 'The Rise of a Money Economy', *Economic History Review*, XIV (1944); M. Postan and E. Rich (eds.), *Cambridge Economic History of Europe*, II (Cambridge 1952); R. de Roover, *Money, Banking and Credit in Medieval Bruges* (Cambridge, Mass. 1948).

[2] 'Natural and Money Economy as Illustrated from Swedish History in the Sixteenth Century', *Journal of Economic and Business History*, III (1930–1), reprinted in F. C. Lane and J. C. Riemersma (eds.) *Enterprise and Secular Change* (London, 1953). The essence of this had already appeared in articles in Swedish and in German, and was subsequently embodied by Heckscher in his *Sveriges ekonomiska historia* (Stockholm, Part I, 1935–6, Part II, 1949), see especially I, i, Chap. 3.

[3] *Mercantilism*, II, 139, and II, 145.

[4] Ibid., II, 177.

perhaps scarcely surprising that he was later moved to observe that 'the transition to a money economy never occurs at once and can hardly be assigned to any definite period whatsoever'.[1] He demonstrated instead that the 'mercantilists' wanted bullion for a set of theoretical reasons, the exposition of which by contemporary writers was substantially later than the supposed transition from natural to money economy and the influx of precious metals from the West.[2] And so, again, 'the circumstances of the time were not decisive'.[3]

If the continued concern with natural economy makes the new edition of *Mercantilism* seem rather old-fashioned, so also does its invocation of 'medieval universalism'. The latter still has a tight hold on history, but its grip is slowly being loosened.[4] To Heckscher, however, it was real enough:

> the medieval combination of universalism and particularism. . . . (I, 22)
> the fundamental unity of medieval culture. . . . (I, 327)
> those universalist factors such as the Church and the empire which had fashioned medieval society. . . . (II, 13)
> the Middle Ages with their universal static ideal. . . . (II, 26)
>
> As for the general conception of society, a sharp division obtains between the Middle Ages and the following period. . . . (II, 271)

Once again, because of his unwillingness to take into account the differing elements of continuity or of change in economic circumstances, he was led to adopt mutually confusing positions. Though he attributes to the medieval world and 'the medieval mind'[5] these especial and temporally limited qualities, he also endows them with remarkable staying powers in themselves and irrespective of that transition from natural to money economy which is otherwise supposed to have transformed

[1] *Mercantilism*, II, 219.   [2] Ibid., II, 177, 219, 221.
[3] Ibid., II, 177.
[4] See, e.g., G. Barraclough, *History in a Changing World* (Oxford, 1955), esp. pp. 128–30.
[5] *Mercantilism*, II, 112.

medieval conceptions. Thus if middlemen in the trade in food-stuffs were attacked in Tudor and Stuart England it was not because of special circumstances but because of a 'medieval conception';[1] and the general reason for the persistence or recurrence of elements of the 'policy of provision' was to be found not in any external conditions but because 'municipal economic principles stood out as almost the only clear principles of economic policy, and remained so for centuries, even after the political influence of the cities had ceased'.[2]

Heckscher emphasized the need to distinguish between economic conditions or economic reality and the attempts made by governments to influence or alter those conditions. This distinction is made briefly in *Mercantilism* and more clearly in the *Sveriges ekonomiska historia*, where he further stresses the dangers of using information about policy as a means of getting to know about economic reality.[3] Acts of economic policy are statements of intention and not descriptions of reality. They will be a reflection of what is not to be found in the economy rather than what is. This is important and salutary advice when considering the development or structure of a country's economy, but it does leave policy as an entity in itself, exogenous, a determinant rather than in any way determinate. Heckscher admitted that the policy and conditions were 'inextricably bound up', but his approach is most clearly stated thus: 'economic policy is determined not so much by the economic facts as by people's conception of those facts'.[4] Now Heckscher had a low opinion of the economic perception of those who lived in the 'mercantilist' era. Consequently, because of his reluctance to concede that the ideas and policies of the time might owe something to contemporary awareness of economic reality, however crude or empirical, Heckscher did not bring out at all clearly certain fundamental distinctions both in ideas and in circumstances in the so-called 'mercantilist' period. He stressed the importance, for example, of the static conception of economic life, of economic resources and activity so evident at that time; he emphasized that this provided one reason for

---

[1] *Mercantilism*, I, 267.   [2] Ibid., II, 102.
[3] Ibid., I, 20; *Sveriges ekonomiska historia I*, I, 12–13.
[4] *Mercantilism*, II, 59.

the many commercial wars; implicit in the 'tragedy of mercantilism' was the belief that what was one man's or country's gain was another's loss.[1] Yet, vital as this is, as he himself says, to an understanding of the attitudes of the time, he nowhere asks why men should have believed it to be true.

But is it in fact a surprising notion in the pre-industrialized economy? It was, after all, a world in which population remained remarkably static; in which trade and production usually grew only very gradually; in which the limits of the known world were expanded slowly and with great difficulty; in which economic horizons were narrowly limited; and in which man approximated more closely than today to Hobbes' vision of his natural state: for most men most of the time, life *was* 'poor, nasty, brutish, and short'. The pervasive conception of a prevailingly inelastic demand, not readily capable of expansion, changeable not so much by economic forces as by the dictates of authority, is not unreasonable in a political world of absolute monarchs and an economic world in which population and trade did not move rapidly and in which the purchasing power of the overwhelming majority of men and women remained very low and changed very little. Nor were informed contemporaries unaware of such matters. When Botero commented on static population,[2] when Gustav Vasa or John Wheeler defended the merits of 'passive trade',[3] or when Colbert observed that the trade and shipping of Europe could not be increased 'since the number of people in all the states remains the same and consumption likewise remains the same'[4] – is it not reasonable to suppose that their conceptions of economic reality may have approximately coincided with the facts? Conversely, when Heckscher simply assumed that the demand for English cloth was necessarily elastic and chided the mercantilists for not being 'alive to the consequences of this elementary fact of everyday life'[5] – does this suggest a necessarily appropriate conception of economic reality?

[1] *Mercantilism*, II, 23–6.

[2] G. Botero, *The Reason of State* (1589, translated from the Italian by P. J. & D. P. Waley, London, 1956), p. 155.

[3] *Mercantilism*, II, 61, 62 n.; J. Wheeler, *Treatise of Commerce*, ed. G. B. Hotchkiss (New York, 1931), pp. 69 *et seq.*

[4] Quoted Cole, op. cit., I, 363.   [5] *Mercantilism*, II, 241–2.

These characteristics of the pre-industrialized economy, as well as others too numerous and complex to be considered here,[1] were true not simply of the 'mercantilist' times but of earlier centuries. The continuity of ideas which Heckscher was eager to stress was paralleled by a continuity of basic conditions which he ignored. It is upon these substrata of economic life that are built the general conceptions of economic life which men hold. These conceptions are not necessarily the same as what is commonly distinguished as the 'economic thought' of the age. They are the latent assumptions of belief and action, counterparts in the economic sphere to those which underlie philosophy or religion or art.[2] Contemporaries often did not bother to note them because they were too obvious to need noting. The historian has to dig for them. Sometimes, on the other hand, contemporaries did write down such things, and then the problem is to distinguish this from attempts at systematic, rational analysis of economic phenomena. Colbert was an administrator of genius, but he had the ordinary man's view of economic life. Is his vision of reality the same as that of Petty or North or Davenant? This was a distinction which Heckscher did not make. And it is an important one, for he viewed the economic thought and policy of an age in which no systematized body of economic analysis existed through the spectacles of an age in which it does. Consequently, apart from his unwillingness to take into account the special circumstances in which tracts were written or enactments made, he also failed to distinguish between: (*a*) limited descriptions of observed phenomena (e.g. descriptions by contemporaries of exchange movements); (*b*) accounts or explanations drawing upon the long-held, deeply embedded economic preconceptions of the day (e.g. notions embodying the static view of economic activity, or the labour theory of value); and (*c*) attempts at rationalized analysis or calculation (e.g. some of the work of the 'Political Arithmetic' writers). By his methods all were implicitly given the same weight and influence. Implicitly he

[1] For an examination of some aspects of the 'mercantilist' attitude to labour, see D. C. Coleman, 'Labour in the English Economy of the Seventeenth Century', *Economic History Review*, 2nd series, VIII (1956).

[2] Cf. Basil Willey, *The Seventeenth Century Background* (London, 1934), p. 2 and *passim*.

identified a 'conception of economic reality' with the classical
or neo-classical economists' conception. And he did not consider why they might be different.

At the same time as certain basic characteristics of economic
life remained the same during these centuries so also were forces
of change gradually making themselves felt. Two main channels through which they made themselves felt were the great
expansion of trade, to the East, to Africa, and, above all, to the
New World; and the growth of industry in many nations of
Europe. As the economic implications of these new developments gradually became apparent the old ideas of fixity and
limited horizons became intolerable. In the course of the
seventeenth century, for instance, imports from American sugar
and tobacco plantations grew at rates unprecedented in the
economic development of the era;[1] by the end of the century
imports of Indian textiles were creating severe problems for
existing European textile industries. Is it unreasonable to
suppose that such developments left a mark on thought and
policy? Much of the policy of the later seventeenth century is
an attempt to deal with the new developments in terms of old
conceptions; the so-called 'Old Colonial System' is one
example. And the anticipation of 'Free Trade' ideas in late
seventeenth-century England was partly a product of Indian
textile imports.[2] But just as the old lingered with the new in
economic circumstances, so it did in ideas. Faced with the decay
of Dutch trade, the Amsterdam merchants, who in 1751 drew
up proposals for its rejuvenation, still built on old and familiar
conceptions: 'by these general amendments, we shall put ourselves in a condition to *reduce* the trade of Hamburgh, Bremen,
Lübeck, Denmark, and other places; at least to prevent them
doing us a further prejudice'[3] (my italics). Though they put
forward the idea of a free port, the idea of mutual benefit from
general expansion was not present; one port's loss was another's

---

[1] See R. Davis, 'English Foreign Trade, 1660–1700', *Economic History Review*,
2nd series, VII (1954).

[2] P. J. Thomas, *Mercantilism and the East India Trade* (London, 1926), p. 68 and
passim.

[3] Translated and printed as 'Proposals for Redressing and Amending the Trade
of the Republic', 1751 in *A Select Collection of Scarce and Valuable Tracts on Commerce*, ed. J. R. McCulloch (London, 1859).

gain. And this in the country 'less affected by mercantilist ideas'.

Here, then, is another sort of distinction which Heckscher's treatment tends to obscure: the counterpoint of old and new conceptions. It developed particularly in the century from approximately 1650 to 1750, as the implications of European expansion made themselves felt. To compare the prolific 'mercantilist' writings of this period with their far fewer counterparts a century or more earlier can be dangerous if it leads one to believe that because men in the earlier period were not attempting formal analysis of economic life they did not know what was going on in the economic world. Colbert thought it 'in the natural order of things' that each nation should have its share of ships and commerce in proportion to its power, population, and sea-coasts.[1] But the course of economic change was to show that this was an untenable concept, just as the birth of modern scientific ideas was to put an end to that other 'natural order' which was the inheritance of the natural philosophy of Aristotle.

The converse of Heckscher's unwillingness to grant much weight to current economic conditions in the formulation of policy was his insistence upon the importance of economic ideas, and their continuity in informing the actions of policy. How realistic is this for 'mercantilist' Europe? Today, faced with particular economic problems, the governments of advanced societies draw upon the advice not only of business-men or trade unionists but also upon that of professional economists. Moreover, governments are increasingly coming to include men who have either had some formal training in economics or at least are acquainted with its teachings. Until comparatively recent times those teachings have been primarily those of classical economics, extended, modified, refined, but in essence the political economy of *laissez-faire* England. Eli Heckscher was peculiarly a product of this situation. An admirer of England and English economic institutions, an eminent theoretical economist, accustomed to handling prob-lems of government economic policy, he had grown up in a rapidly industrializing Sweden in which various economic

[1] Quoted Cole, op. cit., I, 344.

questions came more or less quickly to the forefront of discussion, and which threw up a number of economists of outstanding ability. It is perhaps hardly surprising that he should have exaggerated the role of economic thought in the formulation of policy.

It would be absurd to suggest that the ideas which men held about economic life had no influence on policy. But they are only one element in policy formulation, and their relative importance varies from place to place and time to time. The great value of Heckscher's work lies in its broad and searching presentation of the nature and complexity of those ideas, in spite of the fact that it is less successful in fitting them into the historical context of practical policy. George Unwin's dictum on policy in action, although going too far in the opposite direction, offers a useful antidote:

> Policy, as actually found in history, is a set of devices into which a government drifts under the pressure of practical problems, and which gradually acquire the conscious uniformity of a type, and begin, at last, to defend themselves as such.[1]

Heckscher's broad and synthesizing approach to mercantilism left virtually no element of economic and social policy 'between the Middle Ages and the end of *laissez-faire*' that could not somehow be brought within its comprehensive embrace. Many acts of policy considered by him under the heading of 'unification' had little in common with each other and sometimes still less to do in practice with 'unification'. It is, for example, only by dint of this vast concept that Heckscher is enabled to write as he does, that 'The French tariff of 1664 ranks with Elizabeth's Statute of Artificers as one of the two unquestionable triumphs of mercantilism in the sphere of economic unification'.[2] But is this true in historical reality? Did the English Statute aim at or achieve unification in the same way as Colbert's enactment was concerned to unify and co-ordinate in matters peculiarly requiring unification and co-ordination? And what are the real links between these two,

[1] Unwin, op. cit., p. 184.   [2] *Mercantilism*, I, 103.

with a century separating them, and all the other edicts, be they about bullion, gilds, patents, cloth inspection, trading companies or catching herrings, which can, by Heckscher's definitions, be labelled as 'mercantilistic'?

Using a shorter historical focus, the Statute of Artificers can be seen as 'a classic example of the restrictive legislation which great depressions tend to produce'.[1] In this context, it was one of various measures taken after the collapse in the English boom in woollen cloth exports during the first half of the sixteenth century. It was part of the reaction to falling trade, increased unemployment, and anxiety about home food supplies following upon much conversion of arable land to sheep pasturage; it was at once a naturally conservative reaction to the problem of public order and poverty as well as a move in the sharpening politico-economic conflict between Burleigh and Granvelle. Using a still shorter focus to examine the details of its enforcement, we find that in practice one of its important clauses – that demanding a seven-year apprenticeship — was enforced more by the pressure of private interests than by the force of public policy.[2] The trading jealousy of competition during periods of declining trade and the greed of the professional informer during the booms were the effective agents of such enforcement as there was of this particular item of 'mercantilism'. The government – central and local – showed itself to be more concerned with the pressing realities of an economy of widespread underemployment and periodic unemployment, with its poverty, vagrancy, and inherent threats to public order. The 'really efficient central administration'[3] of the years of Charles I's personal government meant in practice, so far as the enforcement of apprenticeship was concerned, prosecutions by professional informers and trade rivals, most of which were inconclusive or ineffective in their results.

This was the reality of 'mercantilism'. It is a long way from simple *Staatsbildung*. And does it suggest the intention or achievement of unification in the Statute of Artificers?

[1] F. J. Fisher, 'Commercial Trends and Policy in Sixteenth Century England', *Economic History Review*, X (1940), 113 and *passim*.
[2] M. G. Davies, *The Enforcement of English Apprenticeship*, 1563–1642 (Havard, 1956), p. 268 and *passim*.
[3] *Mercantilism*, I, 256; Davies, op. cit., p. 239.

It was by dint of his synthesizing treatment that 'mercantilism' in Heckscher's hands became, as Professor C. W. Cole observed, 'a real entity . . . which manifested itself through the centuries in various countries'.[1] Heckscher noted this criticism in the new edition, denied knowledge of what was meant by it, and observed that no specific quotation had been given.[2] It is not difficult to find such quotations:

> mercantilism in its struggle against the disintegration within the state . . . (I, 137)

> the incapacity of French mercantilism to master even the particularization of municipal policy . . . (II, 209)

> mercantilism had to leave much of its work of unification for its successors to complete. (I, 456)

> mercantilism would . . . have had all economic activity subservient to the state's interest in power. (II, 15)

> mercantilism often arrived at more erroneous conclusions on economic questions than the medieval mind had ever done. (II, 112)

> we are concerned with the tasks which mercantilism imposed on itself . . . (II, 272)

> mercantilism was indeed a new religion. (II, 155)

In the preface to the first edition, Heckscher voiced his disapproval of 'the method of treating all sorts of disconnected tendencies . . . under the name of "modern capitalism" ': he tended to put 'capitalism' in quotation marks; he spoke of it as a 'Protean conception'.[3] However true these strictures may be, they are equally applicable to his own treatment of mercantilism, though in truth there is little meaning in any comparison between 'mercantilism' and 'capitalism'. Capitalism has been written of and fought about in its own time, rightly or wrongly. It has come near to being a religion; Communism has come far nearer. But no man recognized and defended the cause of mercantilism during its supposed reign; no war was fought under its banner. Mercantilism was *not* a 'new religion'.

---

[1] C. W. Cole, 'The Heavy Hand of Hegel', in *Nationalism and Internationalism*, ed. E. M. Earle (New York, 1950), pp. 74 ff.

[2] *Mercantilism*, II, 59 n.   [3] Ibid., I, 14, 191 n., 221.

So again we come back to asking what was this 'mercantilism'. Did it exist? As a description of a trend of economic thought, the term may well be useful, and worth retaining. As a label for economic policy, it is not simply misleading but actively confusing, a red-herring of historiography. It serves to give a false unity to disparate events, to conceal the close-up reality of particular times and particular circumstances, to blot out the vital intermixture of ideas and preconceptions, of interests and influences, political and economic, and of the personalities of men, which it is the historian's job to examine. It was in 1923 that G. N. Clark (Sir George Clark as he has since become) stressed the dangers of using the concept of the 'mercantile system' in dealing with the protagonists in international politico-economic conflict in the seventeenth century.[1] Heckscher's further inflation of the balloon of 'mercantilism' did much to obscure that admirable advice.

As a contribution to the history of economic thought, there can be no doubt whatsoever that Heckscher's work remains outstanding, still invaluable to the student of the period. Nor can the economic historian afford to ignore it. Nevertheless, for the economic historian, although packed with valuable information, it is curiously unrealistic. Taken as a whole, it is unquestionably a brilliant and stimulating study, a product of scholarship, immensely wide reading in several languages and intellectual ingenuity of a very high order. Yet at one and the same time as its range, subtlety, and learning are formidable and impressive so also is it misleading, a signpost built upon strangely unreal assumptions, pointing to an historical no-man's-land. In real life, policy is carried out by governments and governments are composed of men who, whatever their preconceived ideas and whatever their ultimate aims, deal in particular contexts with particular problems. In *Mercantilism*, Heckscher shunned particular contexts and particular problems: he ignored the composition of governments; and with the significant exception of Colbert, most of those mentioned in his pages were concerned less with governing than with writing economic tracts or with trading.

[1] G. N. Clark, *The Dutch Alliance and the War against French Trade*, 1688–97 (Manchester, 1923), p. 7.

5 The Other Face of Mercantilism

CHARLES WILSON

[This article was first published in the *Transactions of the Royal Historical Society*, fifth series, Vol. IX, 1959.]

'In England,' Sir John Seeley once wrote, 'it is our custom to alter things but to leave their names unaltered.'[1] Anyone who wished to test the truth of the dictum historiographically might examine the history of the word 'mercantilism'. It has borne many, sometimes oddly conflicting, meanings, but they have had at any rate one thing in common: they have all been in some degree unpalatable to those reared in the traditions of English liberal thought. It was as the conspiracy of a mercantile minority out to line its pockets at the expense of the rest of the community that the system was first depicted by the classical economists.[2] The interpretation of the German school of historical economists a century later was certainly no less distasteful to the liberal mind. To Bismarckian Germans it might appear seemly to condone the pursuit of aggression and covet its rewards. But even Chamberlainites – like W. A. S. Hewins – among English historians had their doubts, and to George Unwin state 'policy' was simply a sham – the supreme illustration of the evils of bigness. The economic actions of the political body were not even the early thrustings of a lusty infant, but the morbid twitchings of disease. And Unwin, who believed that historians should be concerned with the life of communities, not with the actions of states, found more sympathizers in his profession (one suspects) than Cunningham, who was nearer to the German tradition. Others, misliking what they took to be the moral and intellectual confusion of mercantilists and their works, agreed to deny any title of coherence to

[1] Sir J. Seeley, *Science of Politics* (1896), p. 298.
[2] A. Smith, *The Wealth of Nations*, Book IV.

folly so diverse and deplorable.[1] Thus the history of national policy was persuasively represented as a series of contests from which greed and stupidity emerged monotonously victorious.

No period or society came out of the inquiry with fewer honours than that of Restoration England and the century that followed: the years when (according to Adam Smith) the principles of the mercantile system were devised and applied in legislative form. When the inquiring beam lighted and focused on the ruling classes it found them treating the wage-earners – I am quoting from Professor Tawney's *Religion and the Rise of Capitalism* – in the same way as coloured labour was treated by the less reputable colonists, consigned to 'collective perdition'. This, Professor Tawney explained, was 'partly the result of the greatly increased influence on thought and public affairs acquired at the Restoration by the commercial classes, whose temper was a ruthless materialism, determined at all costs to conquer world markets from France and Holland and prepared to sacrifice every other consideration to their economic ambitions'.[2] Professor Tawney's verdict was echoed by Mr Beloff when he came to write his study of *Public Order and Popular Disturbance* 1660–1714 in 1938. Again, ruthless mercantile ambition is linked in guilt with the destruction of the central machinery of welfare: the Privy Council. The Civil War brought social *laissez-faire*, and the Restoration failed to restore an independent social policy. 'Rarely indeed,' writes Mr Beloff, 'can national wealth, as opposed to welfare, have predominated to such an extent as it did in the minds of the ruling class of the period.'[3]

The picture that has been created is that of a ruthlessly materialistic ruling class which did not merely neglect but actively exploited the poor. 'Mercantilists,' an authority on economic thought writes, 'if they held any wage theory at all, believed in an economy of low wages.'[4] For Miss Margaret James the social legislators of the Restoration 'aimed at nothing less than making the poor a source of profit to the state by

[1] See A. V. Judges, 'The Idea of a Mercantile State', *Trans. Roy. Hist. Soc.*, 4th series, XXI (1939).

[2] R. H. Tawney, op. cit. (London, 1926), p. 268.

[3] M. Beloff, op. cit., p. 18.

[4] E. Roll, *A History of Economic Thought* (London, 1939), p. 99.

E

forcing them to work for reduced wages'.[1] The presence of a few nobly philanthropic exceptions to this general rule was not enough to soften the indictment. Firmin, the London mercer of Socinian leanings, who experimented in social reform or the Quaker, Bellers, whose *Proposals for a College of Industry* (1695) showed deep concern for social welfare, emerge as entirely exceptional figures, quite untypical of their age. How far is all this a just and representative account of the aims and attitudes of the governing classes of Britain in the years that followed the Restoration?

There is no reason to question the belief that the wealth and power of the state represented the twin objectives of much of the thought and policy of the time, inseparably joined in the contemporary mind. It was deemed by most writers the function of government to intervene in the operation of the economy to secure economical ends that could, they thought, be secured in no other way, and the great majority of those who have made a study of mercantilism would, I think, agree with Adam Smith that the apparatus of legislative intervention consisted of those 'two great engines', the manipulation of exports and imports according to certain principles which would nourish native manufactures. The motive principle of both 'engines' was the same: the balance of trade. The efficacy of the entire system was to be measured by the condition of the 'balance'. Recent over-elaboration of the concept of mercantilism has reawakened old scepticism, raising afresh the question whether it is not merely an arabesque woven by the imagination of historians upon the facts of history. It seems to me as dangerous to deny that certain principles informed both thought and policy in this period as it is to apostrophize those principles and exaggerate their effects. It is equally fallacious to suppose that thought and policy were distinct activities that can and should be treated separately. No body of economic literature was ever more closely related to interest and policy than the writings of the mercantilists. Much (though not all) of it represents the skirmishings of interested parties round the political lobbies; and of all the writers mentioned in this paper

[1] M. James, *Social Policy during the Puritan Revolution* (London, 1930), pp. 344–5.

I can think of only two of whom it could be said that they did not in their own persons exercise some practical influence on economic policy or institutions. The mercantilist writers were neither scribblers nor idealists. They were not sophisticated or labyrinthine. Even their *Utopias* were earthy ones, and it was not accidental that they frequently spelt the word as *Eutopia*. meaning a place where all was well.[1] They felt no call to disguise the material character of their aims. They have little relevance to any times but those in which they lived. Unlike the Diggers, the Levellers, and the other social revolutionaries, they have not attracted the devotional attentions of those historians whose preoccupations are really political rather than historical. If they sin, it is not in being heartless or materialist, but in being a bit dull.

In the early formulations of policy the virtue of a favourable balance was held, quite uncomplicatedly, to reside in the net influx of bullion, which was assumed to be its necessary consequence. This doctrine was still powerful in the period of which we are speaking. Indeed, Mun's classical statement of it, though written perhaps forty years earlier, was published for the first time in 1664. It was in the following year – the year of the Plague – that there was sketched out the first draft of an economic tract which, in its various revisions, was to exercise a powerful influence on thought and policy, not only in England but in many European states also, especially in Italy, France, Germany, and Austria. This was Josiah Child's *New Discourse of Trade* as it became known in later editions. When it first appeared in print, in 1668, it was as a very short affair under the appropriate title of *Brief Observations*, and it dealt principally with problems of interest rates and usury. Attached to it by way of appendix was a note by Culpeper on the problem of usury which contained a section on the relief of the poor. Its general theme will be evident from this text: 'He that is weary of his life fears neither axe nor gibbet: and to prosecute such by the methods of Justice I will not say it is like the Excommunication of Rats but I am sure it resembles the Outlawing of Tories.' Child's work, which is not mentioned by Professor Tawney,

[1] Harold Child, 'Some English Utopias', *Transactions of the Royal Society of Literature*, III (1933).

went into five editions between 1668 and his death in 1699. As edition succeeded edition, two themes grew in importance: the relief and employment of the poor, and the relationship of employment to the national welfare as reflected in the balance of trade. From Culpeper's text, Child develops the theme that it is man's 'Duty to God and Nature to provide for and employ the poor, whose condition is sad and wretched, diseased, impotent, useless'. In the later editions this crystallizes into his famous proposal for an assembly of 'Fathers of the Poor', endowed with powers to buy land, build workhouses and hospitals, and to set the poor on work, with a special *non obstante* to overcome obstructive patents. Simultaneously, Child modified the existing conception of the balance of trade. Sharing the doubts of that considerable body of persons who despaired of ever measuring accurately the volume of imports and exports, Child came to the conclusion that the balance might be judged better by measuring the general volume of trade with reference to the 'number of hands' employed. The juxtaposition of ideas might well begin to look suspicious: on the one hand, proposals for organized charity; on the other, a theory that comes near to equating national prosperity with the effective value of its labour. Add that Child was a City merchant with a reputation for tough and none-too-scrupulous bargaining, who hated competition, Dutch or English, and did not conceal his contempt for the booby squires who muffed the nation's affairs at Westminster, and the liberal mind is prepared for the worst. What emerges, somewhat surprisingly, is an impeccable exposition of the virtues of high wages on the Dutch model. 'Wherever wages are high, universally throughout the whole world, it is an infallible evidence of the riches of that country; and wherever wages for labour run low it is proof of the poverty of that place.'

That the views of Child and his followers did not by any means extinguish the older view of the trade balance or the hopes of those who believed it could be calculated is seen from the contemporary debates on the establishment of the Board of Trade and the Inspector-General of Customs, and from the title of Brewster's *Fifth Essay* of 1702: *That the full employment of All Hands in the Nation is the Surest Way and Means to bring*

Bullion into the Kingdom – a theoretical umbrella under which all shades of opinion might happily sit. But Child's proposals proved to be a matrix of opinions and policy on both of his two main counts. Over the wisdom of providing workhouses and similar institutions, many took issue sharply with him. The great debate on the poor raged for over half a century, between those who believed in workhouses and those who did not; and under interrogation by the liberal historians, neither side could escape the fate of the witness who is asked whether he has stopped beating his wife. To believe in workhouses was to invite suspicions of exploitation; to disbelieve in them is to invite the charge of callous indifference to suffering. Consider, for example, Daniel Defoe, spokesman for what he himself called 'the Middle State or – the Upper Station of Low Life', the author of *Giving Alms no Charity* (1704) and the stoutest opponent of organized charity, often condemned as the arch exponent of selfish, middle-class prejudice. Defoe was too passionate, too inquisitive an observer of the human scene to be guilty of much consistent theorizing. Yet if he had a theory to solve the contemporary and social problem it was a theory of a large population and high wages. To this extent he followed Child: 'All the wealth of the nation and all the trade is produced by numbers of people,' he wrote. His observations of the habits of workmen might be thought to point to the dangers of conspicuous consumption by the poor: he describes how he saw workmen take their wages to the ale-house, 'lie there till Monday, spend it every penny and run in debt to boot and not give a farthing of it to their families, tho' all of them had wives and children'.[1] Yet he did not draw the conclusion that the remedy lay either in lower wages or in poorhouses. Defoe wobbled on many things: on one he was rigidly consistent – that England's commercial prosperity depended on the quality of her export goods. To lower wages would reduce 'the value and goodness of the manufacture' and make them less competitive. 'If you expect the poor should work cheaper and not perform their work slighter and more overly (as we call it) and superficially, you expect what is not in the nature of the Thing – This therefore is beginning at the wrong end of

[1] Quoted in J. Sutherland, *Defoe* (1950), p. 130.

trade . . .'[1] He objected to workhouses for the same reason: their subsidized inferior products would damage that reputation for quality on which English prosperity rested. Logically, he raised no objection to welfare schemes that provided for destitute women or half-wit children. It would, of course, be as false to suggest that everything that was said in the debate of the poor can be regarded as pointing to the Welfare State of the mid-twentieth century as it would to condemn the speakers for consigning the poor wilfully to universal pauperdom and Gin Lane. The 'hard tone' presaging the dismal science at its most arid, which even Cunningham detected in the opponents of charity in these years, is not wholly imaginary. 'When a man is perfectly content with the state he is in,' said Locke, 'what action, what industry, what will is there left but to continue in it?' One of Mandeville's works bore the title *Content the Bane of Industry*, while his *Essay on Charity* (1723) made a bitter attack on those tradesmen, like Firmin, who sponsored charitable institutions out of the hope of gain and that satisfaction 'which delights mean people in governing others'. It will be noticed, all the same, that it is not the merchant writers but the philosophers who speak in the sharpest tones. Here, as not uncommonly, it was logic – the logic of clerks who believed that they had discovered the *spiritus movens* of economic action in human egoism – that put the acid into contemporary social thought. When Pope celebrated the new principles of domestic policy and human conduct in the *Essay on Man* he learnt them not from his father, a devoutly Roman Catholic linen draper, but from Bolingbroke and Christchurch. Yet it would be as presumptuous to withhold from the poet and philosopher his claim to sincerity as it would be uncharitable to exonerate the merchant *ex officio* from the charge of compassion. While the spiritual fathers of *laissez-faire* were busily proving the mischief of supposing that anything should or could be done, the tradesmen – Child the Grand Cham of the India Company, Firmin the London mercer, Cary the Bristol sugar merchant, Bellers the Quaker clothier, Nelson the heir to a Levant Company fortune – were pressing on with their schemes for institutions, and helping to foot the bill. And if some, like Mandeville,

[1] Defoe, *Plan of the English Commerce* (1728 edn.), p. 60.

impugned their motives, there were others, like Davenant, who remarked contrariwise on the 'malignant temper in some who will not let a public work go on, if private persons are to be the gainers by it . . .'[1] Not all private vices, it appeared, conferred public benefits.

Historians have underestimated the gravity and oversimplified the complexity of the great debate of the poor. Faced by the difficulty of analysing the relation between states of mind and private interests, between thoughts and actions, they have too often been satisfied with what are fundamentally *a priori* conclusions. It is now apparent that between the Restoration and (say) the end of the Seven Years' War England faced a chronic problem of poverty which affected severely somewhere between a quarter and a half of the whole population. It was not only the large number of real paupers but the high proportion of casual part-time workers in the nation's leading industry, clothmaking, that constituted the problem.[2] Gregory King's Tables included a figure of over a million and a quarter for 'cottagers, paupers, vagrants, gypsies, thieves, beggars' out of a total of five and a half million in 1688. Population growth and industrial change had faced seventeenth-century England with a social problem that the Middle Ages had never known: an army of workers partly or wholly dependent on a great but unstable manufacturing export industry. One of the motives behind the mercantilist urge to diversify the nation's industries had been the consciousness that fluctuations in the demand for cloth might (as Mun put it) 'suddenly cause much poverty and dangerous uproars, specially by our poor people'. Politics and Nature had combined to endorse his warning. At home and abroad wars had continually disrupted markets, and it is at least arguable that at two points – 1652 and 1655 – the decision to fight the Dutch may have been influenced by the belief that the trade depression might thereby be relieved. Vigorous industries in Holland and France were now competing for Europe's shrunken cloth markets, and Colbert had

---

[1] C. Davenant, *An Essay upon the Probable Methods of Making a People Gainers in the Balance of Trade.* Collected Works, II, 214.

[2] D. C. Coleman, 'Labour in the English Economy of the 17th Century', *Economic History Review,* 2nd series, VIII (1956).

placed the forces of the state in the balance. By the end of the century the structure of the industry was adjusting itself to the stresses of the times. The less competitive areas of the West Country were yielding ground to East Anglia, as both these areas were in the eighteenth century to yield to the Yorkshire industry. On an industrial pattern already distorted by human violence must be superimposed the effects of the disastrous harvests which supervened from time to time. 1649, for example, a year of regicide, mutiny, disorder, and upheaval, was also visited by an appalling harvest that drove up grain prices to famine heights and added to the grievous trade depression.[1] On top of the French wars of the nineties came especially bad harvests in 1692, 1693, 1695, 1698, 1708, and 1709. The severity of the hardship created by these conjunctions of normal and exceptional stresses undoubtedly helped to deflect the course of economic thought. The very confusion of 1649 made it an *annus mirabilis* for the literature of social criticism and reform, much of it pivoting upon the problems of poverty. The only one to have achieved any kind of notoriety is Winstanley's *Declaration from the Poor Oppressed People of England* denouncing 'particular property'. For Winstanley, the rebel against reality, there was no question of compromise; to that extent he is less important in this inquiry than others less intransigent – Hartlib, Rice Bush, Chamberlen, or Goffe, for example. Theirs was not the pure milk of utopianism. They were, on the contrary, anxious to come to terms with social reality. Hartlib, the friend of Milton and many of the revolutionary leaders, educationally the disciple of Comenius, had already published in 1641 his *Description of the Kingdom of Macaria, shewing its excellent government, wherein the Inhabitants live in great Prosperity, Health and Happiness*.[2] This remarkable work,

[1] For an account of the depression of 1649 see evidence of Thomas Violet given before Parliamentary Committee of enquiry, *State Papers Dom.*, 1650, p. 178, No. 61. The evidence of depression is discussed in C. Wilson, *Profit and Power* (1957), pp. 147–9. For the depression of the late seventeenth and early eighteenth centuries see Beloff, op. cit., Ch. III, esp. pp. 56–8. For a general discussion of the intellectual ferment of 1649 see Gooch and Laski, *English Democratic Ideas in the 17th Century* (Cambridge, 1927), esp. Ch. VII.

[2] *Harleian Miscellany* (London, 1744), I, 567. I am much indebted to Dr Leon Fuz for allowing me to see the text of his doctoral thesis submitted at the

which followed in the footsteps (as Hartlib said) of More and Bacon and foreshadowed Mandeville and the Physiocrats, was followed in 1649 by *London's Charitie stilling the Poor Orphan's Cry* and in 1650 by *London's Charity Inlarged*. Here he outlines a scheme of Parliamentary provision of workhouses to employ poor people and educate poor children. This in turn reflected the influence of a pamphlet by Rice Bush called *The Poor Man's Friend*, which described the efforts of the 'many worthy citizens of London' to provide for the poor and was dedicated to a group of 'eleven gentlemen' (including Hartlib) who were said to have been active in this work.[1] Peter Chamberlen, the author of *The Poor Man's Advocate, or England's Samaritan*, which appeared in the same year, was, like Samuel Hartlib, of immigrant stock.[2] Here again were proposals, mercantilist in character, for a general increase in wealth which would also provide for the poor and narrow the socially dangerous gap that divided them from the rest of society. It is more difficult to put a certain date to William Goffe's *How to Advance the Trade of the Nation and employ the Poor*, but internal evidence suggests that it appeared at about the same time as Chamberlen's work.[3] Like Chamberlen, Goffe proposes measures by the state of a kind a Keynesian generation was to describe as 'priming the pump'. The principal object was to re-employ the poor, whose numbers he estimates at half a million. 'The poor,' wrote Goffe, 'ought to be encouraged and mercifully dealt with and kindly used, until their slow hands be brought to ready working and ought at first to have the highest price the commodity will bear to themselves.'[4] Most of the reformers were strongly influenced in this, as in so many other matters, by the example of the Dutch, whose provision for the poor offered an obvious model for others.[5]

Rotterdam Hogeschool in June 1951, in which he examines English welfare economics from Francis Bacon to Adam Smith.

[1] See G. H. Turnbull, *Hartlib, Drury and Comenius* (Liverpool, 1947), pp. 65–6.

[2] See W. Schenk, *The Concern for Social Justice in the Puritan Revolution* (London, 1930), pp. 279–80. [3] *Harleian Miscellany*, IV, 366–70.

[4] Quoted by T. E. Gregory in 'The Economics of Employment in England, 1660–1713', *Economica*, I (1921–2). The pamphlet is, as stated above, of an earlier date than the Restoration.

[5] See, for example, *The Dutch Drawn to the Life* (1664), Ch. IV, esp. pp. 55–6.

The profusion of welfare economics of 1649 seems to me to form the basis of almost all later economic thought for more than a century. The recognition that the problems, of poverty, employment, and national welfare are all linked together was never subsequently lost sight of. It was to appear again whenever bad times provoked men to brood on social remedies. 1659, a bad year, brought forth Cornelius Plockhoy's *A Way Propounded to Make the Poor in This and Other Nations Happy*.[1] Between then and the crisis of the nineties writers like Child, Matthew Hale, Robert Harford, Firmin, Davenant, Yarranton, Locke, and others developed the theme.[2] The debate was resumed at full length between 1692 and 1709 with the new editions of Child's *Discourse*. John Bellers published his *Proposals for a College of Industry* in 1695, and two years later his *Epistle to Friends Concerning the Education of Children*. There is a strong general resemblance between these and other writings of the nineties – Dudley North's *Discourses* (1691), *Britannia Languens* (1696), and John Cary's *Essay* (1696).

Some might support and others oppose the idea of parish factories, as Defoe opposed Sir Humphrey Mackworth's Bill for those institutions in 1724, but one idea had come to be firmly established in the popular mind: the potential value of the labour represented by the nation's poor. Nor can the general approach to the problem be dismissed as merely cynical or self-interested. It had become too plain that poverty was the dominant social problem. Post-Restoration mercantilists were no longer so absorbedly preoccupied as their predecessors had been with state welfare measured in the narrow terms of the net amount of bullion gained or lost via the balance of trade. This traditional obsession was now blended with a concern for the social needs of the community, which had its roots in the ideas of 1649. The obstinate core of mercantilist thought can nevertheless be seen in the belief that some activities were

[1] Plockhoy is often referred to as Peter Cornelius (see Gooch and Laski, op. cit., pp. 117–8); Schenk (op. cit., p. 153) describes him as Peter Corneliez Plockboy.

[2] E.g. Sir Matthew Hale, *Discourse Touching Provision for the Poor* (1683). R. Harford, *Proposals for Building in every Country a Working Almshouse or Hospital as the Best Expedient to perfect the Trade and Manufactory of Linen Cloth, etc.* (1677).

beneficial and some harmful to the community and that it was the state's task to discern and separate the two.[1]

At this point I can imagine the critics moving to their second line of defence. 'We may' (they might well say) 'have omitted to count one or two heads, neglected one or two principles. But does this affect the argument? Does not the story remain one of neglect and harshness? Even granting that their motives were less blameworthy than has sometimes been supposed, did not deeds lag a long way behind intentions?' Certainly there is no lack of evidence to substantiate the gloomiest view of society in the hundred years under review. The originals of Tom Nero, Mother Needham, Tom Idle, and the rest may all be discovered in the fearful annals of St Giles, Shoreditch, Drury Lane, and Alsatia. This last century before the Industrial Revolution is near enough the present to invite comparison of its social and moral standards with those of a later day. Even now that it is a commonplace to say that the civilization of the Augustan Age was but a veneer, it comes as something of a shock to read the Report of the Commons Committee on the Care of the Poor in the Parish of St Martin-in-the-Fields in 1715. Three-quarters out of the twelve hundred babies born every year in the parish died, many being exposed or overlaid by 'nurses'. Money was stolen, accounts were falsified, paupers were starved and in some cases murdered. Consider the later inquiries of Jonas Hanway, Russia merchant and social reformer, founder of the Marine Society, the Magdalen House, and the Foundling Hospital, and one of the most indefatigable and splendid bores of English history. His seventy-four separate works on charitable problems seem, again, to underline the failure of private enterprise to find any solution to the social problem. In the fourteen parishes investigated by him he calculated that the death-rate among infants entering or being born in the workhouses that had sprung up since 1720 was 88 per cent. Some parishes (it was said) acknowledged that 'no infant had lived to be apprenticed from their workhouses'.[2] Under the system by which the poor were hired out to a contractor, the workhouse had become a place of vice, a catchall for the infant and the infirm,

[1] See John Cary, *Essay in the State of England, etc.*
[2] See J. H. Hutchins, *Jonas Hanway 1712–86* (London, 1940), pp. 47–75.

the able-bodied idle and the criminal alike. Some of this may have been exaggerated, but much was undoubtedly true. Is the true explanation to be found (as some historians have suggested) in a decline of charity, in a harsher and more censorious attitude towards poverty and misfortune? The title of Professor Tawney's chapter on this period – 'The New Medicine for Poverty' – gives a suitably sinister twist to the theme. Statistical comparisons of virtue, whether of individuals or societies, are not a promising branch of historical inquiry. But there exists one source of information as to the extent, if not the quality, of charity in England which has not (so far as I am aware) been analysed. Under the provisions of Gilbert's Act of 1782 the Ministers and Churchwardens of the parishes of England and Wales were required to make a return of all the Charitable Trusts then existing, with the date of creation, the name of the donor, the object, the capital and annual income, and the title of the Trustees responsible for administering the charity.[1] In all, some sixty or seventy thousand separate donations, mainly of seventeenth- and eighteenth-century origin, were recorded. They yielded a total annual income of £258,700 spread over all the counties of England and Wales. All but £6,236 came from English returns – a capital value all told of some £5 million in the ratio of £5 worth of land for every £1 of other types of investment. The majority of the benefactors defined their intentions only in general terms: food and clothing or fuel for the poor. A few were more specific. These poor were to have beef, those herrings; some got linen, others woollens. Poor men were to have coats, or shirts and shifts, poor women to have gowns. There was to be provision 'to marry poor maidens'. The poor here were to have Bibles, the poor children there to have books. This village was to have an almshouse, another a charity school. Mr Tomkins of Abingdon would relieve 'poor Dissenters (but not Papists)'. And so on. Obscurities abound. Many charities have no date. Many no doubt were omitted. There are hints at misappropriation. Of many a benefaction the authorities could only observe: 'but we do not apprehend that it was ever received'.

[1] *Abstract of Returns made by Ministers and Churchwardens of the Several Parishes and Townships of England and Wales. Ordered, by the House of Commons, to be printed,* 1816.

To interpret reliably the enormous volume of information contained in the return calls for an intimate knowledge of local economic and social history. But by a combination of random sampling and parochial analysis some pretty reliable impressions can, I believe, be obtained. The incidence of charities is related broadly to the size and character of the geographical areas, the density of the population, and the general prosperity of the town or parish. As one might expect, the City of London, the Home Counties, and Midlands were relatively generously endowed. Large areas like the West Riding and rich counties like Kent come top of the income-by-county analysis. To prepare any definitive analysis would require far more study than I have been able to give for the purpose of this paper. The brief survey that has been undertaken does not, however, provide any warrant for supposing that the well-to-do were left any less charitably disposed by the social, economic, and religious changes in the half-century that followed the Restoration. There was undoubtedly some gradual decline – perhaps 10–20 per cent – between the *average* number of trusts created in the half-century before, and the half-century after, 1660. A similar fall occurred in the following fifty years. Josiah Child has himself remarked that 'formerly in the days of our pious ancestors the work was done but now charity is decreased'; but he goes on to explain that this did not proceed from any decline in charitableness, so much as from doubts whether it was proper that private gifts by the benevolent should reduce the poor rate levied on those with less tender consciences.[1] It could indeed hardly be expected in a period when the yield from the poor rate was raised from £665,000 to £900,000 in fifteen years (1685–1701) that private donations should not in general be affected.[2] We have seen the same phenomenon in our own day as the welfare state has extended its functions. But even this trend was not universal. Suffolk, which comes after the West Riding in the volume of charity endowment, was not among the largest shires, and was if anything less densely populated than a number of surrounding areas.[3] Is it unreasonable

---

[1] Child, *New Discourse* (1694), p. 84.   [2] Figures from Beloff, op. cit., *passim*.
[3] H. C. Darby, *Historical Geography of England before* 1800 (Cambridge, 1936), p. 524, fig. 83.

to suggest that its position was probably related to the presence of those *entrepreneurs* of the local draperies, Old and New, of whom Unwin himself wrote so eloquently? And what of Bristol with its noble record of over six hundred charities? A high proportion – almost a third – date from the half-century after the Restoration. It was no accident that Cary was a Bristol man: Bristol was surely the most benevolent place in England. The City of London had well over a thousand trusts, of which about one-third were created between the Restoration and the Peace of Utrecht. At Norwich, too, nearly a third of the 160-odd trusts likewise dated from this period. The collective charge that a whole class was through several generations guilty of social irresponsibility must, I think, be rejected as non-proven. The social conscience of the trading classes seems to me to have been no less tender than that of their feudal predecessors in office, and may in some respects have been more sensitive. For the merchant did not move in society with the unselfconscious ease of the landed magnate nor speak with the confident voice of the learned clerk. He was in general a little more anxious than they to stand well with his fellow men, and for this, less fortunate members of society had cause to be thankful. Charity might go on breaking in. His habit of discriminating between deserving and less deserving beneficiaries may register a spiritual decline when compared with that medieval almsgiving that aimed only at the moral betterment of the donor; but it is by no means certain that the change brought any one material loss.

Among the many uncertainties in the returns of charities one trend emerges clearly: the growing proportion of donors who felt moved to endow some form of active apprenticeship or instruction for the juvenile poor, as distinct from the passive forms of relief common in earlier periods. It is a reminder that these were the early years of that remarkable movement for charity schools which was co-ordinated from 1699 by the S.P.C.K. Hundreds of thousands of children, for whom no other means of education existed, received in the thousands of such schools the rudiments of education, religion, and practical training that gave them a chance to earn a living.[1] At the peak

---

[1] M. G. Jones, *The Charity School Movement: A Study of 18th Century Puritanism in Action* (Cambridge, 1938), *passim*.

of the movement the boys went as apprentices into every kind of trade, the girls became sempstresses or domestic servants. Again, it is easy to put a cynical motive to the work, to point to the drift away from literary and religious studies to technical training and utility. Some falling away of standards there may have been. Yet the Charity Schools remain a notable instance of that principle of voluntary association which historians like Unwin and Tawney have rightly enjoined on us to behold and admire as a vital element in social development. No previous age had faced such a formidable social problem, and none certainly had attempted to relieve, employ, or educate an army of poor already alarmingly enlarged by natural increase. These improvisations in social service failed or fell short of their object not because of a shortage of good intentions or of money but because the supply of those capable of organizing and administering them with reasonable efficiency, honesty, and compassionate understanding was totally inadequate. To read the replies made by parish governors to Hanway is to realize how appalling were the difficulties encountered in the organization of poor relief, how rarely a parish could find a treasure like the splendid Nurse Howe of St Mary Whitechapel, how few were the Humphrey Clinkers, how numerous the Tom Neros. To endure the continual proximity of the poor a man needed to be either especially saintly or especially impervious to human suffering, cruelty, filth, and corruption. In such a situation it was not unnatural that men should lose faith in the efficacy of high principles and take refuge in the reflection that 'whate'er is best administered is best'. Yet the art of administration was equally elusive. Administration, as the modern world understands it, is a Victorian invention resting on Victorian values: it ran counter to much that was characteristic of eighteenth-century society. Enough of the bad old days remained in 1857 to provide Charles Dickens with material for his classic satire on bureaucracy: the Circumlocution Office in *Little Dorrit*.[1] He would not have been entirely at a loss for material a century later.

[1] See Leo Silberman's introduction (1957) to *The Statesman*, by Henry Taylor, especially pp. xx to xxv. The original title of *Little Dorrit* was to have been *Nobody's Fault*.

The apathy, indifference, and chaos of the eighteenth-century poor law was the product not of a new capitalist ethic, but of the frustration, failure, and occasional panic of a generation faced by a problem beyond its power to control. The heart of the matter was contained in the title of Defoe's famous pamphlet: *Everybody's Business is Nobody's Business* (1728). This applied not only to the condition of the institutions but to the Settlement Laws themselves. Few historians today accept Adam Smith's famous strictures on the Laws at their face value, but it was a fact that they gave local authorities powers of ejectment that at first might appear ruthless. Yet here again, the preamble to the Act which explains why the powers were deemed necessary puts the problem in a different light.[1] The provision of relief for the unemployed differed greatly between one parish and another and those parishes 'which endeavoured to do their duty in this respect were inundated by distressed paupers'. In short, what came to be regarded by later critics as a system of calculated brutality and repression arose in the first place not from unconcern or harshness, but out of a desire to protect the efforts of those local authorities who were trying hardest to improvise remedies.

Those who do not trust interventionism are apt to inveigh alternately against its wickedness and its futility. It cannot have been both. The influence of 'policy' on the labour situation in the seventeenth century may have been exaggerated;[2] certainly 'policy' was to an important extent a reflection of social facts. Yet it seems an oddly misplaced modesty in scholars to disown the historical importance of ideas. The great Debate of the Poor conducted in Press, pamphlet, and Parliament had helped to elucidate the importance of labour – skilled labour in particular – to the community. The facts of unemployment and poverty had joined with the ideas of educational reform that stemmed originally from Comenius and Milton, and the junction stimulated a new emphasis on apprenticeship, training, and skill. Later theories of labour value have their roots in these

[1] E.g. E. M. Hampson, *The Treatment of Poverty in Cambridgeshire* (Cambridge, 1934), pp. 125–6.
[2] Coleman, 'Labour in the English Economy of the 17th Century', *Economic History Review*, VIII (1956).

years. Yet though the debaters had broadened and socialized their criteria of the nation's economic welfare, they remained mercantilists to a man. Hartlib, for all his precocious concern with technology, monetary substitutes, and the like, was not free from the orthodox preoccupation with shipping and 'dominion on the sea and thereby the strength and renown and flourishing estate of the nation'.[1] Defoe has sometimes been credited with precociously free-trade views on the strength of the part he played in Harley's *Mercator*, but in fact his views remained conventionally mercantilist and protectionist.[2] Firmin was among the stoutest opponents of the import of French textiles. Mandeville, for all his scorn of bullionism, remained firmly anchored to the old principles, enjoining upon politicians that 'above all, they'll keep a watchful Eye over the Balance of Trade in general and never suffer that all the Foreign Commodities together, that are imported in one year, shall exceed in value what of their own growth or manufacture is in the same exported to others'.[3] The principles of *Machtpolitik* had no more single-minded disciple than Jonas Hanway, who dedicated one of his principal works to Anson, the victor of Finisterre.[4] John Cary, the great Bristol merchant and philanthropist, exemplified perfectly the union of mercantilist principles with ideals of social reform. The theme of his famous *Essay* of 1695 was that some trades were profitable to the nation and should be encouraged; others were harmful and should be discouraged. In making its decisions between the two, government should be guided not so much by the net effects on the bullion flow as by the results in terms of manufacture and employment. As an economist, Cary was heir to the ideas of Child – balance-of-trade mercantilism modified by considerations of employment. His influence was exercised equally on trade policy and on social reform. But it was not only in England where his writings were widely distributed and read

[1] Samuel Hartlib, *Legacy of Husbandry* (London, 1655), p. 292.

[2] See especially *An Humble Proposal to the People of England* in the *Works* (Oxford, 1841), XVIII, 27, 41, 45.

[3] B. Mandeville, *The Fable of the Bees*, ed. F. B. Kaye, 2 vols. (Oxford, 1924), I, 116.

[4] *Historical Account of the British Trade over the Caspian Sea* (London, 1754), I, 421.

down to the mid-eighteenth century. This type of mercantilism – what might not unfairly be called 'social mercantilism' – was the most powerful formative influence on continental mercantilism in the eighteenth century. Two of the founding Fathers of German *Kameralwissenschaft* – Becher and von Schroeder – were resident in England in these years (J. J. Becher fled to England in 1680 and remained here till his death in 1685; von Schroeder lived in London from about 1663 to 1674 when he returned to Germany), and the resemblance between the 'equilibrium of occupation' of Schroeder's *Fürstliche Schatz und Rentkammer* (1686) and the ideas of Child and Cary is too close to be accidental. From this, three-quarters of a century later, came Sonnenfels's theory of the two trade balances by which economic health must be judged: the 'monetary' and the 'employment' balance. The genealogy of mercantilism in Italy is equally clear. When Genovesi came to establish a flourishing school of economics at Naples in the 1750s he began by translating John Cary's *Essay* for his pupils' benefit, while relegating Mun's earlier work to an appendix. His own doctrine that distinguished between the 'useful commerce' which exported manufactures and the 'harmful' which brought in foreign manufactures was the word precisely as Cary had preached it. There can be little doubt that the social and economic policy of Enlightened Despotism in Eastern Europe owed most of its theoretical foundations to English 'social mercantilism'. Even in France, the new synthesis was not without influence. De Gournay, then an *intendant* for commerce, who stood between the extremes of mercantilist and physiocratic dogma, published in 1754 a French edition of the works of Child and Culpeper.[1] In some sense, England was only paying back an intellectual debt owed to Europe. For it is a remarkable fact that not a little of the 'welfare' element in that doctrine may be traced to thinkers of European origin. Hartlib was a Pole, something of a cosmopolitan who spoke several languages including Dutch.[2] Comenius, the source of much of

---

[1] A. Oncken, *Die Maxime Laissez Faire et Laissez Passer* (Berne, 1886), pp. 87–9.

[2] Turnbull, op. cit. See the same author's *Samuel Hartlib. A Sketch of His Life and Relations to J. A. Comenius* (Oxford, 1920); also Brit. Mus., Sloane MSS. 654, fos. 345–8.

the educational controversy of these years, was a Czech. Chamberlen was by origin French; Plockhoy, a Zeelander. Mandeville came from Rotterdam. That the debate which had begun round the theme of wealth and conquest had broadened into a debate on social ends was not a little due to their intervention. It was not only English economic and technological organization that was leavened by immigrant influence but English social ideas, too.[1]

At their weakest, the criticisms of the social arrangements in the post-Restoration age to which I have referred imply that at the time human nature among the ruling classes took a distinct turn for the worse. More charitably, we might take the theory to be that in the social situation of that time the worst side of human nature found more opportunities to exhibit itself. The evidence of the creation of charitable trusts seems to me to dispose of any sweeping allegations of this kind. It is rather evident that, on the contrary, local experiments and experiences grew into something like a social philosophy which grafted new social ends on to the older strategic and monetary objectives of mercantilist thought. There was no unanimity about the means to be employed: there was indeed a bitter and protracted debate between those who believed, with Child, that the problem of poverty demanded direct treatment – the workhouse and the spinning school – and those who believed, with Mandeville and Defoe, that this was a problem which could be dispersed only through an accelerated rate of economic activity in general. The alignment of supporters, it is plain, can in no way be explained in terms of economic interest; and the ranks of those who took what has often been regarded as the tough line included many (like Dr Johnson) who qualify neither as Capitalists nor as Puritans and who can hardly be accused of inhumanity. Both sides recognized that the employment of the poor – and especially their skilled employment – was an objective to be pursued as a means to the prosperity of individuals and of society; but many recognized that it was, besides, a social and religious duty. Here was, in fact, not the monotone of repression but the antiphony of a genuine debate in which

[1] For the influence of immigrants on technology, etc., see, e.g., W. Cunningham, *Alien Immigrants* (Cambridge, 1897).

the claims of material interest and social welfare were mixed in proportions not discreditable to the age. To administrators and thinkers in the less fortunate, more backward states of Middle and South Europe such arguments seemed to be the talisman of English progress. Writing later in the eighteenth century, Hannah More described the period we have been examining as 'an age of benevolence'. Perhaps the *Bas Bleu* was predisposed in favour of the paternalism for which her native Bristol was famous. But her verdict is entitled to respect, especially as it seems that the opposite conclusion has been reached by the device of peopling the post-Restoration scene with selected cartoon figures more appropriate to the comedy of Congreve or Wycherley than to serious historical study. As historians we might do well to ponder what an eminent critic has written of this technique of caricature as it was employed by the dramatists of the Restoration: 'It is in a sense prig-drama. It flatters the vanity of the spectator for whose amusement the weaknesses of his friends are held up.'[1] It is true that there is weighty authority for the view that it is the historian's task to sit in judgement. 'Morality,' said Sir Thomas Browne, 'is not ambulatory', and Acton invoked his support for the view that the historian should err on the side of severity rather than risk the moral perils of leniency.[2] But Acton also saw the dangers that arise from haste and prejudice. The 'weighing of testimony' was for him the vital part of the historian's task.[3] There is not, after all, much fundamental difference between that and Professor Butterfield's injunction: 'to surround the man with all that can be gathered in the way of historical explanation'.[4] When Acton spoke,[5] the impact of the social sciences on the study of history in England was but recent. When historians spoke of moral judgements they still thought of the actions of individuals, and principally of rulers and statesmen who were conceived to have shaped the course of events. It is different with the sociologized history of our own day, which is less concerned with individuals and more with men as members of social groups. It is

[1] Bonamy Dobrée, *Restoration Comedy 1660–1720* (Oxford, 1924), p. 11.
[2] *Lectures on Modern History* (1930 edn.), p. 28.
[3] Ibid., p. 16.
[4] *History and Human Relations* (1951), p. 119.
[5] June 1895.

curious that the socially scientific historians began by glibly ordering men's characters according to their occupations and ended by dispatching to collective perdition whole classes of men throughout several generations on the strength of evidence which the late Judge Lynch might have hesitated to regard as adequate. So far from reducing the need to weigh the testimony, this new sociological trend in historical technique makes it all the more imperative, lest history should sink to the rough justice and intellectual shallowness of a standardized political conflict.

6 Fiscalism, Mercantilism and Corruption[1]

JACOB VAN KLAVEREN

[This article is a translation of 'Fiskalismus – Merkantilismus – Korruption', which was first published in the *Vierteljahrschrift für Sozial- und Wirtschaftsgeschichte*, Vol. XLVII, No. 3, 1960. The translation is by George Hammersley.]

Fiscalism, mercantilism and corruption were neither with equal impact nor with equal inevitability part of the *ancien régime*. Corruption existed in classical times and in the Middle Ages. The 'honest administration', historically exceptional phenomenon as it is, emerged as part of the modern state only from the French Revolution or, at any rate, as a result of the insights due to the Enlightenment.[2] A chronological limit for that subject therefore possesses significance mainly for the most recent era. The phenomenon of fiscalism, on the other hand, may be regarded as virtually timeless. As here defined it is the endeavour of the state to increase government revenues regardless of the objectives of economic or social policy. It is artificial to restrict it, as has been done here, to the *ancien régime*: even today economic and social policies which have been well publicized may be sacrificed in the name of national objectives of greater importance than the economy. Fiscalism, however, is

[Translator's note: I am grateful to the late Dr S. H. Steinberg for assistance in preparing this translation. G.H.]

[1] This article is intended as a contribution to the discussion of mercantilism which has recently developed in Britain, Scandinavia, and Holland. For this see the review of periodical literature in *V.S.W.G.* (*Vierteljahrschrift für Sozial- und Wirtschaftsgeschichte*), XLVII (1960), No. 2, Hermann Kellenbenz in the *Scandinavian Economic History Review*, and the present writer, ibid., p. 429, in *Tijdschrift voor Geschiedenis*. The present article was, however, written independently of this international discussion. As the latter seems rather to have died down, I hope I may be helping it to the revival which it deserves.

[2] In general, see my series of articles on 'Die historische Erscheinung der Korruption', *V.S.W.G.* (1957), (1958), (1959).

concerned only with the revenue of the public treasury and has nothing definite to say about its expenditure. Sometimes its purpose is nothing more than the accumulation of treasure to augment princely power. Equally well it can be aimed at specific expenses for political, dynastic or other purposes. Fiscalism may indeed benefit the economy, even if unintentionally.

Mercantilism apparently fits more naturally into the period of the *ancien régime* than either corruption or fiscalism.[1] The bounds of mercantilism are most easily determined if it is taken to refer to the accumulation of writings on economic doctrine which became numerous in the seventeenth and eighteenth centuries. The novelty of their expositions, however, consists less in the economic policies they recommended than in their attempt to investigate relationships in the economy as a whole. Undoubtedly they initiated important steps towards the formulation of an economic theory at this time, though these have been properly acknowledged only since John Maynard Keynes. During the whole of the nineteenth century they were overshadowed by classical theory because the doctrines had not been developed into a properly integrated structure. Nevertheless, the precepts of the mercantilists were never forgotten altogether. Indeed, they much influenced politicians and businessmen, especially in France and in the United States, where they left their imprint on the tariff policies of these countries.[2] This holds true rather more for the customs tariffs

[1] Hence, for instance, the 'age of mercantilism' has been so called. The chronology of this age, as seen by different writers, appears to be in a state of oscillation. For this see Heinrich Bechtel, *Deutsche Wirtschaftsgeschichte*, II (Munich, 1952), p. 18. All suggested chronologies agree though in excluding the nineteenth century.

[2] For these countries with high protectionist duties in the nineteenth century see, in general, Henri Sée, *Französische Wirtschaftsgeschichte*, II (Jena, 1936) and F. W. Taussig, *Tariff History of the United States* (New York, 1888), and many subsequent editions. Though this is usually described as 'protectionism', the tariffs were still designed on the mercantilist pattern. The same was true of the *Zollverien* tariffs, which thus resulted in the move of Bremen tobacco factories and of Swiss cotton factories into *Zollverein* territory. Cf. Ludwig Beutin, *Bremen und Amerika* (Bremen, 1953), pp. 36, 97, 125, and Wolfgang Fischer, 'Ansätze zur Industrialisierung in Baden', *V.S.W.G.* (1960), p. 199. Beutin, op. cit., p. 242, speaks expressly of 'mercantilist measures' at that time, and one cannot but agree with him.

than for the orders and prohibitions of mercantilism. In the Middle Ages, on the contrary, it was generally not the customs duties but the orders and prohibitions which corresponded to those of the so-called age of mercantilism. The objective is always the development, from an agrarian base, of an industrial, commercial, and maritime superstructure coupled with the attempt to secure a bigger share in the profits of international commerce for one's own citizens.[1] The chronological limits of mercantilism are therefore especially difficult if the criterion is to be concrete economic policy, since this is decided not by doctrines and laws alone but by their effective execution.

Both corruption and fiscalism could obstruct such execution. The present article will therefore show that the attempt to find a period during the *ancien régime* which can be characterized as 'mercantilism' is somewhat one-sided. The main emphasis of this paper will be upon connections of mercantilism with corruption rather than with fiscalism. I will deal with fiscalism first.

I *Fiscalism and Mercantilism*

Fiscalism may be defined as the endeavour to maximize the public revenues at all times for other than economic purposes. As a rule, therefore, it is obviously incompatible with mercantilism. For the development of national productive potential, mercantilism sometimes requires recourse to foreign exports at the expense of the public treasury; they may have to be exempted from taxation at first and might even have to be assisted with subsidies. In the long run this may produce a higher yield from taxation, but fiscalism, in the proper meaning of the word, cannot, by definition, exercise foresight of this kind.[2] There may often also be a background of national emergency. Such times

[1] This should serve as the criterion of mercantilist economic policy, regardless of the period at which it was applied.

[2] Bechtel, op. cit., II, p. 71, maintains that a narrow policy of fiscalism favoured by most of the small German principalities after the Thirty Years' War incapacitated them when it came to initiating a policy of reconstruction to repair the ravages of war. For the principality of Osnabrück this is shown by Klaus Winkler, *Landwirtschaft und Agrarverfassung im Fürstentum Osnabrück nach dem Dreissigjährigen Krieg* (Stuttgart, 1959), pp. 119, 138, 140.

frequently lead to the violation of mercantilist customs duties, for instance by the imposition of tariffs on the export of manufactured goods. France took such a turning after Colbert's death when export duties were placed on linen, hats, and paper to finance Louvois's war policies. True, there were discussions as to how much duty the foreigners could be made to bear without producing too great a reduction in exports. These, however, underestimated foreign competition. As a result of the Sun King's Wars, the exports of French industry declined because of the fiscal increases in duties, although the English embargoes on trade also contributed.[1]

Occasionally, of course, fiscalist and mercantilist attitudes may be linked in one measure. A differentiated customs tariff which discriminates against foreigners may allow the domestic merchants to take over the business of foreigners. When that happens, however, the advantage for the public treasury disappears. This naturally presupposes that the native merchants were advanced enough to respond when a stimulus was provided. Thus, in the export of cloth from England to the Netherlands, the English Merchant Adventurers managed, at least to some extent, to dislodge the Hanseatic merchants, while discrimination was still being practised in the opposite direction, i.e. against the native merchants. This trend was reinforced first by the equalization of duties in 1557 and then by discrimination against the Hansards which followed under Elizabeth.[2]

In Norway, however, duties which discriminated against the Hanseatic League had no mercantilist effect at all: the native merchant class was too undeveloped and backward to respond to the stimulus.[3] The duties were certainly borne by the Norwegian public which, in theory, could therefore have been taxed to that same extent. But it was more convenient to levy

[1] Albert Girard, *Le commerce français à Séville et Cadiz au temps des Habsbourgs* (Paris, 1932), pp. 352, 361, 367, 373 f., 384.

[2] Richard Ehrenberg, *Hamburg und England im Zeitalter der Königin Elisabeth* (Jena, 1896), *passim*.

[3] Only in the eighteenth century was there some kind of Scandinavian awakening, but the bourgeoisie emerged so slowly that Denmark continued under absolutist government until 1849. Cf. Axel Nielsen and others, *Dänische Wirtschaftsgeschichte* (Jena, 1933), pp. 95, 193, 362, 409; O. A. Johnsen, *Norwegische Wirtschaftsgeschichte* (Jena, 1939), pp. 308, 313 f.

taxation by a duty on foreigners which did not even require the consent of the provincial diets. It was precisely because such duties, in a backward country, are either pointless or harmful that Friedrich List demanded the greatest possible freedom of trade in the initial stages of economic development; this would permit the natives to learn most rapidly in active collaboration with the advanced foreigners.[1]

Disregarding corruption for the moment, discriminatory duties act fiscally in backward countries, mercantilistically in advanced countries though with a transitory fiscal effect. In special conditions a general increase in customs duties could be mercantilist as well as fiscal. This requires, first, that the foreign commodities imported and the domestic commodities exported are both of a kind which allows the payment of the duties to be shifted abroad; and, second, that the volume of trade does not decline in proportion to the increase in duties. This produces an improvement in the balance of trade because either the deficit will be decreased or the surplus increased. Thus it will augment the quantity of money circulating inside the country and also promote the expansion of domestic production. But states were then small and more divided than today: it was probably the exception for an increase in customs to produce a wholly favourable effect while manufactures were being exported or raw materials and semi-finished goods imported.

Here I conclude this section. There remain for consideration the relations between fiscalism and corruption and between mercantilism and corruption.

II *Fiscalism and Corruption*

Exceptionally and briefly, fiscalism and mercantilism may be conceived as compatible: as defined, fiscalism and corruption cannot be so. Corruption aims at the maximization of the officials' own incomes, which must necessarily prevent the maximization of government revenues. Regarded thus, the connections are quite clear and simple. Reality, though, is more complex, because hybrid forms of both may often be found in

---

[1] Friedrich List, *Das nationale System der politischen Ökonomie*, ed. H. Gehring, 3rd reprinted edn. (Jena, 1950), p. 64.

the *ancien régime*. It is easy to imagine a renunciation of maximal government income, but a corresponding renunciation by individual officials does not occur. Rather there occur complex and pugnaciously contested shifts within the body of the civil service. Such internal conflicts occur within the authorities, even when the interests of the public treasury are not involved. In that case their subject is simply the distribution of the spoils of corruption either among the civil service hier archy or between the members of a 'collegiate' authority. When, however, the interest of the public treasury is involved it may produce symptoms which can deceptively simulate mere fiscalism. In fact, it will be semi-fiscalism – which is quite compatible with corruption. The explanation of this curious phenomenon is that defalcations affected both the receipts and the issues of the exchequer. Tax and customs authorities were placed at the receiving end, military and court administration at the issuing end. Where spending was concerned, an artful surcharge was added to the cost of procurements, and this concealed difference divided up when payment had been made. As for receipts, here the income was fraudulently understated and the resulting difference split. The ministers of finance straddled both sides of the line: not only did they let out tax farms at undervaluations but they could also demand a discount before settling due payments or let the creditors wait.[1] The issuing authorities depended for the extent of their defalcations on the amount available in the treasury, hence they exerted continuous pressure on the receipt. Apart from these officials there were also the courtiers who, by insinuating themselves into pensions and other favours, committed effective defalcation without offending against the letter of the law. Equilibrium was further affected by the need to perform at least some of the functions of government effectively if the state was to survive at all in the arena of nations.

Under the *ancien régime* the equilibrium between these three

---

[1] In this way they creamed off some of the excess available for corrupt purchasing officials. In England around 1666 this was called 'fee of the office'. Cf. Samuel Pepys, *Diary*, Everyman edn. (London, 1950), I, pp. 108 f. On 13 February 1663 [in fact it was 1661–2. D.C.C.] Pepys reported that the treasury rarely ever paid out except at a discount of 10 per cent (*Diary*, I, p. 225).

forces was deliberately maintained. The machinery of government under the *ancien régime* cannot be regarded as completely
hamstrung or rudderless, though it must be admitted that,
compared to a modern state, direction was but fitfully maintained. There was a delicate equilibrium between, on the one
hand, the departments, cohering but tenuously and operating
each on its own account and, on the other, the needs of the
treasury: this has been described excellently and in detail in
R. H. Tawney's book about Lionel Cranfield, the lord treasurer
of James I.[1] It was his task to adjust the equilibrium in the
treasury's favour because the Thirty Years' War required an
increase in military preparedness. Cranfield developed a form
of semi-fiscalism by making severe inroads into corruption on
both sides of the exchequer; he dealt with the receipts by taking
over tax and customs farms himself and with the issues by
doing the same with procurements. This injured subordinate
offices and officials, who became Cranfield's implacable
enemies. With royal consent he also countermanded, as far as
possible, surreptitiously acquired pensions. That this was far
from genuine fiscalism, however, is made evident by the manner
in which Cranfield managed to secure juicy morsels for his
patron the Duke of Buckingham and himself.

This, then, is semi-fiscalism but not genuine fiscalism, which
is so defined as to exclude corruption. Of all the possible
relationships between the three aspects of financial and economic policy, only that of mercantilism and corruption remains
for examination.

III *Mercantilism and Corruption*

Corruption so curiously illuminates the manifestations surrounding not only fiscalism but also mercantilism that some of
them may easily be mistaken for the genuine substance. The
fisc renounced the maximization of its income in favour of the
officials. One and the same bulk was divided between both, but
the proportion falling to either share altered from time to time

---

[1] R. H. Tawney, *Business and Politics under James I; Lionel Cranfield as Merchant
and Minister* (Cambridge, 1958). See also my review in *V.S.W.G.*, XLVII (1960),
p. 127.

for extraneous reasons. What changes occurred then affected mainly the quantities. Mercantilism, however, is not quantitatively but qualitatively modified by corruption: corruption destroys it. We speak therefore of 'semi-fiscalism' but, on the other hand, of 'pseudo-mercantilism'.

The pretences of pseudo-mercantilism are often the more easily accepted because people concentrate on the text of laws but lose sight of their execution, which is what really matters. This happens the more easily because the laws remain explicit in the sources, whereas reports of actual implementation are much rarer and often hard to interpret. Moreover, such reports in their original form are always highly suspect because they strive to conceal much and intentionally foster uncertainty. The reports of civil servants were really produced like 'une vaste comédie', as Chaunu found during his work on Spain.[1] This is how he characterizes the official correspondence:

> . . . relentless dialogue of the deaf. Nobody wants to get to the root of problems, everybody conceals his interests under considerations of a general kind . . . (I, 233) . . . The wording is deliberately obscure and full of evasiveness . . . (V, 331 f.) . . . A comedy like everything there . . . nobody takes it seriously (V, 436).

Chaunu is one of the very small number of historians who have perceived this. But this alone does not facilitate the interpretation of the material. This can be achieved only from an understanding of the system underlying corruption. The application of this systematic knowledge can turn the material into a gold mine; too trustful a reliance on it will produce wrong and even grotesque results. Below I shall attempt to demonstrate, by the use of some examples, the need to revise mistaken views in the field of mercantilism, with due regard to corruption. It is also necessary, in dealing with actual examples, to take into account whether a country is backward or advanced, because this profoundly affects its capacity to respond.

[1] Huguette et Pierre Chaunu, *Séville et l'Atlantique 1504–1650*, 8 vols. (Paris, 1955–9).

(A) BACKWARD COUNTRIES

Relying on the literal text of the laws would make their orders
and prohibitions seem to testify to the existence of unadulter-
ated mercantilism in the Middle Ages. This applies, for
instance, to the Norwegian prohibitions directed against the
Hanseatic League. It may be appropriate, though, at this point
to begin with a description of the economic background.[1]

The conflict between the rudimentary bourgeoisie of the
Norwegian towns and the Hansards may be observed in
Norway into the sixteenth century. The Hansards insisted on
their privilege of selling at retail ells of cloth, jugs of wine, etc.
In addition, they claimed the privilege called *Landkaup*, to sell
and buy outside the towns. But the citizens demanded for
themselves this privilege of collection and distribution in the
inland trade. They wanted to confine the role of the Hansards
to importing and exporting. Yet because of the small capacity
of their ships and the low turnover of the individual Hanseatic
merchant, the Hansards would not agree to such a restriction:
they could only hope for an adequate return if they could
command the profits of internal trade as well. Had the law
restricted them to foreign trade alone, they would either have
had to withdraw from that commerce altogether or extract a
higher rate of profit from it. Norway, however, relied on the
continuation of the trade to feed its population; hence the
Norwegians would have been made to pay for the higher profits.
The activities of the native merchants would thus have acquired a parasitical character: peasants and landlords therefore
always sided with the Hansards.[2] A mercantilist economic policy
would have been thinkable only if legal provision could have
ensured the replacement of the Hansards in foreign trade as

[1] For this I have in general relied on O. A. Johnsen, *Norwegische Wirtschaftsgeschichte*, and on Ewald Bosse, *Norwegens Volkswirtschaft vom Ausgang der
Hanseperiode bis zur Gegenwart*, I (Jena, 1916). The interpretation is my own.

[2] O. A. Johnsen, op. cit., p. 121. The Hansards paid more for the peasants'
produce and sold to them more cheaply. When at the beginning of the seventeenth century King Christian IV reserved the Icelandic trade for the Danes, the
Icelanders similarly complained about the 'racked prices' of the Danes. Cf. Axel
Nielsen, op. cit., pp. 270, 279. The Danes in any case remained merely the agents
of the merchants of Hamburg, which simply meant less advantageous prices for
the Icelanders.

well. This was not possible owing to the comparative back-wardness of the Norwegians and to the discrimination prac-tised against aliens in Hanseatic towns.[1]

We must then suppose that contemporaries realized the insubstantial nature of a mercantilist policy. If the Hansards thought it necessary to obtain explicit privileges establishing their right to *Landkaup* and retail trading and if the govern-ment at Copenhagen continued nevertheless regularly to vio-late these privileges by granting contrary privileges to its burgesses, this must have been determined by other than mercantilist intentions. While their privileges were operative, it seems clear that the Hansards were vigorously attacked by civil servants and urban magistrates for reasons of nationalist economics. The reports, however, also indicate that the same officials continued to permit the practice of *Landkaup* even when it had been prohibited.[2] It was at these times that they suddenly stopped complaining about the Germans, whereas the Hansards began to complain because they, of course, had to pay for favours granted, while the burgesses complained of the failure to enforce the prohibitions. *Landkaup*, then, con-tinued, with or without prohibitions, only with larger or smaller bribes in each case. The prohibitions must therefore be regarded as the basis for the enrichment of local dignitaries. The privileges were not needed by the Hansards to facilitate the trade itself but as a safeguard against this form of extortion. The Crown co-operated with them, naturally for some tangible return, by granting or renewing privileges at the expense of the local officials.[3] The grant of contrary privileges to the towns subsequently permitted a repetition of the same bargain. In the modern period too prohibitions and orders existed, supposedly to create openings for the native burgesses and directed against the Dutch, yet these never possessed a genuinely mercantilist character either. They were never seriously enforced.[4]

This then is pseudo-mercantilism, whose laws read exactly

[1] O. A. Johnsen, op. cit., p. 118. The purchase of rye was prohibited to aliens.
[2] Ibid., pp. 125, 165.
[3] Magnus Erikson even expelled the Hansards in 1342, only to readmit them in 1343 when he had been granted a 'loan' of 49,000 Marks (Johnsen, op. cit., p. 161).
[4] Ewald Bosse, op. cit., p. 209.

like those of genuine mercantilism. Nobody really expected mercantilism to succeed in these backward countries, hence the absence of sincere determination in enforcement is easily demonstrated. High customs duties might perhaps have been interpreted as fiscalism; orders and prohibitions only facilitated corruption.

A similar situation existed in another backward country: Spain in the sixteenth and seventeenth centuries. Here, too, the absence of genuine mercantilism can easily be established despite the mercantilist orientation of legislation. No Spanish official really believed that Spaniards could conduct the American trade themselves, but the prohibition against the participation of foreigners remained. Again, these prohibitions served simply as the basis for extortion. The so-called 'merchants' of Seville had become mere appendages of officialdom. The prohibitions against the export of money fitted into exactly the same pattern: they neither did nor were they ever intended to inhibit the export of money, but they functioned exclusively to ensure as essential the paid co-operation of the officials. The civil service probably knew, but certainly did not mind, that the cost of this corruption fell on the Spaniards themselves as well as on the Spanish colonies.[1]

In backward countries it appeared to make little difference whether they employed orders and prohibitions or perhaps seemingly mercantilist customs tariffs. As a rule, they were intended as a basis for corruption and only exceptionally for a fiscal purpose.

These simple examples may suffice to deal with backward countries. In the more advanced countries, of course, conditions were far more complex.

(B) ADVANCED COMMUNITIES

Mercantilism becomes meaningful only in a community which has attained the necessary maturity to react positively when stimulated by economic policy. Pseudo-mercantilism is the variety always met in backward countries, but it is by no means unknown in the more advanced countries. Because the

[1] Cf. the present writer's *Europäische Wirtschaftsgeschichte Spaniens im 16. und 17. Jahrhundert* (Stuttgart, 1960), especially Chapter IV.

relationships in this case are rather more complicated, it is therefore preferable to discuss orders and prohibitions separately from the customs tariffs.

1. *Orders and Prohibitions*. Pseudo-mercantilism in connection with orders and prohibitions is more easily unmasked than for tariffs. The imperial decree of 1 August 1597, intended to expel the Merchant Adventurers from the Empire, may serve as a first example. The affair is familiar and was excellently treated by Richard Ehrenberg. The decree was not only justified in mercantilist terms but in terms of international law and economic morality as well. The convoying of the cloth fleet by English men-of-war violated international law; the practice of monopoly offended against the canonical prohibition of usury, which the Lutherans accepted. But, at least as it was worded, it was a mercantilist complaint that Hanseatic privileges had been infringed, which had diminished the German merchants' share in international commerce and hence their profits.[1] When the English penetrated farther, to Frankfurt, Augsburg and Nürnberg, they even began to impinge upon the German share of their own internal trade. The active German trade in cloth imports had been converted into a passive trade when the Merchant Adventurers established their staple in Germany and, in the mercantilist canon, this sort of change was always abhorrent. Under superficial examination, then, the imperial decree could be interpreted as a mercantilist measure.

Closer consideration, however, forces upon us the question whether the decree was from the beginning intended to serve other ends, not made explicit, but in any case not mercantilist ones. Ehrenberg has treated the affair so thoroughly that the answer is readily discernible. Despite Spanish backing, the Hanseatic league could overcome the indifference of the imperial commissions only by the liberal greasing of palms.[2] This is quite inconsistent with the mercantilist purpose. Even

[1] Ehrenberg, op. cit., p. 195, cites the plaint of the imperial decree that the English were trying continuously 'to enfeeble, emaciate, and pull down' the German merchants, as 'a complaint wholly mercantilist in conception'.

[2] Ibid., p. 194. As early as 1579, when the Hansa wanted to appeal for assistance to the emperor, Hamburg opined that emperor and Empire would remain indifferent unless they obtained an 'exceptional douceur'. Indeed, it was necessary to 'grease' imperial departments at every stage. Cf. op. cit., pp. 154, 164.

F

so, the decree deliberately left an opening, as only the Merchant Adventurers, and not English merchants as such, were expelled. A second gap was opened by the issuing of imperial licences which produced a rewarding sideline for the emperor and his courtiers. No sooner had the Merchant Adventurers, disguised as free merchants, started up their old accustomed trade in Stade again and complaints about this begun to mount up, than the imperial chancery made use of these circumstances. Elizabeth I had facilitated the disguise by throwing open to all merchants, even the so-called 'interlopers', the trade in cloth to the ports between the Weser and the Elbe, in March 1601. Next, Elizabeth addressed to the emperor a request that he might repeal the decree which applied only to the Merchant Adventurers: now after all there no longer was any question of a monopoly. The emperor and his courtiers, though, wanted neither effective execution nor repeal of the prohibition on which their corrupt gains rested; hence Elizabeth received a refusal in October 1601. The reason for their refusal became obvious only in the next month, November: an imperial councillor was sent to Stade to investigate whether disguised Merchant Adventurers were really continuing to trade there. This inquisition soon degenerated into a 'shakedown'. The commissioner negotiated in a series of secret conferences with the men of Stade and eventually gave out that he could discover nothing for certain.[1] There was no change in the state of affairs which the Hansards had denounced, but they were handed a bill of 4,200 imperial Thalers for expenses. This, then, had no connection with mercantilism but much with pure extortion and corruption, based on the imperial decree.

This is not a criticism of Ehrenberg, who may have emphasized the mercantilist justification of the decree[2] but who rejected the possibility of applying any such notion as 'imperial mercantilism' to a loose federalist structure such as the Empire.

---

[1] Ehrenberg, op. cit., pp. 213, 215. Ingomar Bog, *Der Reichsmerkantilismus* (Stuttgart, 1959), claims that Minckwitz returned without having achieved anything; he explains this by saying that 'he did not know how to conduct such investigations'. But Hanseatic complaints were voiced immediately that Minckwitz had taken bribes: proof of how well this gentleman knew his trade. Cf. Ehrenberg, op. cit., p. 213.

[2] Ehrenberg, op. cit., p. 195.

In his *Reichsmerkantilismus* (pp. 64, 65, 66), Ingomar Bog also denies the mercantilist character of this imperial decree. While this is correct, Bog apparently overlooked the mercantilist justification of the decree, inasmuch as it was directed against the by-passing of the German merchants. Ehrenberg had drawn attention to this,[1] but did not see it as a measure of imperial mercantilism for all that. But the distinction between the imperial decree of 1 August 1597 and the later imperial embargoes, interpreted as 'imperial mercantilism' by Bog, is therefore less great than he appears to think. Surely none of the imperial trade embargoes mentioned can thus be interpreted as an effective implementation of mercantilism, even if they are justified in mercantilist terms.

This is not to say that the then generally prevalent corruption ruled out mercantilism altogether. It was quite feasible if only government were prepared to eliminate corruption, at least partly, so as to facilitate the execution of the required measures. This is best illustrated by reference to England under Elizabeth, where corruption was also a regular feature. The queen was determined to make her counter-attack effective. When the Merchant Adventurers were expelled from the Netherlands in 1563 she also stopped the interlopers from exporting there. To ensure that the prohibition would be observed she set the Merchant Adventurers to supervise the customs officials.[2] At that time the success of mercantilist measures often depended on having them supervised by parties interested in their observance.

Officials were probably inclined to be interested in circumvention of the rules; it was therefore much more difficult to compel them to do their duty. On the whole, the spirit of the age found corruption acceptable, so that such compulsion required special exertion. Diplomacy was concerned with national and dynastic interests, which were highly regarded: here the rulers were usually prepared to exert themselves as required, rather than in economic affairs which were allowed less importance. Thus Elizabeth could tolerate abuses of regulations for the grain trade and of supervision of the bakers by the very justices of the peace who were to control them.[3] The

---

[1] Cf. above, p. 151, n. 1.   [2] Ehrenberg, op. cit., p. 70.
[3] E. Lipson, *The Economic History of England*, II (London, 1931), p. 430.

Statute of Apprentices was obviously quite unsuitable for its
purpose: it was neither abolished nor firmly enforced, but
violations, by an abuse, were made to produce a revenue from
extortion.[1] Under Elizabeth's successors, and especially under
Charles I, who confronted parliament as the sole executive
power, effective execution was simply inconceivable. Matters
improved only towards the end of Charles II's reign when
parliament, with growing success, supervised the executive and
even sat in judgement on officials.[2] The 'glorious revolution'
of 1688 created a firm basis for parliamentary rule and initiated
the period of so-called 'parliamentary Colbertism'.[3] Mercantilism obviously needs a strong central authority: in parliamentary
England it found more favourable conditions than in the German empire with its imperial authorities. A comparison of the
structure of both states might be instructive.

The English House of Commons consisted of representatives
of the landed gentry and of the city merchants. The gentry were
presumably an aristocracy, but there were so many of them that
only a minute proportion could occasionally obtain a remuner-
ative place in government. As they were the most important
tax-payers, they always objected in parliament to corruption at
government level. The city merchants, always the first victims
of corruption, similarly opposed it. Not their virtue but their
large numbers caused the classes represented in parliament to
superintend and guarantee, as far as possible, the execution of

[1] Margaret Gay-Davies, *The Enforcement of English Apprenticeship; a Study of
Applied Mercantilism 1563–1642* (Harvard, 1956). The author sees little of the
general picture, but has brought to light an uncommon wealth of archival
sources. This makes it possible to follow in some detail the tug-of-war between
the Crown, which farmed out the powers of search with their profits, and the
law courts, which anticipated the farmers' loot by secret compacts; at the
same time the different courts of law competed among themselves.

[2] Samuel Pepys mentions repeatedly in his *Diary* that he had been summoned
before a parliamentary committee to testify as to the employment of naval
finances and that great apprehension was caused by such summons. Yet Pepys
was then only a minor secretary of the Navy Board. One can appreciate that the
representatives of the city merchants would rapidly summon any officials who
had permitted circumvention of the navigation laws. Supervision was, of course,
made easier because of the concentration of a very high proportion of commerce
in the port of London.

[3] W. Cunningham, *The Growth of English Industry and Commerce*, 5th edn.
(Cambridge, 1912), II, thus entitles the chapter which deals with this period.

mercantilist legislation, exerting for this their hard-won predominance in the state.[1]

This differed altogether from German conditions. Here agreement about a common imperial economic policy could be but rarely attained; measures here were drafted and operated by men who were more interested in by-passing than in successfully executing them. This is not surprising where 'community' stood only for the least common multiple, was only the resultant vector of independent forces pulling powerfully against each other. Parliamentary decisions, of course, tended to result from a similar play of forces; once decisions had been taken the difference arose from the manner of their execution and from the extent of their territorial reach. Germany differed from England because resolutions adopted in the former were effective only in those federated territories which had actually voted for them. One imperial prince might accede, another might stand aside or even enter the opposite camp. Cologne, Münster, and Bavaria fought on the side of the Sun King in his wars. Naturally they did not support the trade embargo imposed by the empire. Can one rightly speak of 'imperial' mercantilism just because measures originated on the side where the emperor happened to be, although they did not become effective for the whole imperial territory? Even in the principalities which were his allies the emperor possessed no police powers. Each imperial principality executed resolutions or embargoes in its own territory as it wanted. Since consistent implementation was the decisive criterion of mercantilism, 'imperial' mercantilism could exist at all only in exceptional circumstances. It would merit our special attention as a historical exception if it were really possible to establish the existence of an imperial mercantilism, even only for a brief span. This accounts for the interest of Ingomar Bog's book on *Reichsmerkantilismus*, which has deservedly attracted much attention and which has already been cited in this article.

---

[1] Such a difference in numbers was responsible for the entirely different courses of the speculative scandals of 1719 and 1720 in France and England. For this see my article 'Rue de Quincampoix und Exchange Alley', *V.S.W.G.*, XLVIII (1961), pp. 329–59, and my 'Die Korruption in den Kapitalgesellschaften', ibid., XLV (1958), p. 456.

As a discussion is soon to be held based on this work of a colleague, I should here like to confine my remarks about it to a few sentences. Under its main title, 'Imperial Mercantilism', the book is not acceptable; under its subtitle, 'Studies in the Economic Policy of the Holy Roman Empire in the Seventeenth and Eighteenth Centuries', it will be welcome indeed because the valuable material it contains will help towards a better interpretation. At present I merely want to set down briefly a suggested interpretation of the events.

The three import embargoes directed against France during the Dutch War, the War of the League of Augsburg, and the War the Spanish Succession were demanded by the allies. The emperor had the greatest difficulty in meeting the expenses of war; the embargoes served two different fiscal functions for him. First, he obtained subsidies from the allies in return for his show of accession to the boycott; second, the prohibitions served as a point of departure for the creation of *quasi* customs duties, for the emperor did not possess the right to levy these outside his own territories. This camouflaged customs levy of the emperor's did not affect the empire but only the imperial cities, which were militarily weak but powerful in trade. Viennese courtiers were at once dispatched there to act as contraband commissioners. Obviously an effective embargo of the kind demanded by the allies, as well as by any mercantilist circles that there were, could not have produced the yield which the emperor wanted for the treasury: hence no effective embargo had been intended from the beginning.

In the first war the import embargo degenerated in this manner, viz. that goods, allegedly confiscated, were 'auctioned', undoubtedly to be bought back by the importers who had been caught. The proceeds were to be transferred into the imperial coffers. But the yield disappointed the emperor: it turned out that the commissioners were compounding privately with the merchants. Furthermore, there existed a clash of interests between the commissioners, who enriched themselves on the spot, and the courtiers in authority at Vienna. According to then accepted convention, the latter were entitled to a share in the receipts of their subordinates. At the considerable distances involved, however, they could not maintain control and therefore suspected that their shares might not be properly transmitted.

In the second and third wars therefore new methods were adopted: the imperial towns compounded directly with leading ministers and the emperor. In return for large payments into the imperial exchequer and of unknown amounts to the ministers, the embargo was partly converted into a customs tariff. Moreover, in the second and third wars the mere import embargo demanded by the allies was supplemented, in order to increase the yield of this conversion, by an embargo on exports which contradicted mercantilist precepts. This export embargo, which had not been demanded by the allies, was converted into a customs tariff; the import embargo, however, had to be retained, at least in outward show, for diplomatic reasons. Nevertheless, its effectiveness was reduced by several regulations favouring the merchants. In the second and third wars, then, what happened was as follows:

(1) the augmentation of the total income of treasury and officials by the extension of the embargo to exports;

(2) the transfer of the profits of corruption from the contraband commissioners to the leading courtiers in Vienna;

(3) a shift favouring the treasury at the expense of corruption in general.

In short, we have here semi-fiscalism and corruption but not mercantilism.

It is easier to unmask pseudo-mercantilism where 'imperial mercantilism' is concerned, because here prohibitions are involved. The emasculation of such prohibitions by corruption and semi-fiscalism confirms the insincerity of any mercantilist intention, and hence the absence of any 'imperial mercantilism'. Where customs duties are involved it becomes much harder to uncover pseudo-mercantilism.

2. *Customs Duties.* Corruption converts a prohibition into an individual kind of customs duty. From the point of view of mercantilism it is, of course, immaterial whether these 'customs' fall to the lot of the officials rather than that of the public exchequer. Could a prohibition which is abused for corrupt

purposes conceivably be regarded nevertheless as a mercantilist measure? Could mercantilist customs tariffs remain 'mercantilist' despite their corrupt execution?

Colbert was the first statesman who rigorously drew up and executed a comprehensive mercantilist customs tariff. The same Colbert also organized an honest administration in France in the service of Louis XIV. Adam Smith, who lived in the age of corruption and who presumably looked upon such honesty not as the norm but as an exception, wrote about Colbert:

> Mr Colbert, the famous minister of Louis XIV, was a man of *probity*, of great industry and *knowledge of detail*, of great experience and acuteness in the examination of public accounts, and of abilities in short, every way fitted for introducing *method and good order* into the collection and expenditure of the public revenue.[1]

This is the light in which we must examine mercantilism in France under Louis XIV and Colbert; it had one of its rare successes there and at that time, and was therefore justifiably described as 'Colbertism'. Three essential conditions had to be fulfilled for this: (1) the integrity of the ministers themselves; (2) the minute investigation of actual conditions of marketing and production to determine specific rates of duties; (3) the customs tariff, which was thus constructed to correspond to the general nexus of economic relationships between internal economy and foreign trade, must be observed without deviation by the customs officials. The whole success of the customs tariff depended on 'method and good order' in the actual levying of duties, because the customs schedule had been exactly designed to obey mercantilist principles and would have been distorted by corrupt execution.

It is not sufficiently well acknowledged that official customs tariffs under the *ancien régime* did not normally mean very much. According to the law, customs duties were uniform in the republic of the United Netherlands. In reality, though, they differed profoundly, from one 'admiralty' to another and even

[1] Adam Smith, *The Wealth of Nations*, ed. Seligman (Everyman edn., London, 1957), II, p. 157. The three groups of words here italicized by me stand for the three essential conditions of an effective mercantilism as set out below.

between different offices of the same admiralty.[1] Moreover, the tariff ordinances were deliberately left indeterminate so that merchants could not really know exactly what rates of duties applied to their goods. In Hamburg in the sixteenth century the book of rates was indeed deliberately kept secret.[2] In sixteenth- and seventeenth-century Norway 'duties' payable for identical goods differed from one port to another.[3]

The categorization of goods and of classes of goods was also upset because the orientation of corruption differs completely from that of mercantilism. Customs duties are arranged in the mercantilist sense by referring them to the state of imports and exports and to the stage in manufacture of the goods; for corruption private gain is the sole criterion. Only by sheer accident would corrupt execution leave the effect of a customs tariff fundamentally unchanged: the extent of corrupt 'duties' depended only on the costs of by-passing the customs.

Not even the superior officials knew how and to what extent customs were levied. In the conflict between superiors and their subordinates over the spoils of corruption the former employed the armoury of dismissal, transfer, and judicial proceedings, the latter simple secretiveness about their subterfuges. It was a general rule for subordinates to share their emoluments with their superiors, but uncertainty about the amount of the spoils produced much lasting suspiciousness and an underlying mood of conflict. The directors of the *Casa de la Contratación* did not know the tricks of their subordinates; when the council of the Indies in Madrid demanded information on this subject they had to attempt very cautiously, 'con toda disimulación', to obtain some clues from the officials.[4] R. H. Tawney found identical conditions in England during the time of James I.[5]

[1] Joh. De Vries, 'De ontduiking der convooien en licenten in de republiek tijdens de achttiende eeuw' , *Tijdschrift voor Geschiedenis* (1958), pp. 349–61.
[2] Ehrenberg, op. cit., p. 91.
[3] Bosse, op. cit., I, pp. 124, 126, 130.
[4] Chaunu, op. cit., I, pp. 77, 82; III, pp. 120, 174. In 1751 Austria concluded a commercial treaty with Spain in which it was to be given most-favoured-nation treatment; neither the Viennese nor the authorities in Madrid knew what this most-favoured-nation status might comprise. Cf. Bechtel, op. cit., II, p. 353, and his reference there to A. Beer, *Handelspolitik*, p. 74.
[5] Tawney, op. cit., pp. 156, 165.

It is even doubtful whether discrimination by flag or nationality was effectively maintained. The officials at least were interested in their receipts rather than in differences of nationality. In the republic of the United Netherlands foreigners who journeyed independently to the Amsterdam wholesale market were generally made to pay much more than the native firms of merchants not because they were foreign but because they were less well protected and could be squeezed more easily.[1] In Spain the situation was reversed. The Spaniard sending his goods overland *via* Seville to Cadiz on an effectively controlled route paid many times more than the foreigners whose ships lay in the open roadstead of Cadiz: they, always with the connivance of the commanders of the Spanish ships, could trans-ship directly from their own vessels to those of the *flota*.[2] Even if the customs tariff had been devised for mercantilist purposes, corruption would still have transformed it into anti-mercantilism.

Retrospect and Summary

In this paper I have tried to show that orders, prohibitions and customs duties, however strongly mercantilist their express intention, lose their character with corrupt execution. Under the *ancien régime* corruption was allied to semi-fiscalism and both militated against mercantilism.

Until now the problem of responsibility has not been discussed. I have deliberately avoided it in the body of this paper. If I now say something about this in principle, I would be happy if these remarks were to be read as a statement of my own views, which can be accepted or rejected without implying the necessity for modification of the general conclusions derived from the main part of the paper.

[1] De Vries, op. cit., p. 358 n.

[2] Chaunu, op. cit., IV, p. 443; Albert Girard, *La rivalité commerciale entre Séville et Cadix* (Paris, 1932), p. 45. G. de Uztariz, *Teorica y Practica de Comercio* (Madrid, 1742), pp. 241–2, tries to blame the customs farmers or at least the system of farming the customs for this. However, matters had been no different when the customs were still being levied directly by the state; this is made evident by Chaunu, loc. cit., which deals with the year 1615, before the lease. Farming became the rule only after 1647. Cf. Girard, op. cit., p. 46.

As I have suggested in my articles on corruption,[1] the ruler had it in his power to insist on as rigorous an execution of mercantilist measures as was his wont in the case of dynastic measures and foreign policy as a whole. Ministers, too, had power enough at their disposal to enforce compliance with the mercantilist measures they had planned, against the opposition of subordinate officials. This, if true, would suggest that the depreciation of such measures by corruption or fiscalism was due to the intentions and disingenuousness of at least the leading politicians. That the ruler tolerated this where fiscalism was concerned is intelligible; when it involved corruption it must have been either weakness or the implicit assent to contemporary assumptions which granted to economic policy significance of only subordinate rank as compared with dynastic, religious or military affairs.

Finally, it must be remembered that, where this paper deals with the relationship of mercantilism and corruption, its conclusions, strictly speaking, apply only to those aspects of mercantilism concerned with foreign trade. Other aspects, such as the construction of roads and canals and the foundation of manufactories, will also have to be examined in the complete context of the financial and economic policies of the *ancien régime*. They present problems which will have to be approached in a similar manner.

[1] [See above, p. 140, n. 2. D.C.C.]

7 Mercantilism in Germany[1]

INGOMAR BOG

[This article is a translation of 'Der Merkantilismus in Deutschland', which was first published in the *Jahrbücher für Nationalökonomie und Statistik*, Vol. CLXXIII, 1961. The translation is by George Hammersley.]

Every field of knowledge needs some symbols, so that communication may be possible. Students within that field agree on these indicators, representatives so to speak of a rich and highly articulated inner meaning which gain definition by general use over long periods. No single mind can do justice to the total range of meanings; none of these symbols fully describes the totality of ideas for which it supposedly stands. It is its very nature to convey nothing to the uninformed. Meaning and symbol in the natural sciences correspond far more closely

[Translator's note: I am grateful to the late Dr S. H. Steinberg for assistance in preparing this translation. G.H.]

[1] *Note to the original German version by the editor of the* Jahrbücher für Nationalökonomie und Statistik:

As here printed this contribution is the slightly revised version of a paper which the author read on 9 December 1960 in Heidelberg at a session of the commission for economic history of the Gesellschaft für Wirtschafts- und Sozialwissenschaften (Verein für Sozialpolitik), to introduce the discussion. The problem to be considered was the justification for the use of the term *Reichsmerkantilismus* [Imperial Mercantilism]; the author had already affirmed his attitude by thus entitling his book *Der Reichsmerkantilismus* (Stuttgart, 1959). J. van Klaveren criticized this concept and designation in his article 'Fiskalismus – Merkantilismus – Korruption' [Fiscalism, Mercantilism, and Corruption (see Chap. 6)], *Vierteljahrschrift für Sozial- und Wirtschaftsgeschichte*, XLVII (1960), No. 3. The meeting in Heidelberg probably helped to clarify a number of points, but naturally it left many questions still open. The present paper would seem suitable as a stimulus for further discussion. It would be useful if other aspects also were now to be considered. The fundamental question, after all, is not the justification of the term *Reichsmerkantilismus*; it is rather the substance of the present international learned discussion regarding the significance of that historical phenomenon which we have customarily called mercantilism. The present paper, and that of J. van Klaveren already referred to, should offer a valuable contribution to this problem too.

than they do in the technical language of economics. There they still coincide more closely with reality than do the verbal signals of the literary disciplines such as history. Such signals have never been regarded as wholly satisfactory. The humanists created the compact term 'Middle Ages' for the dark 'period in between' of indigenous Gothic and barbarian development when the spiritual paradise of the ancient world had seemingly been lost: the humanists, of course, were once again revealing it to a mankind redeemed. Few other concepts have aroused the hostile criticism of historians as did this creation of the ephemeral spirit of that age. In fact, the verbal formula 'Middle Ages' is nothing more than a temporary designation in a roughly sorted archive. It is the indeterminate middle in the tripartite progression of periods from a world wholly past to the humanist present, and this is no longer our present: it is no longer that last contribution of experience which then determines the whole of present existence.[1] The humanists were thus right to sense their age as an epoch.

World historians, art historians, economic historians: all have tried to reconcile the word and the historic reality. The boundary which was marked by Martin Luther has been shifted from its position, backwards or forwards in time. Economic historians have seen landlordism [*Grundherrschaft*] as the characteristic feature of a millenium; and they have set the end of the Middle Ages in 1848. The more suggestions, the more failures. Whether stretched to the farthest limit or squeezed together, the Middle Ages have still continued, in the consciousness of experts and laymen alike, to occupy the period which the humanists first allocated to them and to fill it with their unmistakable aura.[2]

Other symbols have aroused the same kind of antagonism.

[1] Hermann Heimpel, *Der Mensch in seiner Gegenwart*, 2nd edn. (1957).

[2] Who would deny the emergence of a new spirit, for instance in the fate which befell defenders of Copernican doctrines? *De revolutionibus orbium coelestium* appeared in 1543, after the author's death. On 17 February 1600, fifty years later, Giordano Bruno was burnt because he held firm to Copernicus's doctrine. Another fifty years on, in 1642, Galileo Galilei died a natural death in his villa at Arcetri although under surveillance. They did not dare to execute the sentence of the inquisition and to incarcerate the man who had in 1623 dedicated his literary defence of Copernicus to Cardinal Barbarini, the Pope Urban VIII. The weft in this century's texture, the spirit of the time, are new: it is a new age.

'Early capitalism' was sacrificed to the general antipathy towards the concept of capitalism. Yet even those who, parenthetically as it were, ridicule 'early capitalism', derive benefit from it. The suggested alternatives, such as commercial or financial capitalism, are without exception worse. Capitalism stands for a type of economy in which the means of production do not belong to those who actually perform the work and remain unattainable for them. Early capitalism, then, stands for the time when this type of economy began until, by the end of the sixteenth century, circumstances make it difficult not to rank the capitalist above the craft sectors of the economy. The search for the characteristic marks of capitalism must certainly not be confined to the great commercial firms. Those workers in the southern, central, and eastern economic regions of Germany, who owed their raw materials and their tools to the putter-out, are closer to the wage labourer than to the craftsman.

These few examples from the history of concepts have not been imported into the present context for their own sake. They have been adduced to substantiate the proposition that the membership of a discipline, its self-critical whole, does not erroneously choose and assent to its general terminology. Put the other way round: given the linguistic deficiencies made inevitable by the gap between language and history, only the least inadequate stands any chance of general acceptance.

It is evident from the history of historiography that virtually every generation debates the traditional concepts. A new aggregation of life inspires a new historical picture. Old concepts, too, are summoned to the bar of the new generation. However, like any other subject whose methods of distinguishing truth and error can be taught, history disposes of a basic stock of what are virtually categorical certainties. Content and concepts of the basic stock, its substance and its notations are fully formed, and only their details may be changed. Debates which question them root and branch will of necessity have to return unsuccessfully to their point of departure. The 'Middle Ages', for instance, is one of these certainties. And so is 'mercantilism'. The mercantilists evoked the new social and economic ideal of their age. This dominated the rulers, and with them society, at least in its acknowledged aspirations towards economic objectives. A symbol in the philological sense acquires meaning only in the context of a sentence: similarly the historical symbol takes on flesh and blood in the total context of an age.

II

At present mercantilism is being discussed in Sweden, Britain,[1] and Holland,[2] while in Germany Jacob van Klaveren has contributed to the discussion with his article 'Fiskalismus – Merkantilismus – Korruption'.[3] What follows will be concerned only with propositions which deny that the theory of mercantilism also underlay the principles guiding economic activity. The proposition of the Englishman, D. C. Coleman, reduced to its most rigorous version, regards the concern of government for the economy as so obviously dominated by political purpose as to leave no room for anything that can properly be called economic policy. In other words, absolutism devours mercantilism.[4] The second statement I want to discuss here is the thesis of Jacob van Klaveren. According to him, all striving after the common weal by the economic and political administration is overshadowed by general and dominant corruption. This degrades fiscalism to semi-fiscalism and, even more, mercantilism to pseudo-mercantilism. This would make 'somewhat one-sided' the attempt 'to find a period during the *ancien régime* which can be characterized as "mercantilism"'.[5] Both these contentions deny mercantilism any reality; along-

[1] Cf. E. F. Heckscher's criticism of J. M. Keynes in the second English edition of *Mercantilism* (1953).

[2] J. G. van Dillen, 'Betekenis van het begrip Mercantilisme in de economische en politieke Geschiedschijving', *Tijdschrift voor Geschiedenis*, LXXII (1959).

[3] *V.S.W.G.*, loc. cit.

[4] D. C. Coleman, 'Eli Heckscher and the idea of mercantilism', *Scandinavian Economic History Review*, V (1957). Cf. van Dillen's summary in 'Betekenis', p. 191:

Coleman is quite willing to accept mercantilism as a term for a certain 'trend of economic thought' but not as a label for a definite economic policy. As such the term is in his view misleading and confusing, in that this gives an appearance of unity to measures that in reality were very different from each other. [For my comments on this statement, see above, p. 4. D.C.C.]

[5] See above, p. 142.

side them we may cite T. W. Hutchison's article on Keynes and the history of classical economics,[1] where he wrote: 'It would certainly be a great advantage if it were possible to avoid the concept of "mercantilism" altogether: surely it is one of the worst and vaguest "isms" in the dictionary.' Hutchison maintains that despite all the discussion it has never become quite clear what exactly can be regarded as the central core of mercantilism, i.e. of mercantilist doctrine.

Students of Anton Tautscher's writings, especially of his *Staatswirtschaftslehre des Kameralismus*, which appeared in 1947, would not agree with Hutchison. In a further book, *Die öffentliche Wirtschaft* (1953), Tautscher confessed that the teachings of cameralism meant more to him than a mere historical phenomenon. The economists who reviewed his book would not agree to accept Tautscher's thesis as a compelling principle for the predominantly neo-liberal economic policies of the present day. He had formulated this thesis to mark the core of mercantilist doctrine thus: 'the management of the state's economy is no mere housekeeping ... with the government's own resources to cover its needs ... more than that, it is the management of the total national wealth.'[2]

Tautscher's notions of economic policy may be accepted or rejected. Regardless of this, it remains his merit to have utilized a whole century's accretion of learning to disclose the rigorously logical structure of mercantilist economic policy. That Tautscher discusses cameralism and not mercantilism makes little difference. He sees cameralism as the specifically German variety of mercantilism: because of the federal structure of the empire, its theoreticians substantiated their propositions with experience garnered in the principalities, in their travels, as administrators or even as entrepreneurs. Well-known historians of doctrine have accepted as quite a matter of course that mercantilism and cameralism 'realize two phases of the same development and represent the same principle'.[3]

[1] 'John Maynard Keynes und die Geschichte der klassischen Nationalökonomie', *Zeitschrift für Nationalökonomie*, XVII (1956), No. IV.

[2] A. Tautscher, *Staatswirtschaftslehre*, p. 27. Very regrettably, Tautscher's most fruitful arguments have not hitherto been used in the discussion.

[3] E.g. Eduard Heimann, *Geschichte der volkswirtschaftlichen Lehrmeinungen* (1949), p. 43, citing the work of Luise Sommer and of Kurt Zielenziger. Admittedly

The central core of cameralist doctrine, sought in vain by Hutchison, is the common task which the German cameralists prescribed for themselves 'to reduce the different kinds of productive activity to a just equilibrium and due proportion one with another'. And Justi also tells us to what end the search for due proportion is intended. 'If commerce, manufactures, trades, and production together gain and flourish, and if countries are to become ever more populous, more must without fail flow into the coffers of the government.'[1] Johann Joachim Becher speaks of the 'populous nourishing community'; in Johann David Eulner we read:

> One may frequently observe how a prince will grant exemption from all imposts to wealthy and well-endowed persons who establish factories. Why is this so? Assuredly for no other cause but that such persons thus put out much work and with this they help to nourish many hundreds of people, so by that means they come to be of more use to the prince than if all their capital were paid in as taxes.[2]

The cameralists subordinated their doctrines about government economic policy to their general economic doctrines. Even the first significant theorist, Johann Joachim Becher, recognized two kinds of economic organization 'the structural order of the different kinds of productive activity ... as a pattern of mutually interdependent demand ...' and, on the other hand 'the order established by the state' to the intent 'of reducing different kinds of production to the necessary proportions'.[3] The economic activity of the state is 'the reins by which the state must guide all commerce to its own designs for the true welfare of the state'.[4] Joseph von Sonnenfels deliber-

---

other historians of doctrine, such as Gerhard Stavenhagen, 'Geschichte der Wirtschaftstheorie', *Grundriss der Sozialwissenschaft*, II (1951), have not troubled to do justice to the German mercantilists.

[1] J. H. G. Justi, *Staatswirtschaft*, 2nd edn. (1758), IV, Part II, p. 63.

[2] J. D. Eulner, *Practische Vorschläge, welcher Gestalt Steuer und Contributionen zum Nutzen eines Landesherrn und ohne Nachteil der Untertanen einzurichten seyn*, 2nd edn. (1741), p. 50.   [3] A. Tautscher, op. cit., pp. 114 ff.

[4] J. F. Pfeiffer, *Lehrbegriff sämtlicher ökonomischer und Kameralwissenschaften* (1778), IV, Pt. I, p. 195. 'Commerce' here stands not merely for trade but for the whole economy, and 'state' means the whole community, not just the budget of the government.

ately prefaced each chapter of his maxims by a quotation from Rousseau; he maintained that:

> In the nicest understanding there cannot even be a contradiction between the true private and the true common welfare: a more exacting enquiry will always show that either apparent individual welfare will not last long if it conflicts with the common weal or that alternatively something was seen as derogating from the common weal which did not do so in fact.[1]

The discussion about mercantilism was sparked off by the work of Eli F. Heckscher.[2] His ideas owed less to the German cameralists Johann Joachim Becher, Philipp Wilhelm von Hörnigk and Wilhelm von Schröder than to Davenant, Mun and Child, and to the French practitioners. Consequently, participants in the discussion have also mainly drawn upon the English theorists and the French example.[3] In contrast to the state of the German empire after the Thirty Years' War these thinkers and economic practitioners were familiar with flourishing national economies engaged in world-wide foreign trade distinguished by strongly active groups. In his *Inquiry into the Nature and Causes of the Wealth of Nations*, Adam Smith blamed the companies, the merchants, the entrepreneurs and their specific interests for the plethora of protectionist measures which characterized the 'mercantile system'. It was to be expected that directors of the East India Company, Thomas Mun[4] and Josiah Child,[5] should have formulated the balance-of-trade theory as the original English contribution to mercantilist theory. The German mercantilists, serving a less productive economy without a strong export trade, had to concentrate all their attention on the '*consumptio interna*', the domestic market. They were faced by reality which demanded

[1] J. von Sonnenfels, *Grundsätze der Polizey-, Handlungs- und Finanzwissenschaft* 3rd edn. (1777), Pt. I, p. 17.

[2] *Mercantilism* (Swedish original, 1931; German translation, 1932; first English translation, 1935; second, 1955; second Swedish edn., 1953).

[3] E.g. J. G. van Dillen, 'Betekenis', *passim*.

[4] *England's Treasure by Forraign Trade, or the Ballance of our Forraign Trade is the Rule of our Treasure* (1664).

[5] *Discourse Concerning Trade* (1668).

from them a closed system of national economics: the doctrine of political economy called cameralism.[1]

The differences are obvious. Nevertheless, J. G. van Dillen's observation about the mercantilists in general, not excepting the Germans, may retain its validity: 'they after all had more common sense than Heckscher supposed'.[2] 'The entire economy is seen as a whole';[3] there is an awareness of the static nature of the world economy: it is accepted 'that the world holds a supposedly stable quantity of commodities and that a growing national economy can acquire a greater share of this only in economic conflict at the expense of another country'.[4] The quoted statements undoubtedly nowhere justify the belief that the mercantilists were exercised about the prosperity of the people solely because it formed an inexhaustible source for revenues which reinforced the power of the state.

In the context of the discussion with Hutchison, this seems the point at which to insist on the real contribution of the mercantilists to the development of economic theory. Obviously nobody can formulate a system of economic policy without a clear picture of the complete pattern of economic relationships. Whoever abstracts, from the wildly tangled totality of life, those economic data which can be organized into cause and effect, creates theory. Many mercantilists drew a sharp distinction between empirical data and perceptive insights. Johann Joachim Becher and his successors admittedly did not construct a theory of prices or an exchange mechanism regulated by price. This, the core of classical theory and of its derivatives, was undoubtedly neglected by the mercantilists. Nevertheless, this does not detract from the validity of Eduard

[1] Ingomar Bog, *Der Reichsmerkantilismus*, Forschungen zur Wirtschafts- und Sozialgeschichte, ed. Friedrich Lütge, I (1959), pp. 14 f. The same explanation serves to account for the difference between the ideas of Adam Smith and of Gustav Schmoller which J. G. van Dillen places in juxtaposition. Schmoller saw the state handling the range of mercantilist notions in all the German principalities. It is, of course, true that: 'The English eighteenth-century liberal did not admire the powerful state as much as did the nationalist German professor of the time of Bismarck and William II.'

[2] J. G. van Dillen, 'Betekenis', p. 188.

[3] F. Lütge, *Reich und Wirtschaft. Zur Reichsgewerbe- und Reichshandelspolitik im 17. bis 18. Jahrhundert* (1961), p. 6.

[4] I. Bog, *Reichsmerkantilismus*, p. 66. Van Dillen repeatedly stresses this conviction, pp. 181 f., 182, 198.

Heimann's statement that: 'The theory and practice of mercantilism were eminently dynamic.'[1] The mercantilists owed their insights to their observation of ordinary economic processes, and especially of the market. Their minds were unencumbered by the assumptions associated with notions of harmony derived from natural law: it is not surprising that they were impressed by the disequilibrium of the real situation. They are therefore properly enlisted among the forebears of the new economics. Rudolf Gunzert only recently emphasized in his article 'Was ist Konzentration?' how, in mercantilist doctrines, one 'comes across problems which still retain their significance in the present. Awareness of these can save many a wrong turning.'[2] They not merely pioneered a theory of types of market but they also adumbrated a theory of distribution. Why, then, should we avoid the concept of mercantilism, as Hutchison demands, when it identifies something unique which cannot be mistaken for its predecessors or its successors?

III

When they wished to justify their doctrines mercantilist theorists evidently gave little thought to the priority due either to political objectives or to economic welfare. '... power is essential to wealth, ... wealth is essential to power.'[3] The spirit of the age may have spoken through the merchants of Ulm in mid-June 1677 when they wrote to the town of Nürnberg that it was the business of the state rather than of individual merchants to introduce new manufactures. In the same year the merchants of Augsburg agreed: 'manufactures require knowledge, continuous experience and much capital. Any merchant can invest his money better and with more certainty in commerce; it is more fitting for the public interest so to employ itself than for the private individual.'[4] The need for mercantilist

---

[1] E. Heimann, op. cit.

[2] *Wirtschaftssoziologische Studien*, ed. Rudolf Gunzert, I (1960), pp. 19 ff.

[3] Jacob Viner, 'Power versus Plenty as Objectives of Foreign Policy in the 17th and 18th Centuries', *World Politics*, I (1948). [See above, p. 71.]

[4] I. Bog, 'Die kaiserliche Kommission Johann Joachim Bechers in Nürnberg 1677', *Jahrbuch für fränkische Landesforschung*, XI–XII (1953), where the source references will be found.

endeavour to promote a flourishing economy was recognized, but the state was to be charged with it. Only greater power and improved finances would enable the state 'to adjust the productive activities in their properly proportioned pattern' (Tautscher). We must then agree with van Dillen that, as far as the doctrines are concerned, it is idle to discuss the primacy of either power or welfare.

D. C. Coleman, it is true, is not interested in the doctrine but in the actions and omissions of responsible authorities. With complete justification he stigmatized Heckscher's work as theoretical, as 'curiously unrealistic'.[1] Let us disregard the distaste of the liberal Heckscher for the element of economic planning implied in mercantilism. He shared this antipathy with Adam Smith, and this misled him into the belief that the balance-of-trade doctrine resulted from a fundamentally erroneous theory. A second criticism is equally valid – 'It is a marked feature of Heckscher's work that his book "inflates" the concept ... so that the concept becomes approximately identified with the entire policies of European monarchies in the seventeenth and eighteenth centuries.'[2] But it is Coleman's criticism that Heckscher has lost sight of historical reality which carries the most weight. Simultaneously Charles Wilson[3] reminded us that Mun and Child, the originators of the balance-of-trade theory, were themselves in a position to observe the outflow of English gold to India, Russia, Scandinavia and the Near East. The balance-of-trade theory was therefore not just a 'fallacious theory'. If, however, historical reality fails to justify Heckscher it does as little for Coleman's view, which accepts the existence of a 'trend of economic thought' but not of an economic policy inspired by mercantilism. A look at the circumstances of German states should teach us better.

'A policy of economic management meeting the needs alike of the state and of the national economy': this we have by definition accepted as the meaning of mercantilism.[4] It is the

[1] See above, p. 117.
[2] J. G. van Dillen, 'Betekenis'.
[3] C. Wilson, 'Mercantilism: some Vicissitudes of an Idea', *Economic History Review*, 2nd series, X (1957).
[4] [See above, p. 166. D.C.C.]

form in which it can be identified in the actions of its practitioners, to the letter in the German principalities and, modified by its federal structure, in the Empire too. On behalf of the elector of Brandenburg, the envoys of the principalities of Halberstadt, Kammin, Eastern Pomerania, and Gminden made the following representations to the imperial diet in 1675. The power and reputation of states are based on people and abundance of money. Of neither reputation nor temporal happiness is there enough in Germany. The best of our manhood is lured away by foreigners, and all Europe makes use of German soldiers, even against Germany. Money is sent away for numerous imported manufactures. 'Both of these evils might be cured at one stroke.' In Germany there are towns without people because the manufactures do not flourish, craftsmen without work, and journeymen in their hundreds travelling about and collecting bread from door to door. They all explain that they could find no employment. If one could manufacture oneself all those things which there is now an opportunity to keep out of the Empire, then another hundred thousand people might be sustained in the country and the money saved to the Empire. All who valued things foreign ought to be willing to introduce, here in Germany and for the gain and benefit of the realm, whatever they thought of so highly in Italy, France, and other places.[1]

In 1680 Peter Philipp von Dernbach had read out before the imperial diet what 'great and noticeable benefits' he expected from 'the rejection and prohibition of foreign manufactures' because this would stimulate the imitation of foreign products.[2] In 1677 Count Wilhelm Ludwig of Württemberg sent to consult Johann Joachim Becher in Nürnberg as to how the cloth industry of Calw might be promoted by excluding from the German market the foreign textiles, 'Cadis'[3] and bolting cloth.[4] When the emperor Leopold I married Claudia Felizitas

----

[1] Haus-, Hof- und Staatsarchiv Wien (henceforth referred to as HHStA Wien), Reichstagsakten (henceforth referred to as RTA), Reichsfürstenratsprotokolle, Fasc. 233, 1675-6. Cf. I. Bog, *Reichsmerkantilismus*, pp. 84 f., 99, also for what follows below.

[2] HHStA Wien, RTA, Reichsfürstenratsprotokolle, Fasc., 240, 29 December 1680.

[3] [A type of cheap woollen or worsted. D.C.C.]

[4] HHStA Wien, Mainzer Erzkanzlerarchiv, Zollsachen, Fasc. 21, fo. 81.

in 1673 he boasted that he wore not a stitch on his person which had not been made in the lands of his inheritance. It was in 1673 that the admonitory patents (*Warnungspatenten*) of 29 November introduced the change of course towards a rigid protectionism.[1] Economic references are admittedly rare in the minutes of the secret conference which was the imperial cabinet. It is therefore all the more significant that the emperor himself so frequently contributed with his vote on economic matters. When the aulic council wished to report to the emperor the objections of the imperial cities to the first imperial mercantilist edict of 7 May 1676 it was, contrary to all custom, refused an audience, because the emperor himself insisted on this law. In the customs ordinance of 22 January 1721 his son, the emperor Charles VI, was to write: 'We recognize and know how indissolubly the promulgation of these taxes is connected with the promotion of trade.' In the autumn of 1675, immediately before the first phase of imperial mercantilism, Lorenz von Crockow, Brandenburg's envoy in Vienna, reminded the emperor of the Swedish example. Regardless 'of its closer association with the crown of France,' wrote Crockow, French manufactures had here been prohibited, 'for the salvation of the state and the prevention of the total ruin of the same'.[2] By 'state' here is meant, of course, the whole of Sweden, the king, the institutions of government, and the society.

None of these sources lends itself to the conclusion that rulers and practitioners were without interest in the economy for its own sake.

Closely related to the question of the pre-eminence of political objectives is the problem of fiscalism. To accept van Klaveren's terminology, this is, by definition, not endowed with the foresight to sacrifice immediate utility for the prospect of greater future gain.[3] A government which recognized only its obligations in respect of the problems of internal and external politics might be prepared to exhaust every financial source without thought for the fiscal needs of the future, to say

[1] Wilhelm Roscher, 'Die österreichische Nationalökonomik unter Kaiser Leopold I', *Jahrbuch für Nationalökonomie und Statistik*, II (1864).

[2] HHStA Wien, RTA, Dictata, Fasc. 279, 1675, Diktat der Prinzipalkommission of 20 November 1675.   [3] Cf. above, p. 142.

nothing of the requirements of the economy. Historians owe to van Klaveren the suggestion that in theory pure fiscalism and mercantilism are mutually exclusive: this has offered them a more refined analytical equipment. Conceivably some fiscal measures might produce results which mercantilists would normally aspire to; this would require the kind of favourable economic environment for the fiscal measure which a purely financial technician would be incapable of interpreting within the accustomed considerations of his field. If, for instance, special duties were to be imposed on the commerce of foreigners and if native merchants could fill the gap thus left, internal wealth, and hence the yield of taxation, would increase too. The immediate yield of the customs, however, would not change. This quasi-mercantilist success would not, of course, have been foreseen, and hence would not have been derived as a planned verification of firm theoretical conclusions. The example therefore cannot properly be used to demonstrate the possibility of an occasional alliance between theoretically pure fiscalism and mercantilism.[1]

Such considerations could be justified as theoretical speculations. History, however, deals with the activities of men of widely differing convictions.[2] In a principality one central department of state could cherish fiscal tenets, a second mercantilist ones. The conflict between those two interests has a profound effect on the economic history of the mercantilist era. It had not been finally decided by the time the old Empire ended, yet it left its unmistakable marks upon an entire age.

The German principalities emerged from the Thirty Years' War not only with the formal *jus superioritatis* but with a second invaluable gain; this was a capable generation of princes and public servants equipped with an insight into the structure of the economy which became gradually more penetrating, and with a firm determination to employ this youthful discipline effectively.[3] Many principalities, it may be suggested, turned themselves into proper states only as the result of such

[1] J. van Klaveren has overlooked this point.

[2] F. Lütge, *Reich und Wirtschaft*, has recently expressed some doubt whether fiscalism can indeed be isolated in van Klaveren's sense.

[3] I. Bog, 'Die Dorfplanungen im Nürnberger Raum des 18. Jahrhunderts', *Mitteilungen der Altnürnberger Landschaft*, VI (1957), Pt. I.

efforts.[1] War and plague, high mortality and low birth rates had excessively diminished the labour force, and the first need was therefore the restoration of a reasonable ratio of labour to land. This was to be achieved by a suitable population policy, the *Peuplierung* (peopling); it was vigorously promoted by the diversion of ample public funds towards the individual peasant economy, partly as cash and partly as capital goods. This was intended to procure optimum productivity, within the limits of natural fertility and contemporary techniques – which hardly advanced at all. Here is the explanation for the official preference for such commercial crops as tobacco or hops, madder, woad, and the like, which give a better return from labour and land. At least in grain-producing regions this was quite a new preference. Before the war there had been fierce opposition to any change which threatened to diminish the amount of arable under grain, even when a higher individual return could have been expected. The fisc relinquished momentary gain and smoothed the path to a happier future with gifts of wood, rebuilding subsidies, premiums, rent-free years, forgiven dues and moratoria: this played no small part in overcoming the dreadful consequences of the Thirty Years' War.[2] Intimate contact with an economy which had to be reconstructed from miserable beginnings created in the ablest members of the civil service and of the academic bourgeoisie a common-sense belief in the validity of the reversible equation state power = economic power. Thus the spirit of the mercantilist age was born.[3]

Admittedly, the birth of this new spirit had not yet decisively

[1] F. Lütge, *Reich und Wirtschaft.*

[2] F. Lütge, *Deutsche Sozial- und Wirtschaftsgeschichte* (1952), pp. 241 ff.; for the principality of Öttingen-Öttingen, August Gabler in *Jahrbuch des Historischen Vereins für Mittelfranken*, LXXIX (1960-61); for mid-Franconia, I. Bog, 'Die bäuerliche Wirtschaft im Zeitalter des 30 jährigen Krieges', *Schriften des Instituts für fränkische Landesforschung*, IV (1952). For Brandenburg, Coburg, Oldenburg, and Württemberg similar data may be observed. Convincing evidence for Westphalia in Bruno Kuske, *Wirtschaftsgeschichte Westfalens in Leistung und Verflechtung mit den Nachbarländern* (1948).

[3] Oswald Redlich, 'Der Dreissigjährige Krieg und die deutsche Kultur', *Ausgewählte Schriften* (1928); I. Bog, *Bäuerliche Wirtschaft mit Quellenbelegen aus dem Fränkischen*; F. Lütge, 'Die wirtschaftliche Lage Deutschlands vor Ausbruch des Dreissigjährigen Krieges', *Jahrbuch für Nationalökonomie und Statistik*, CLXX (1958).

impinged upon the traditions of the fiscalist treasuries, of the princely financial authorities. But the question of how many disciples this new creed attracted, especially in the eighteenth century, is not one to be shirked. Cameralism was made a subject of systematic instruction in Germany alone; in 1727 chairs in it were founded at Halle and at Frankfurt-on-the-Oder, and henceforth the universities transmitted the doctrine to many generations of prospective civil servants.

In the decades which immediately followed the Thirty Years' War, however, the mercantilists found it hard to prevail against the fiscalists in the German states. 'Government and revenue board guarded their rights jealously and well understood how to derive and buttress them with legal argument down to the last detail.' Hence the mercantilists agitated 'for the official institution of a purely economic policy'.[1] 'It is the merit of the mercantilist, . . . trend alone that, from the last third of the seventeenth century, the new responsibilities of economic policy were ever more frequently delegated to newly founded commercial authorities.'[2] Originally they were derived from 'the welfare aspects of police jurisdiction',[3] like the councils for the affairs of police and commerce instituted by Maximilian I of Bavaria between 1610 and 1640; they gradually developed into independent institutions. The great Johann Joachim Becher still chose a 'police ordinance' as the vehicle for his economic plans in 1661 for electoral Mainz, and even in the spring of 1664 for the electoral Palatinate.[4] In the summer of 1664 he was won over by the example of the Amsterdam Commercial College founded in 1663. At once he submitted a plan for a commercial college to the elector of Bavaria. The project failed, and Becher was invited to Vienna, where, after unceasing effort, the commercial college (*Kommerzkollegium*) was founded on 22 February 1666; it was the official buttress of the entire economic policy which he inspired, and especially

---

[1] Friedrich Facius, 'Wirtschaft und Staat. Die Entwicklung der staatlichen Wirtschaftsverwaltung in Deutschland vom 17. Jahrhundert bis 1945', *Schriften des Bundesarchivs*, VI (1959), p. 8.

[2] F. Facius, op. cit., p. 18.   [3] ibid., p. 20.

[4] Cf. above all Herbert Hassinger, *Johann Joachim Becher, 1635–1682*, Veröffentlichungen der Kommission für Neuere Geschichte Österreichs, XXXVIII (1951), pp. 23 ff.

of the five projected manufacturing and trading companies.[1] He hoped thus to liberate the policy from fiscal influence. The notion of the college survived for more than a century, especially as Becher immortalized it in his famous and frequently republished *Politischer Discurs*.[2]

Most German principalities followed in the footsteps of the Habsburg dominions. Between 1710 and 1790 there were two false starts in Baden-Durlach, and the commercial council (*Kommerzdeputation*) for Baden-Durlach and Baden-Baden was active in Karlsruhe from 1790 to 1805. The appointment of the mercantilist Johann Georg Förderer Edler von Richtenfels in the year 1710 is closely linked with the foundation of Karlsruhe as a commercial city.[3] At five different times between 1689 and 1788 colleges and councils were set up in Bavaria; Brandenburg-Prussia, simply among the central authorities, had eleven colleges, commissions, and councils from 1677 to 1796. Brunswick-Wolfenbüttel attempted three times between 1674 and 1714 to establish a consultative commission of economic practitioners which, in 1681, was intended to act as representation for the commercial interest. In Hessen-Kassel five authorities were being actively considered or founded between 1710 and 1782; so were three in the imperial town of Lübeck between 1740 and 1814, while nine projects were discarded during preliminary discussions. Electoral Mainz set up four commissions for the territory of Erfurt between 1687 and 1782, Austria established six central authorities between 1666 and 1765, to say nothing of the colleges for Silesia, Bohemia, Moravia, Trieste, Görz, etc. The Palatinate fits into this pattern of German principalities, with five councils, chambers, directorates and commissions between 1681 and 1768; and

[1] F. Facius, op. cit., p. 21.
[2] This book is essential for an understanding of German mercantilism. It appeared under the title *Politischer Discurs von den eigentlichen Ursachen, des Auf- und Abnehmens der Städt, Länder und Republiken*, Frankfurt (1668); 2nd edn., Frankfurt (1673), the best one for historical purposes; 3rd edn., Frankfurt (1688); 4th edn., Frankfurt (1720, 1721). Cf. Herbert Hassinger's excellent monograph, op. cit., p. 266.
[3] F. Facius, op. cit., Exkurs IV, gives a list of commercial authorities in German principalities in the seventeenth and eighteenth centuries which is most useful.

finally the kingdom of Saxony offers four foundations between 1711 and 1764.

The rise and decline of all these authorities is a commentary on the embittered conflicts between the mercantilist spirit and an inflexible fiscalism. The disciples of the mercantilist spirit were not so much overwhelmed by pettifogging accountancy as depressed by the Empire's over-extension during half a century of war on two fronts between 1660 and 1715, yet they girded themselves to ever-renewed endeavour.[1] They retained an audience because their spirit was the ferment in the economic consciousness of the age. The fate of Johann Joachim Becher and of his foundations may serve as a parable.

Becher had demarcated a field of work for the Viennese commercial college of 1666 'which was not merely derived from those of existing authorities'.[2] The

> survey of the whole of commerce, of changes in prices and consumption, the survey and promotion of industry and of industrial technology (Becher displayed glass and ceramics to the delegation of the Nürnberg council which he had developed in his manufactory on the Tabor)[3] ... and of companies outside the gilds, as well as the gathering of information about economic conditions abroad from commercial correspondents.

The commercial college was charged with all of this. The great imperial ministers, the lord high steward [*Obersthofmeister*], the lord high chamberlain [*Oberstkämmerer*], and the lords of the treasury [*Hofkammerpräsidenten*] were to be restricted to a loose general supervision and to the giving of advice. Five great manufactory companies were to be founded; the principal office of their managing directors was to be that of commercial councillor, and they were to be called upon to conduct an economic policy in economic terms.

Becher's promising intentions were thwarted by the jealousy of court authorities, above all of the treasury, but especially

---

[1] I. Bog, 'Christoph de Royas y Spinola und die deutschen Reichsstände', *Jahrbuch für fränkische Landesforschung*, XIV (1954).

[2] F. Facius, op. cit., pp. 22 ff., and for what follows.

[3] Staatsarchiv Nürnberg, Differential-Akten, No. 505, 14 March, 1677.

by the envy of the president of the aulic treasury, Georg Ludwig Count Sinzendorf, with his petrified fiscalism.[1] As president of the aulic treasury he also obtained jurisdiction over the commercial college, while most of its members were primarily officials in other departments of the court. The real commercial councillors, the merchant experts, remained in a minority. The college was left without a secretariat or authoritatively delegated powers of control; it expired of its own weaknesses in 1674. Becher himself fell a victim to his fiscalist enemies when, in 1677, he tried to drive out the devil with brimstone: he used his own brain child, the first imperial mercantilist law against the import of French goods, to score a fiscal success. He conjured up before the emperor the prospect of five millions worth of loot in French contraband from the imperial towns alone. Five million gulden was one and a half million more than the treasury's peace-time revenue from the whole of the state.[2]

The city councils, well instructed by the merchants, confronted Becher with his own mercantilist teaching: from town to town mercantilist reactions flooded in, more and more overcoming him. As fiscal intent disappeared, so did the prospect of fiscal success and with this went the favour of the Viennese treasury. Becher did not return to Vienna, but left the Empire at the end of his travels.[3] The fate of Becher and his foundation was shared by many commercial colleges and their begetters. In Baden-Durlach, Förderer von Richtenfels fell under the bitter opposition of the treasury. The Bavarian commercial college of 1689 yielded itself up to subjection by the treasury in 1699; weighty concessions to the supreme council and to the revenue chamber undermined the commercial council of Württemberg of 1709.

Nevertheless, the idea conquered rigid fiscalism. Progress occurred in three stages. The founding ventures, originating between 1666 and 1700, did not prosper. The second stage lay

---

[1] Heinrich Ritter von Srbik, *Der Staatliche Exporthandel Österreichs von Leopold I. bis Maria Theresia* (1907), pp. 68, 77 ff.; H. Hassinger, *Johann Joachim Becher*, p. 146.

[2] H. von Srbik, op. cit., pp. 193 ff.

[3] I. Bog, 'Becher in Nürnberg', for the sources.

in the first third of the eighteenth century, and some of its
foundations survived with only brief interruptions: the commercial commission of electoral Mainz in Erfurt (1704–16), the
commercial council of Württemberg (1709–30), and the commercial authorities in several Habsburg territories, Silesia
(1716–40), Inner Austria (1716–49), Bohemia (1717 and
1724–49), Austria above and below the Enns (1719 to *ca.* 1740),
Trieste (1731–35).[1]

Around 1740 new foundations and revivals at last grew more
numerous and, to quote Friedrich Facius, they were distinguished 'generally by their persistence or by a tendency to
healthy innovation, lasting into the nineteenth century'. In
1740 the fifth department of the Prussian general directory was
established as a purely commercial authority; it survived until
the overthrow of all traditional arrangements in 1807. From
1746 to 1776 Austria possessed a commercial administration
which did not lack uniformity either at the centre or in the
territories.

All these colleges strove for independence and struggled for
control over their own administration. They provide a substantial argument against D. C. Coleman's proposition, which
views mercantilism as a vehicle for power politics rather
than for economic policy.[2]

Many, perhaps most, of the enterprises of these mercantilist
commissions failed, as did those of the 'entrepreneurial'
nobility. Merit for the later successes may have to be shared
between the contemporary advocates of economic policy and
the secular improvement in the economy during the second
half of the eighteenth century,[3] for which economic policy did
not perhaps bear primary responsibility. Equally, though, it
cannot be made to bear the sole blame for the failures of the
first decades after the Thirty Years' War: these were partly

---

[1] F. Facius, op. cit., pp. 190 ff., 205, and for what follows.

[2] [For my comments on this statement, and that on p. 165, see above p. 4.
D.C.C.]

[3] This problem is illuminated by the seminal work of Wilhelm Abel, *Agrar-
krisen und Agrarkonjunktur in Mitteleuropa vom 13. bis zum 19. Jahrhundert* (1935).
The author is obliged, for important suggestions, to Professor Abel's contributions to the discussion at the meeting in Heidelberg which was devoted to the
topic of *Reichsmerkantilismus*.

due to the secular depression. Yet it was the mercantilist spirit which stood godparent to the towns built mainly for economically well-qualified immigrants: Hanau and Freudenstadt, Mannheim, Karlsruhe, the new towns in Ansbach and Erlangen, and many others. Notable industries flourished therein.[1]

Is it, then, right for Jacob van Klaveren and others like him to judge mercantilism by its successes and to deny its existence if they have been tried and found wanting?[2] Who would refuse to include the century after the death of Descartes in the age of enlightenment because thousands of pyres roasted witches in every country? In German territory the age of mercantilism spans the period from the end of the Thirty Years' War to the end of the Napoleonic era. The responsible prince, the discipline of cameralism, and the initiators of economic policies, the councillors in governments and commercial colleges: all paid obeisance to one socio-economic ideal. It was the state made powerful by the 'populous nourishing community' (Becher); a 'populous nourishing community' made thus by the state's care. All who were economically active at the time, even the urban merchants, breathed this atmosphere, whether it helped or hindered.[3]

[1] Helmut Erbe, 'Die Hugenotten in Deutschland', *Volkslehre und Nationalitätenrecht in Geschichte und Gegenwart*, 2. Reihe (2nd series), I (1937).

[2] J. van Klaveren, above, pp. 155ff.

[3] Hans Mauersberg, *Wirtschafts- und Sozialgeschichte zentraleuropäischer Städte in neuerer Zeit* (1960), p. 248, n. 2. He here objects that 'solely on the strength of these imperial or princely decrees it is not possible to explain away the liberal economic policy of the towns which in fact remained widely practised despite decrees; this was especially true of the economic operations of the major towns, which must after all indisputably be regarded as the originators of decisive economic trends in the higher echelons of economic activity during the seventeenth and eighteenth centuries'. None will deny, in particular, that the diplomacy of the imperial towns sought, at the emphatic request of the mercantile patriciate, to protect the free exchange of commodities from disturbance. It must not be forgotten, however, that old business ties, e.g. with France, were dissolving under the pressure of imperial protectionist decrees from 1676 onwards and that new links were being forged. It has long been known, too, what severe damage the protectionism of the principalities inflicted on the urban economy. Cf. Georg Schrötter, 'Nürnbergs wirtschaftlicher und finanzieller Niedergang', *Historischpolitische Blätter für das katholische Deutschland*, CXL (1907), and *Reichsmerkantilismus*, Exkurs.

IV

As we have seen, it needed a severe and extended struggle against predominantly fiscal modes of thought to tilt the balance within the commercial authorities towards the advocates of mercantilism, especially for the internal economy. The imperial constitution had entrusted the internal economy to the principalities. Mercantilist doctrine naturally also offered rules for a policy on foreign trade. In fact, a policy for foreign trade was not only implemented by individual territories in their intercourse with their equals, but also by that association for political action on the part of the German states, i.e. the Empire.[1] The federalist structure of the Empire obviously presented a severe obstacle to attempts of that kind. It was surmounted by the powerful revival, between 1660 and about 1715, of that sense of imperial unity which, assisted by the nations of Europe, saved the Empire from the fatal menace of eastern Islam and of Louis XIV's aspirations for western hegemony. The decades of war were punctuated by mercantilist laws which were debated and passed by the imperial diet at Regensburg and approved by the emperor. The import of French and Genevan commodities was prohibited in 1676, 1689 and 1702-3; in Leibniz's estimate these had swallowed up a tenth of the German national income. It was expected that this would release extraordinary purchasing power, thus stimulating demand for German substitutes, not least for the manufactures of the French immigrants; this in turn would cause them to prosper greatly, to the use and benefit of society at large.

It matters little if a few of the principalities were not allied with the emperor in some of the wars.[2] The first imperial law remained without immediate effect precisely in those years when Ferdinand Maria's Bavaria and Johann Friedrich's Hanover were linked with France. In the War of the League of Augsburg Max Emanuel of Bavaria was the emperor's supreme

---

[1] F. Lütge, 'Aussenwirtschaftspolitische Massnahmen des Deutschen Reiches im Zeitalter des Merkantilismus', *Festgabe für Friedrich Bülow*, eds. Otto Stammer and Karl C. Thalheim (1959), summarizes the data; Lütge, *Reich und Wirtschaft*.

[2] J. van Klaveren makes much of this factor. [See above, p. 155.]

commander; the emperor's friend Ernst August had inherited
Hanover in 1679; exactly as in the War of the Spanish Succession, the territories of Cologne were occupied by the armies and
their commissioners-at-war had been charged by the council of
war at Vienna to execute the law as official contraband commissioners. They obeyed strict military orders.[1] In the War of the
Spanish Succession Max Emanuel lay abroad while the emperor
held his Bavaria.

That the laws were adapted to fiscal ends would be a graver
objection. They were demanded by the allies and thus earned
subsidies for the emperor; they made extensive confiscation
possible and thus created imperial 'incidental customs'. They
had not been intended as an economically effective embargo
because that would not have procured the fiscal yield desired by
the emperor.[2] The history of these laws however does not
permit this interpretation.

The first imperial edict of 1676 sprang from the mind of
Johann Joachim Becher, who can certainly not be suspected of
fiscalism. The text of the imperial law itself reproduces Becher's
turn of phrase.[3] The ambassador of Brandenburg at the imperial
court, Lorenz von Crockow, promoted it through the official
stages; the secret conference at Vienna did not deny his
competence as a mercantilist.[4] Long before the beginning of the
Dutch war, i.e. before 1672, Brandenburg had discussed
similar plans with the States General.[5] What personal advantage
could Crockow have expected from the edict? The edict itself
was explicitly mercantilist, following in the footsteps of its
Austrian precursor of the year 1673 when Leopold I had
boasted that every stitch on his body had been manufactured in
the lands of his inheritance.[6] Explicitly mercantilist, too, were
the reasons advanced by the imperial estates to justify this law

[1] Kriegsarchiv Wien, Hofkriegsratsprotokolle, Nos. 389, 392, 398, and attached
papers.
[2] J. van Klaveren, above, pp. 156–7, claims this but offers no proof.
[3] J. J. Becher, *Politische Discurs*, 2nd edn., pp. 786 ff., and especially pp. 814 ff.,
for the text of the decree.
[4] HHStA Wien, Geheime Konferenz, Kanzlei- und Konferenzvota, Fasc. 21,
12 January 1675.
[5] I. Bog, *Reichsmerkantilismus*, p. 82; the prohibition is also discussed in J. G.
van Dillen, 'Betekenis', but the problem of its interpretation is not yet settled.
[6] Cf. p. 173, above.

G

to the imperial diet.[1] The emperor himself, in opposition to the vote of the aulic council, insisted in 1677 on retaining the law.[2] The law lost its effectiveness in 1678: more will be said about this below. In closest consultation with the highest court offices the emperor immediately essayed a new initiative in imperial mercantilism: a plan for something like a 'common market' of the imperial estates; in 1678 Christoph de Rojas y Spinola submitted this to the princes and the urban magistrates.[3] The envoy of Nürnberg reported in 1690 from Vienna that the secret conference, in the presence of the president of the aulic council, the imperial vice-chancellor, the lord-chancellor and others, had decided to implement that law and had obtained 'the highest authority of the emperor'. The aulic council speaks of 'the emperor's policy'.[4] One could find countless additional proofs which all exclude the assumption that the embargo was imposed for fiscal rather than for mercantilist purposes.

True, the imperial mercantilist edicts shared their formulary with the proclamations and prohibitions customary in a state of war which exposed all property of enemy subjects to confiscation. It was an unfortunate decision to instruct commissioners, dispatched to the estates to implement the imperial edict against the import of French commodities, with the confiscation of enemy property under the laws of war as well. They fell foul of the law of the Empire.[5] Johann Joachim Becher had aroused exaggerated fiscal expectations for his commission, hoping thus to escape at last the hostility of the president of the aulic treasury; he was crushed by this conflict. It is, however, an unjustifiable suspicion that the commissioners, one and all, were corrupt or in particular that they indulged in collusive embezzlement with their Viennese superiors.[6] What could have been Becher's motive in proposing to enrich his arch-enemy, the president of the aulic treasury, Count Sinzendorf? On the other hand, the commission in

[1] See above, pp. 172–3.
[2] Staatsarchiv Nürnberg, Differential-Akten, No. 505, 29 April 1677.
[3] See above, p. 178, n.1.
[4] Staatsarchiv Nürnberg, Differential-Akten, No. 507.
[5] I. Bog, *Reichsmerkantilismus*, Exkurs.
[6] J. van Klaveren, above, pp. 156–7.

Frankfurt in 1677 was sent by electoral Mainz, not by Vienna. In Nürnberg there officiated in 1690 a Wallerstein official (*Amtmann*) whose honesty impressed even his opponents, the town council of Nürnberg.[1] In Hamburg the law of 1676 was executed by the incorruptible Habbaeus von Lichtenstern.

The problem of imperial mercantilism is evidently not exhaustively settled by a confrontation of mercantilism and fiscalism or of mercantilism and corruption. Admittedly the president of the aulic treasury in 1678 sold the right to punish the town of Hamburg for its infringement of the imperial law. This was wrong, and in consequence the law was undermined in the whole Empire. There was some excuse, though, for this piece of pure fiscalism: just at this time lack of all means had compelled the secret conference to recommend to the emperor the consideration of an early peace.[2] Long after Sinzendorf's death, however, when Hamburg hoped in 1690 to buy exemption from the imperial law with 50,000 Gulden, the imperial vice-chancellor count of Königsegg wrote to the resident of Hamburg 'even with such a considerable sum it will not be possible to obtain anything from the emperor'.[3]

The first law of 1676 failed. Its inspiration survived, borne up by the wave of patriotism which was a feature of this period. When the War of the League of Augsburg started, the ledger of leading Nürnberg houses show that Saxon, Dutch, English, and Swiss goods had replaced French ones in the decade of peace with France.[4]

What is corruption? Does it include the hospitable gift, the 'donative' presented by the imperial towns to every personage of standing passing through, to every imperial councillor, to every civil servant of rank, and thus to the imperial commis-

[1] Cf. p. 184, n. 5, above.
[2] H. von Srbik, *Exporthandel*, p. 204; Hofkammerarchiv Wien, Hoffinanz, 1 December 1677.
[3] Staatsarchiv Hamburg, Classis VII, Lit. K^d No. 1, Vol. Ib varia, Prod. 3, fos. 19–37.
[4] Staatsarchiv Nürnberg, Differential-Akten, No. 507, 1689-90. The council had examined the books of the great merchants at the request of the imperial commissioners. This intervention was regarded as highly improper and as gravely damaging to the international reputation of the trade of Nürnberg.

sioner Johann Joachim Becher too? Did most of the 'gratifica-
tions' which disappeared into ministerial pockets really buy
consciences? Did they not rather buy time, the privilege of
speedier dispatch? Did not the jealousy of rival authorities
produce that useful degree of moral anxiety which, fearing
discovery, leaves matters to justice?[1]

The merchants of the imperial towns complained too frequently about goods confiscated and perishing at the frontiers
to support the belief that the mercantilist intentions of the
empire could have been thwarted by the corruption of commissioners and customers. There was the ever-present
reluctance of merchants to expose themselves to criminal or
social risks which might destroy their 'credit' but, quite apart
from this, it must be acknowledged that their rapidly rising
prices placed prohibited commodities out of reach for the
majority of purchasers.[2] In 1693 the imperial ambassador and
head of the contraband control organization in Switzerland was
offered 15 per cent *ad valorem* plus customs duties for illicit
certificates of passage.[3] To Germany, too, may be applied the
statement of the inspector general of the English customs in
1668 that '. . . every Maid-Servant in England became a standing Revenue to the French King of the half of her Wages'.[4]
French fashions had universal currency. Even if corruption
had opened the empire's gates as the Swiss merchants had
wanted, the expectations of those Augsburg merchants who, in
1679, expected that high rates of duty on commodities 'would

---

[1] A good example is provided by the behaviour of the imperial vice-chancellor
Count Königsegg in 1689 when Hamburg tried to buy its exemption from the
mercantilist imperial laws. I. Bog, *Reichsmerkantilismus*, p. 115.

[2] J. van Klaveren is difficult to understand on this point. He writes (above,
p. 157): 'it is easier to unmask pseudo-mercantilism where "imperial mercantilism" is concerned because here prohibitions are involved. The emasculation of
such prohibitions by corruption and semi-fiscalism confirms the insincerity of any
mercantilist intention. . . .' As the legislators and the corrupters are not identical,
the statement lacks logical cohesion. F. Lütge, *Reich und Wirtschaft*, p. 24,
similarly emphasizes that mercantilism and fiscalism can be distinguished only in
theory but not in practice.

[3] Herbert Lüthy, *Die Tätigkeit der Schweizer Kaufleute und Gewerbetreibenden in
Frankreich* (Zürich, 1943), p. 72.

[4] A. Anderson, *An Historical and Chronological Deduction of the Origin of Commerce*, II (London, 1764), pp. 135–6. [Transl. note: the author refers to the German translation of 1773.]

restrain at least the lower orders from their purchase', would have been justified.[1]

The Empire preferred embargoes on imports to prohibitive tariffs; this is partly explained by the example of the sea powers, e.g. England, which was familiar to the imperial diplomats. In addition, it heeded the unfortunate experiences of Brandenburg, for instance, with its trial of very high duties. Johann Georg Krünitz in 1782 and Sonnenfels still advocated the advantages of the embargo over prohibitive duties because that avoided the difficulty of having to distinguish between duty-paid and smuggled goods.[2]

The Empire's torment evoked the determination to subdue the enemy at last: the mercantilist purpose was overcome and all traffic with the enemy prohibited in 1689 and 1702-3, including the export of non-military goods. Thereupon the protests of the Netherlands, the Swiss cantons, the imperial towns, and of the district of Swarbia re-oriented policy in the mercantilist sense; in fact, going a little beyond the norm hitherto accepted. The Swiss frontier became the only entrance left open for the products of Geneva and France, and here was developed a customs organization in 1693 and 1705 with its own court of law.[3] The emperor approved a rigorously mercantilist customs tariff, of which the yield was assigned to the Swabian district, which was struggling hard in the west. The export of non-military goods was once again permitted freely, and so was trade with all neutral countries who had an unfavourable balance of trade with the Empire. A system of over-elaborate controls kept enemy goods out of the Empire. Certainly the imperial towns did not purchase this tariff by heavy payments to the emperor and his ministers.[4] These measures were in fundamental conformity with the Empire's

---

[1] Stadtarchiv Augsburg, Commercia, Tom. I, Prod. XXVIII/6, 31 January 1697.

[2] Hugo Rachel, 'Die Handels-, Zoll-, und Akzisepolitik Brandenburg-Preussens bis 1713', *Acta Borussica* (1911), p. 703; Johann Georg Krünitz, *Ökonomische Enzyklopädie* (1782 ff.), Pt. III, pp. 200 ff.

[3] I. Bog, *Reichsmerkantilismus*, pp. 126 ff., 141 ff.

[4] J. van Klaveren, above, pp. 156-7, takes a view of this which is not supported by the sources. For the payments made by the towns and the reasons for them cf. *Reichsmerkantilismus*, Exkurs.

original intention to defend the country against the flood of French goods.

It was no accident that these events took place at the Swiss border. In the west, from the upper Rhine to the sea, the armies confronted each other. English and Dutch privateers beset the Empire's coasts, freight rates rose, and the trade in French fashions, whether clothing or domestic utensils, for rich and poor alike, disappeared as a result. Hence transit via Switzerland alone was left open for these goods.

Imperial mercantilism is a new topic. It will still need much research to verify contemporary opinions; according to them, imperial mercantilism produced a favourable balance of trade with France, severely damaged Genevan industry, and hence aroused unrest in the town. They also claimed that: 'silk manufactures in France have much declined in recent years whereas they have increased in Germany and the Netherlands and that demand had mostly followed it there.'[1]

How close must have been the correspondence between the mercantilist idea and the spirit of the age if it caused so loosely federated a structure as the Empire to bring forth 'imperial mercantilism'.[2] It reinforces our conviction that one may indeed properly speak of an age of mercantilism in Germany.

[1] Quoted from H. Lüthy, op. cit., pp. 28 ff.

[2] We have given reasons to show why it is not proper, other things being equal, to compile statistics of mercantilist successes as a criterion whether an age under the sign of mercantilism existed or not. J. G. van Dillen, too, is cautious about evaluating even the success of Colbert: 'On the other hand it is probable that the French textile industry certainly became more prosperous through the exclusion of Dutch and English cloth by means of very high import duties and the granting of export premiums to the French Levant trade' ('Betekenis', p. 185). Nevertheless he poses the question to Coleman why a common European policy, oriented towards economic unity and welfare, should not be recognized as mercantilism. It is difficult enough to deal satisfactorily with the economic operation of gild regulations covering an easily comprehended area; it is one of the hardest tasks of economic historiography to count the successes of large-scale and long-term economic policy before the end of the eighteenth century. Published research in the archives does not suffice to dismiss mercantilist economic policy as unsuccessful, especially as closer examination shows that many enterprises failed for other than economic reasons. Ortulf Reuter, 'Die Manufaktur im Fränkischen Raum', *Forschungen zur Sozial- und Wirtschaftsgeschichte*, III (1961), emphasized in any case that 'resulting from an imperial edict of 1676 which prohibited the import of French luxuries as a measure of mercantilist warfare against France, a genuine upsurge of new foundations occurred in the Nürnberg region during the decades around 1700'.

This will be quietly acceptable to anyone who refuses to pass the troubled but full stream of history through the excessively fine filter of a logical schema. Too little of the water would reach the historians' mills. For Goethe's word remains true: 'Die Welt, durch Vernunft dividiert, geht nicht auf.'[1]

[1][Literally: 'the world divided by reason will not go,' i.e. as in a division sum. The implication is as in the preceeding sentences of the text, i.e. that reason alone does not provide a definitive solution to the problems of the world. D.C.C.]

8 French Views on Wealth and Taxes from the Middle Ages to the Old Régime

MARTIN WOLFE

[This article was first published in the *Journal of Economic History*, Vol. XXVI, No. 4, 1966.]

The belief that the state should, can, and must contrive to make its subjects wealthier, and that in part this can be done through its taxing powers, certainly is one of the most powerful concepts in modern times. Intuitively it seems that this belief must arise from important and strongly rooted developments starting far back in the history of Western thought and institutions. Economic historians concerned with the history of economic growth ought to be able to demonstrate which developments produced this belief, and when. But work on this highly interesting problem of origins has yet to be begun. The dimensions of the problem, at least, can be presented by sketching in the main developments for one country, France, over the whole period from a time when the concept of a beneficent national fisc obviously was still unborn to that point when it was alive and thriving. Viewed as an essay on the history of economic thought, this paper is a suggestion that some of the concepts concerning French mercantilism found in modern writings need to be improved. The questions to be raised are: At what point did influential persons in France begin to argue that by changing its tax policies the state could promote what we call economic growth? And when can we say that an important part of royal fiscal policy was aimed at promoting the wealth of the king's subjects?

None of us needs to be reminded that what we call Western civilization does not begin with the Renaissance, that our way of life should not be contrasted with that of the Middle Ages, since it is in fact an extension of medieval culture, and that when a person uses the term 'medieval' to mean stagnant, exotic, and otherworldly (and therefore of another civilization) he is only buttressing our medievalists' customary posture of smug despair. For our topic, however, it seems safe to say that a widespread concept of potentially positive relationships between taxing and wealth cannot be found before the late Renaissance. Of course, the ingredients for such a concept did exist in the medieval world. We know that medieval men (or, rather, medieval intellectuals) were able by the thirteenth century to conceive of a national state, of national as well as feudal taxing, and of a commonwealth that could be altered by man-made economic policies as well as by God and nature. All readers of the third volume of the *Cambridge Economic History of Europe* know that even earlier, in many Central European city-states, makers of economic policy obviously were sensitive to connections between fiscal policy and wealth. Possibly we can find the same realization in the more autonomous cities of France such as La Rochelle, Lyons, or Marseilles, although this is not yet established.[1]

However (and this is my first main point), men of medieval and Renaissance France did not combine these ingredients of theory and observation into a concept that under certain conditions the *royal* tax system could improve the wealth of the king's subjects and that substantial improvements in national wealth could help the fisc. This is not to say that discussions of the relations between wealth and royal taxes were wholly lacking until the late Renaissance. But from the late thirteenth century until well into the Renaissance such discussion reflects the prevailing view that regular national taxing – that is, annual royal revenue beyond traditional domanial income and occasional emergency aid – could have only bad effects on the economy. As late as Jean Bodin (around 1576), going theory held that as far as taxes were concerned the prince's gain had to be the people's loss. A favourite Renaissance metaphor was that the fisc was a parasite (*le rat au corps*), growing fat and sleek as its host grew thin and lifeless.

[1] The ability of most French cities to control their economic affairs diminished rapidly after they were absorbed into the royal domain.

There were two associated pivots about which swung all late medieval and early Renaissance arguments on wealth and taxes: the inviolability of private property and the importance of restricting the royal fisc to its sources of traditional revenue. In the Middle Ages the ideal prince was an armed judge – a force useful to society primarily as an arbiter and as a protector of feudal, natural, and divine law. Therefore the men of this era did not regard royal revenues as contributions by participants in a commonwealth to expenditures that would increase the well-being of the people. They thought of the fisc as a house-holding operation, intended to support the royal family in proper style and to provide a small surplus which, when husbanded as it should be, would provide funds for emergency military affairs. The prince's revenues, mainly, were not what we would call taxes but rather were rents, tolls, seigneurial dues, and a host of other items conceived of partly as the ruler's family property and partly as God's method of providing princes with what they needed to fulfil their proper functions. St Thomas Aquinas, as one would expect, had the definitive word here: 'Princes of the earth were instituted by God not to seek their own gain but to look after the common utility of the people. . . . For this reason the revenues of certain lands were established for princes, that, living on them, they might abstain from the despoiling of their subjects.'[1] In an emergency, such as an invasion by enemies or the need to finance a crusade, the prince might approach his subjects and his vassals for a subsidy. But such aid had to be requested rather than forced, intended for 'common utility' rather than selfish schemes, and limited in time to the emergency that had called it up.

One often reads in accounts of the origins of royal taxing that the modern state, born like 'a famished Gargantua' (Michelet), had to invent taxing almost as soon as it drew breath. This is an oversimplification, however, since in France the early modern state is an extension of the medieval state; and the medieval state was firmly established, in fact and in contemporary thinking, long before royal taxes had arrived as a fixed element of royal revenues. In other words, we could say

[1] *De Regimine Judaeorum*, in E. Lewis, *Medieval Political Ideas* (London: Routledge, 1954), I, 111.

that the French state was born self-supporting. The intellectuals of the fourteenth century were convinced that as far as possible it should stay that way; controversy on this matter was only over the degree to which the king could supplement, through taxing, his domanial revenues and feudal aids.

With some exceptions, late medieval political theorists did not reject the idea of a strong state. What they wanted was what we all want – a state that does well what we ask of it and at small expense. There was little feeling, however, that the rising level of expenditures in the fourteenth century reflected an entirely different international situation or that these expenditures represented justifiable claims on the people's wealth in the sense that they provided new and important services. The Middle Ages did permit the king certain functions we would call economic – supervising fairs, maintaining roads and proper weights and measures, protecting French merchants abroad, protecting the country against famine and against the loss of its precious metal, and so on. But these were regarded not as a separate economic branch of royal government but as part of *la police*, the law and order, which was in turn only part of the Crown's functions as the guardian of justice. This is why, when late thirteenth- and fourteenth-century kings were pushed by their higher expenditures to debasing the coinage and to imposing national taxes, they were scolded so often by being reminded of the good king Saint Louis – apart from his 'crusader tithes', this ruler was supposed to have managed very well on his traditional revenues alone.

The belief that a well-ordered state should be funded without taxing, therefore, was an important part of medieval political views before regular taxing became an important issue in the days of Philip the Fair (1285–1314). In the early stages of the Hundred Years' War the debate over royal taxing reached such a pitch that it played a major part in the struggles between the Crown and the French Estates-General in the 1350s and in the even more serious uprising of 1382. The debate was pushed into the background by Charles VII's success in driving out the English during the 1430s and 1440s – decades when royal taxing was being firmly tamped into a permanent place in the royal fiscal structure. But it flared up again during the Wars of

Religion (1562–98), when both Huguenots and Catholic zealots (though at different times) condemned arbitrary royal taxing as a mortal error and a crime against society. All during the sixteenth century the Crown's right to collect national taxes was attacked; and only rarely was it defended, either in official or in private statements, with justifications beyond those of urgent necessity.

We all know that medieval men had little realization of secular change in affairs such as prices, trade, population, production, and so on. But by the late Middle Ages the French did have an agonized conviction that they were being taxed more than in some happier past and that the future looked threatening. The new national taxes, the bruising fiscal expedients, and the hordes of new tax officials brought in by fourteenth-century kings trod painfully on important toes and on established ideas about property. Moralist writers then and in the early Renaissance took up and elaborated Aquinas' findings that private property is itself part of God's dispensation, the very basis of family life and public order, and as important as rulership itself. They taught that any prince who fleeced his subjects so that he might live in pomp or gratify his lust for conquest was committing a deadly sin; the sweat and the blood his subjects needed to produce this taxed wealth would stand as a permanent and vengeful witness against him until the final day of judgement. Another strand of hostility to the rising tax power of the Crown came from the 'feudalists', mainly legal experts working for great barons, who emphasized customary law for its importance in protecting each man in the fruits of his labour, his property, and his rights. For the feudalists a king's property had to be delineated sharply from that of his people; when the king needed funds beyond his traditional revenues he had to request them from the French, both those living in the royal domain and those in the remaining fiefs.

What particularly galled many of the feudalists in this era was that while the tax burden was rising the Crown was absorbing the seigneuries of one French noble family after another. The royal domain lands just before the Hundred Years' War had spread to include virtually two-thirds of all France. Now, surely, the king could 'live of his own' – that is, from his huge numbers of domanial tolls, rents, and seigneurial dues – and cease harassing the French with taxes.

Even the lawyer-administrators (*légistes*) who worked for the king advanced only relatively radical propositions in favour of royal tax power: that in spite of canonical prohibitions the king did have the right to tax the Gallican Church; that in emergencies 'which know no law' individual and provincial liberties had to be subordinated temporarily to the Crown's responsibility for the *défense et tuicion* of all; and that in his law-making powers the prince was above feudal tradition and man-made law: *princeps legibus solutus*. Even the king's men did not claim the king could impose taxes at will or that when taxing was necessary any good would come of it. The spirit of the *légistes*' apologies for royal taxing is nicely conveyed by one of their favourite metaphors, that when the king taxes away his subjects' property he is a surgeon cutting off a limb to save the rest of the body.

While attitudes towards wealth and taxes seem to have remained remarkably fixed all during the late Middle Ages and the Renaissance, the taxing system itself was not only growing luxuriantly but was pushing out strange new limbs.[1] By the reign of Francis I (1515–47) the French fisc was probably the largest and most complex governmental organ in the Western world. It was an 'absolutist' system in the sense that apart from a few provinces (and then only occasionally) the Crown did not consult popular representatives when new taxes or higher rates were imposed – though sometimes, as during the meetings of the Estates-General in 1560–1, a national parliament was helpful in facilitating acceptance of a new source of funds. It was operated by an enormous group of royal officials who functioned at local and provincial levels as well as at the national level and who, from the first *président* of the Chambre des comptes down to the lowliest *sergent* of the salt taxes, were responsible to and appointed by the king – from whom they bought their offices, since these were all venal positions. The Crown could increase the number of these officials virtually as

[1] The following discussion is based on my forthcoming work, *The Tax System of Renaissance France*.

it saw fit or whenever the market would bear it; during the later Renaissance the Crown often ordered that the number of posts in a certain type of office be doubled, thus creating hundreds of additional venal positions to sell off. The Crown could alienate its domain lands as well as its excise and salt taxes; it could squeeze 'free gifts' from the clergy and the towns; it could and often did decree an increase in the chief taxes during the course of a fiscal year. The regular annual national imposts (*tailles, aides, gabelles,* and *traites*) were still called 'extraordinary', but this was only a bit of fiscal nostalgia. No wonder commentators of the period called the fiscal system 'France's Peru'.

It is important to emphasize these characteristics of the sixteenth-century fiscal machine, since they help us understand that in the Renaissance era the term 'mercantilist' can in no useful way be applied to royal policy concerning relations between wealth and taxes.[1] For purposes of this discussion perhaps we can sidestep the hopelessly complicated argument over what mercantilism was and whether there ever was such an animal. Let us simply identify it with Colbertism – that is, with royal economic and fiscal policy in the 1660s and 1670s plus the writings (either policy oriented or theoretical) that approved of such policies. If this is allowed we can express the essence of mercantilist fiscal beliefs as follows: (1) improvements in the structure of taxes, in fiscal administration, or in the burden of taxes can enhance the nation's wealth; (2) of all the devices for increasing royal revenues in the king's fiscal arsenal, the best by far, and the only one not self-defeating, is to improve trade and industry.

It is my belief (and this is my second main point) that the most representative mercantilists caught a glimpse of a sort of fiscal–economic harmony, an identity of interests between the monarch and his subjects. For mercantilists (since the richer the subjects, the richer the king) the success of royal taxation depended on enhancing the people's wealth. Beyond a doubt this gives the essence of the vision on which Colbert based his

---

[1] In a paper given at the Third International Congress for Economic History (Munich, August 1965) I argued that other aspects of mercantilism, also, were absent in France before the last quarter of the sixteenth century.

fiscal reforms. But such a vision had no place in Renaissance fiscal policy. In a vague sort of way, of course, the Crown in the sixteenth century realized that revenues from its indirect taxes would rise and fall in response to prosperity and depression, peace and war; but such fluctuations were resisted as much as possible by the system of farming these indirect taxes, thereby keeping the bid prices as high and as stable as possible. The main tax, the *taille* on peasants, was not a rate on income or production but what the French call an *impôt de répartition*; that is, its global sum was fixed in advance of the fiscal year by the royal council, which directed its officials to follow the principle of *le fort portant le faible*, meaning that lower revenues in one district, for example because of a crop failure, had to be made up by higher revenues in another, and tax concessions forced by general economic distress in one year had to be made up in another. The royal revenues were not regarded by the Crown as the fiscal facet of the nation's economy; at least until the era of Henry IV and Sully the king continued to treat his fiscal system as a domain to be exploited, as machinery for turning his multifarious rights and properties into cash, as 'a field I can mow when I wish' (a statement attributed to Francis I). Scholars who find it difficult to believe in the primacy of revenue considerations for the Renaissance Crown are invited to look hard at venality of offices, a practice which was developed during the Renaissance and which put the needs of the treasury over the most basic considerations of efficiency, of justice, and even of the Crown's ability to control its own bureaucrats.

We would do much better, then, to label the Crown's policies on wealth and taxes in the Renaissance as fiscalist rather than as mercantilist. To put it bluntly, the standard works in modern literature on mercantilism that see the policies of Colbert as an extension of those of the Renaissance are simply wrong.[1] For example, we all know that Colbert did what he could to eliminate France's internal tariffs. But during the Renaissance the

[1] E.g. C. W. Cole, *French Mercantilist Doctrine before Colbert* (New York: R. R. Smith, 1931), Chap. 1; H. Hauser, 'La colbertisme avant Colbert', in *Les débuts du capitalisme* (new edn.; Paris: Alcan, 1931), pp. 181–2; Prosper Boissonade, *Le socialisme d'état* (Paris: Champion, 1927), pp. 16 ff., 96–8, and *passim*; Eli Heckscher, *Mercantilism*, 2 vols.; rev. edn. (London: Allen & Unwin, 1955), II, 266 and *passim*.

internal *traites foraines* were applied not only to additional commodities but also to additional provinces. One gets the impression the Renaissance kings felt that the more tolls and internal tariffs the better; they strongly resisted the efforts of tax farmers to unify the administration of these taxes (as well as those of the excises and some of the salt taxes), giving as justification that when associations of tax farmers were allowed to bid on *grosses fermes* they conspired to keep the bid price down, whereas when tax farms were small and not too expensive more would-be farmers entered the market and forced up the bid price close to its real value. Again, a central tenet of mercantilism was economic unity; but the Valois kings acted as though they had a stake in the continuing disunification of the national economy.

On examining import tariffs in the Renaissance we see that they were few and far between (until the end of this era) and that they appear to be devices to force merchants to buy import licences rather than part of projects to build up French industry. In matters of foreign trade Renaissance tax policy was concerned almost exclusively with *export* taxes, and it is only in the 1580s that import taxes become significant landmarks on the fiscal horizon.[1] The famous mercantilist principle of the balance of trade and its connection with the nation's stock of money is nowhere to be found in Renaissance France – at least not as we see it in Colbert's time. And it was in the Renaissance that the restrictions on interprovincial salt trade (which might have made some sense in the age of medieval scarcity) were frozen into a rigid and harshly policed system in order to protect the grotesquely high *gabelles* the Crown could collect in north and central France.

Heckscher tells us that 'mercantilist statesmen struggled [against] anything that bound down economic life to a particular place and obstructed trade within the boundaries of the state'.[2] Perhaps; but if so, this completely rules out any useful application of the label 'mercantilist' to the fiscal policies of

---

[1] G. Zeller, 'Aux origines de nôtre système douanier: Les premières taxes à l'importation', *Publications de la Faculté des Lettres de Strasbourg*, fasc. 106 (1945–7), pp. 165–217.

[2] Heckscher, II, 273.

Valois kings or statesmen. Of course, the Renaissance king, like his counterpart in the seventeenth century, did exert himself to improve his revenues. But he did so directly – that is, by broadening the base of his taxes, eliminating the remaining constitutional obstacles to his taxing powers, increasing the size and efficiency of his fiscal apparatus, raising the rates of his imposts, and subjecting the country to an astonishing profusion of fiscal expedients – rather than indirectly, through enhancing the wealth of his subjects.

This image of exploitive fiscality is not an exaggeration. It is not too much to say that with the exception of Louis XII (1498–1515) the Renaissance kings were constantly on the prowl for ways to increase their tax revenues. After 1522, in fact, the Crown's effort to increase the number of fiscal windfalls and to search out additional expedients was institutionalized in the form of a fiscal bureau, the office of Parties casuelles. As the sixteenth century wore on the flood of fiscal expedients increased, arousing the French to furious protests and a few serious tax revolts. Not content with the expedients which royal officials and the royal council could devise, the Crown more or less openly invited outsiders to suggest additional ways and means in return for a cut of the profits. Such men were known as *traitants* because they struck an agreement or *trait* with the Crown, usually to take the tax farm of the new revenue or for the new venal office.

Unfortunately for France, the Renaissance fiscal system and the fiscalist policies built up about it were carried over largely intact into the seventeenth century. That mercantilist reformers managed to make some significant changes in this formidable edifice is the chief reason we should honour their memory, since this was a greater contribution to Western civilization than the additions they may have made to deductive economic reasoning.[1]

My third main point is that mercantilist proposals for fiscal

[1] There is no point in compiling another bibliography on French mercantilism here. The indications in the works of C. W. Cole, Eli Heckscher, and J. J. Spengler are more than sufficient. See also the useful notes in Paul Harsin, *Les doctrines monétaires et financières en France du xvie au xviiie siècle* (Paris: Alcan, 1928), and Lionel Rothkrug, *Opposition to Louis XIV* (Princeton: Princeton University Press, 1965)

change had to operate around and through not only what
G. N. Clark, speaking of Louis XIV, calls the Crown's 'high
flying contempt for merchants and their sordid affairs' but also
the formidable and immensely well-entrenched fiscal system,
rooted by innumerable ties to vested interests in every corner of
France and hardened by almost two centuries of successful
operation.

In the area of fiscal policy and theory, if not on other subjects, mercantilism was not an extension of medieval views but
a new departure, a real break with the past. I want to emphasize
this as strongly as I can, since it is easy to get the contrary
impression from modern studies. In fact, some works on
mercantilism give the impression there was no specifically
mercantilist stand at all on public finance. About ten years ago
two excellent articles on mercantilism appeared in the *Scandinavian Economic History Review*, inspired by the appearance in
1955 of the second edition of Heckscher's classic. The first, by
D. C. Coleman, challenges the very validity of our using the
concept of 'mercantilism'; and as part of his demand that we
abandon this concept Coleman points out Heckscher's grave
error in neglecting public finance. He recalls that in 1937
Herbert Heaton attacked the first edition of Heckscher for,
among other mistakes, not adding 'mercantilism as a system of
public finance' to the work's categories, which included 'mercantilism as a system of power', 'mercantilism as a monetary
system', 'mercantilism as a concept of society', and so forth.
A. W. Coats, in his rebuttal and defence of Heckscher, claims
that while Heckscher recognized that 'financial consideration
determined many of the particular applications of mercantilist
ideas ... there was no general theory of public finance in
mercantilist economics'.[1] Heaton and Coleman, I believe, are
nearer the truth than Heckscher and Coats. However, we
do not find convincing statements on just what *was* the
mercantilist position on problems of public finance in

[1] D. C. Coleman, 'Eli Heckscher and the Idea of Mercantilism', and A. W.
Coats, 'In Defence of Heckscher and the Idea of Mercantilism', both in the
Scandinavian Economic History Review, V (1957); Herbert Heaton, 'Heckscher on
Mercantilism', *Journal of Political Economy*, Vol. XLV, No. 3 (June 1937). I have
been told that the study of mercantilism is soon to be blessed by the publication
of a D. C. Heath booklet in the series, 'Problems in European Civilization'.

Heckscher's detractors any more than in Heckscher or his supporters.[1]

Perhaps the reason this feature of mercantilism has received little attention is that it is almost too obvious: what we *mean* by mercantilism, especially in its policy aspects, *is* fiscal–economic relations; as Colbert put it, almost offhand as though its obviousness made explanation unnecessary, 'Commerce is the source of finance, and finance is the sinews of war.'[2] A bald statement of the main points in question, I believe, is sufficient to establish the reality of mercantilist fiscal policy. These points can be located in many sizeable mercantilist tracts, in preambles to royal ordinances, and in pronouncements by Councils of Commerce, Assemblies of Notables, and the like. But they do not have to be patched together from isolated statements or implicit references. They can be found quite explicitly and more or less complete in Colbert's most important single policy statement, his famous *mémoire* on finances of 1670. They can be expressed as follows: The object of economic statesmanship is to provide the monarch with the funds he needs for order and glory; to a large extent any increase in these funds must come from increases in the volume and circulation of cash, the only way to improve the tax-paying capacity of the population.[3] Of course, non-fiscal devices can help to build up taxable wealth: colonies can be planted and nurtured, home manufacturing improved in quality, internal transportation strengthened, the

[1] J. J. Spengler's long and important article on mercantilism, 'Mercantilist and Physiocratic Growth Theory', in Bert Hoselitz and others, *Theories of Economic Growth* (Glencoe, Ill.: The Free Press, 1960), touches only lightly on mercantilist public finance and not at all on mercantilist views concerning relations between the fisc and the economy. Neither does Jacob Viner in his article 'Power *vs*. Plenty as Objectives of Foreign Policy in the Seventeenth and Eighteenth Centuries', in his *The Long View and the Short* (Glencoe, Ill.: The Free Press, 1958). But how does one get from 'plenty' to 'power' if not through royal revenues? The best reference I know to the fiscal elements in mercantilism is Gabriel Ardant's highly stimulating and important study, *Théorie sociologique de l'impôt*, 2 vols. (Paris: S.E.V.P.E.N., 1965), esp. I, 699–708.

[2] P. Clément, ed., *Lettres, instructions et mémoires de Colbert*, 7 vols. (Paris: Imprimerie Nationale, 1861–82), III, Part 1, 37. See also the memoir advising the king not to loan money to the king of Denmark, VI, 231–2.

[3] Apparently, before John Law, mercantilist theories ignored both credit and monetary debasements as approved mechanisms for increasing the ability to pay taxes.

shipping industry expanded, the idle forced to work, and so forth. And reforms entirely within the fiscal system must not be neglected: budgetary control must be put on a sound basis, the domanial revenues must be built up as much as possible, and the quality of the fiscal bureaucracy improved. But the heart of fiscal policy (and the heart of Colbertism generally) is the effort to increase royal revenues indirectly, through economic improvements. 'The universal rule of finances,' according to Colbert, is so to control the economy and the fiscal system that a sufficient quantity of cash will circulate in every corner of the country, giving all the French the opportunity to make profits and pay taxes. The way to lighten the tax load is not to reduce taxes, even if we could, but to 'increase the cash available for general commerce [that is, all transactions] by attracting cash from other countries, keeping it inside the kingdom, and hindering its export, thus giving men the means to profit from it'.[1]

Colbert was no economic philosopher on the right hand of the throne. When the political situation (that is, the king's favour) required it, he could show as little concern for economic welfare as had Mazarin. And his ideas on the economy were not new; we find them more or less worked out in the formulations of Laffemas and Montchrétien around 1600, in the petitions of the Estates-General of 1614, and in the reforms and the *Testament Politique* of Richelieu.[2] Colbert had at hand a set of economic theories and a group of policies concerning economic welfare that were widely known before his time and, in many circles, rather popular. Of course, his main interest in them was that they could be used to consolidate his position at court. But the point is that before the end of the Renaissance such views could never have survived in the suffocating atmosphere of royal fiscalism.

Why seventeenth-century kings were willing to listen to mercantilist arguments on public finance is another problem:

---

[1] Clément, VII, item 15, esp. pp. 235–9, 246. This point is explained thoroughly in our foremost account of Colbertism: C. W. Cole, *Colbert and a Century of French Mercantilism*, 2 vols. (New York: Columbia University Press, 1939), I, p. 340.

[2] See esp. Cole, *French Mercantilist Doctrines*.

perhaps it was because in the days of Henry IV and Sully it was widely understood that new measures were needed to help the country recover from the disasters of the Wars of Religion; perhaps because the English and the Dutch were demonstrating that concern for the economy paid off for the government; perhaps because of increasing Christian sensitivity to human suffering during these days of religious revival. Certainly the king was determined not to make wholesale changes in the 'French Peru'. But his financial needs were great; and he could be expected to pay attention to specific and limited proposals (and to the general arguments on which they were based) that promised to increase his revenues and lessen disaffection among his subjects through amelioration of the economy. We all know about Henry IV's wish to see even his poorest subject with a chicken in the pot every Sunday; without wanting to detract from the warmth of his emotions, we can understand that the *vertgalant* realized quite well that the more chickens in the pot, the more sous in the tax-collectors' money chests.

In his introduction to Vauban's great work *Projet d'une dixme royale* (1708) Emile Coonaert says Vauban 'wrote with his eyes fixed on the king, imploring him prayerfully again and again'.[1] But tracts aimed at the king or at one of his more powerful ministers were even more the rule during the heyday of Colbertism than when Vauban wrote. It was the mercantilist's mission not only to search out areas of mutual benefit to the treasury and the economy but to convince the king that the changes they proposed were indeed worthwhile. If France's Estates-General had not died ingloriously in 1614, or if the rebellions before Louis XIV had accomplished anything except strengthening the Crown's hand, perhaps the French could have obtained a fiscal system more responsive to their needs. But as matters stood in Colbert's time, reform had to come from the top.

Viewing mercantilism as a programme to improve the treasury through the economy helps us understand much about the development of political economy in this period. Take for example the many agitated discussions on the dangers of royal war chests, a topic that is presented in a thoroughly confusing

[1] *Projet d'une dixme royale*, ed. Emile Coonaert (Paris: Alcan, 1933), p. xxxix.

manner in Heckscher.[1] War chests adequate to military emergencies had been a highly desired objective in both theory and
policy during the middle ages and the Renaissance, when they
were regarded as devices to allow the Crown to refrain as much
as possible from laying down imposts. But the mercantilists
pointed with alarm to the bad effects of storing up treasure,
which – like any form of hoarding – would reduce the circulation of cash, cut into consumption and production, and inevitably dry up the springs of treasury revenue.[2] A king should
be extremely careful not to lay up more treasure in any given
period than the increase in precious metal entering the country.
Again, the puzzling diversity of specific proposals for protecting domestic production is explained by the need for advocates
of each reform to convince the Crown that losses in import
tariffs would be more than made up by the increases in taxable
transactions resulting from the growth of home industry.[3]
This emphasis on maximizing taxable transactions also helps us
understand why mercantilists should have been so concerned
with unemployment, how they justified public works on economic grounds as well as on *la police*, and why Colbert insisted
that royal subsidies should flow towards provinces where
revenues were greatest. Even the famous (and largely vain)
campaigns to unify French weights and measures were justified
in part by the hope that this would expedite the collection of
excise taxes. What Colbert meant to concentrate his attention
on, as he told an intendant, was 'exciting the industry of [the
king's] subjects . . . in order to have them to earn back by these
means what they are obliged to give him every year through the
taille and other taxes'.[4]

Mercantilism in general, and mercantilist public finance in
particular, remained the dominant framework of the French
Crown's fiscal policies until after the middle of the eighteenth

[1] Heckscher, II, pp. 209–16 and *passim*.
[2] There are countless mercantilist statements to this effect. An interesting and
very explicit one is attributed by Colbert to the Crown: Clément, *Lettres*, VI,
466–7.
[3] This argument can be found in one of the first clear expressions of mercantilist
attitudes in France, the findings of an Assembly of Notables in 1583; Cole,
French Mercantilist Doctrines, pp. 39–40.
[4] Clément, *Lettres*, III, Part 1, p. 196.

century. Following Colbert's death in 1683, there had been an interesting outpouring of criticism against his work, though often even the critics armed themselves for the attack with mercantilist-type arguments. While these 'anti-mercantilists' gained many followers, including some of the king's own ministers, their programmes were rejected. Mercantilism continued, if not triumphant, at least firmly in command. Even the experiments of John Law, for our purposes, can be labelled 'paper-money mercantilism' – Colbert plus credit. With the collapse of Law's system the government fell back again on seventeenth-century policies and theories. As the vigorous and creative 'Young Régime' of seventeenth-century government hardened into the decrepit and ultraconservative 'Old Régime' after 1720, a seemingly unbridgeable gap appeared between going theory and government policy. It was not until physiocracy captured the imagination of the *philosophes* in the 1760s that the Crown seriously began to consider prying itself loose from mercantilist concepts.

My last main point is that when we know more about the significance of this 'anti-mercantilism' of the three decades 1680–1710, it may well appear that it represents a watershed in the history of French views on wealth and taxes, and perhaps in the history of economic thought generally. Originally the rulers of France had permitted themselves to become committed to mercantilism because of its promises of increased strength. Though no one could have foreseen this in the 1660s, mercantilism contained seeds of dangerous dissent and serious criticism of the government. It was, after all, a definite set of policies associated with a widely understood theory of political economy. These policies were placed in operation by powerful men who persuaded the Crown that these changes were worth the trouble and the dissent they caused. Advocates of mercantilism could take some of the credit for the increase in French wealth during the first two-thirds of the seventeenth century. Quite naturally, then, during the double crisis of deep depression and war disasters after 1688 critics of mercantilism tried to make the mercantilists take some of the blame. The government after 1690 was quite sensitive to these attacks, we know; it was anxious enough to authorize several investigations into the causes of increasing economic distress.[1]

A fascinating example of this new trend in economic reasoning is the anonymous tract, 'The Groans of Enslaved France' (*Les soupirs de la France esclave qui aspire après la liberté*), written in 1689 or 1690 and attributed to one Michel le Vassor. In some important respects this apparently influential and often reprinted tract stands Colbertism on its head. Mercantilists argued that the king must increase his revenues only in proportion to the increase in the stock of money. *Les soupirs*, therefore, could blame France's misery on the fact that the Crown's 'frightful and excessive taxes' had drawn too much of the nation's specie out of circulation and had 'dried up commerce'. Mercantilists promised that if the king promoted economic development his treasury would profit; *Les soupirs* threatened that unless the king lightened the tax burden the economy would collapse completely. Again, the solution proposed by *Les soupirs* for the depression was not additional mercantilist regulation but 'liberty of commerce', since 'the prohibition of foreign goods, far from turning out well for commerce, on the contrary, is that which has ruined it'.[2]

The anti-mercantilists, like the mercantilists, did not form a cohesive school; and since they were engaged primarily in attacking the establishment, they presented their philosophy in an even more disorganized fashion than had the mercantilists. But this does not mean that concepts of men such as Bois-guilbert can be dismissed as extensions of mercantilism, or as a few new ideas 'imbedded in a matrix of the older ideology'.[3] It seems to me that there is a connection between physiocracy and anti-mercantilism, or at any rate between Boisguilbert and Quesnay, though it is not easy to say just what this connection was. Very tentatively, we can characterize the main views of

[1] See Rothkrug's interesting analysis of the attempts by anti-mercantilists to oust the Colbertists from royal favour: *Opposition*, Ch. IV and pp. 374 ff.

[2] *Les soupirs de la France esclave* (Amsterdam, probably 1690), pp. 18–19.

[3] Cole, *Colbert*. One sometimes sees the term 'neo-mercantilist' applied to Boisguilbert and others, but I prefer 'anti-mercantilist', since I want to emphasize their contribution in crying out against the discrepancy between the government's avowed aim to promote economic growth and the strangulating effects of the government's fiscal system.

French anti-mercantilism around 1700 as follows: (1) While the mercantilists saw economic growth as possible only by transfers from abroad, Boisguilbert and others now saw growth as a dynamic process. (2) These men pointed to agriculture, rather than commerce and industry, as the sector which would best repay attention by the Crown. (3) At least some of them (not Vauban) argued against mercantilist regulations and for 'liberty of commerce', by which they meant not only free circulation of goods inside the nation (mercantilists wanted the same) but also fewer trade and industrial monopolies and freer trade with other nations. The objective of state economic policy was still the improving of national wealth – but as a goal in itself and not for the treasury, not at the expense of other nations, and through liberty rather than control.

At least some of the anti-mercantilists, like the mercantilists, were anxious to assure the Crown that their projects certainly would not harm the treasury – indeed, we find echoes of this compulsion in the physiocrats and even in Adam Smith.[1] But there is reason to believe that for anti-mercantilism the needs of the treasury occupy a distinctly secondary place. Perhaps we can characterize the chief significance of anti-mercantilism as a subtle but important shift from increasing royal revenues through economic improvements to using the fiscal apparatus as a device for economic growth. This seems to be their meaning when they attacked mercantilism for pretending concern over economic welfare while really providing the monarch with tools and justifications for tyrannical oppression. Schumpeter lauds Vauban for his 'Gladstonian vision' in recognizing that 'fiscal measures affect the economic organization right to its cells'.[2] But mercantilists had seen the same vision. Surely Vauban's contribution in this field was that his proposals were directed towards improving the economy first and the king's revenues a very distinct second. The king's fiscal policies now were to be judged not by the level of his revenues but by the well-being of his people.[3]

[1] *The Wealth of Nations* (Modern Library edn. of 1937), p. 397.
[2] Joseph A. Schumpeter, *History of Economic Analysis* (New York: Oxford University Press, 1954), p. 204.
[3] *Les soupirs*, esp. pp. 21–40.

The analysis of relations between wealth and taxes found in anti-mercantilism is much more sophisticated than that in Colbert. Boisguilbert, for example, knew that it was not primarily the simple increase of monetary stocks that increased taxable transactions but rather the decisions of consumers and producers who, he felt, were being hamstrung by arbitrary fiscality. Vauban and Boisguilbert argued for an abandonment of the mercantilist emphasis on excises and tariffs and for substituting direct taxes on production, set as a fixed proportion of output or income rather than as a global sum to be repartitioned in advance, as was the *taille*.

In general, anti-mercantilists were much less inclined than were mercantilists to emphasize the harmony of interests between the treasury and the economy; instead they pointed to royal fiscality as one of the main reasons for the economic crisis. While the mercantilists, generally, had seen great virtue in low, stable prices, the anti-mercantilists were greatly concerned to work for higher prices in their era, especially prices for cereals. Many of them, like Boisguilbert, were great landowners; and they were appalled by the decline in their profits and in the value of land and by the frightful distress they found among their poorest peasants. They felt that consumption had to be stimulated, and that this could only be done by a more rational tax system which would end hoarding and would encourage peasants to work harder and to stop directing all their efforts towards thwarting the tax collector.[1]

Finally, we have arrived at a time – that is, around 1700 – when the concept of a beneficent fisc was firmly espoused by an important group of intellectuals. It is a long way from the medieval view of the king as an armed judge to the physiocratic maxim that 'the government should trouble itself less with economizing than with the operations necessary for the prosperity of the kingdom; for very high expenditure may cease to be excessive by virtue of the increase of wealth'.[2] The

---

[1] Pierre le Pesant de Boisguilbert, *Dissertation sur la nature des richesses* (1707?), cited in Eugene Daire, ed., *Economistes-financiers du xviiie siècle* (Paris, 1843), pp. 417–24. This idea is stressed in Boisguilbert's other works and in Vauban.

[2] Quesnay, 'General Maxims for the Economic Government of an Agricultural Kingdom', in Ronald L. Meek (trans.), *The Economics of Physiocracy: Essays and Translations* (London: Allen & Unwin, 1962), p. 237.

mercantilists and the anti-mercantilists, each group in its own way, helped us mightily in travelling that distance. Of course, good understanding of this journey awaits analysis that will take note of many more signposts than were touched on here: the effect on France of fiscal theories and developments in other countries, the relation between ideas on growth and actual economic development, and all the debates on social welfare that come out of the Enlightenment, to name a few. For the questions that were raised at the beginning of this paper are, after all, only partial ones. The real question is: When and why did the conviction arise in Western civilization that a people has the right to hold its government responsible for progress towards established expectations?

Select Bibliography

This bibliography does not include: (*a*) the articles reprinted in this volume; (*b*) contemporary sources of mercantilist ideas. It is confined to the conception and development of the idea of mercantilism; and is concerned mainly with mercantilism as economic policy rather than with its position in the history of economic thought. It makes no pretence of providing a Europe-wide coverage: there is a moderately detailed list for England; much smaller ones for France, Germany, and Holland; for elsewhere no coverage is provided save in so far as their countries' policies are discussed in general works.

(The place of publication is London unless otherwise stated.)

General

ADAM SMITH, *The Wealth of Nations* (1776, ed. E. Cannan, New York, Modern Library edition, 1937).

GUSTAV SCHMOLLER, *The Mercantile System and its Historical Significance* (1895).

ELI F. HECKSCHER, *Mercantilism* (2nd edn., ed. E. F. Söderlund, 1965).

J. VINER, *Studies in the Theory of International Trade* (New York, 1937).

E. A. J. JOHNSON, *Predecessors of Adam Smith* (New York, 1937).

P. W. BUCK, *The Politics of Mercantilism* (New York, 1942).

J. A. SCHUMPETER, *History of Economic Analysis* (New York and Oxford, 1954).

B. F. HOSELITZ (ed.), *Theories of Economic Growth* (New York and London, 1960), especially the chapter by J. J. Spengler, 'Mercantilist and Physiocratic Growth Theory' and that by the editor, 'Theories of Stages of Economic Growth'. Useful bibliography.

G. ARDANT, *Théorie Sociologique de l'Impôt* (2 vols., Paris 1965).

C. H. WILSON, 'Trade, Society and the State', being Chap. VIII of the *Cambridge Economic History of Europe*, Vol. IV (ed. E. E. Rich and C. H. Wilson, Cambridge, 1967).

H. HEATON, 'Heckscher on Mercantilism', *Journal of Political Economy*, XLV (3), 1937.

J. H. DALES, 'The Discoveries and Mercantilism: an Essay in History and Theory', *Canadian Journal of Economics and Political Science*, XXI (2), 1955.

C. H. WILSON, 'Mercantilism: some Vicissitudes of an Idea', *The Economic History Review*, X (2), 1957.

A. W. COATS, 'In Defence of Heckscher and the Idea of Mercantilism', *Scandinavian Economic History Review*, V (2), 1957.

L. HERLITZ, 'The Concept of Mercantilism', *Scand. Econ. Hist. Rev.*, XII (2), 1964.

R. C. BLITZ, 'Mercantilist Policies and Pattern of World Trade, 1500–1750', *Journal of Economic History*, XXVII (1), 1967.

England

W. CUNNINGHAM, *The Growth of English Industry and Commerce* (2 vols., Cambridge, 3rd edn., 1903).

EDGAR S. FURNISS, *The Position of the Labourer in a System of Nationalism* (Boston, 1920).

B. SUVIRANTA, *The Theory of the Balance of Trade in England* (Helsinki, 1923).

P. J. THOMAS, *Mercantilism and the East India Trade* (1926).

G. UNWIN, *Studies in Economic History* (1927).

B. E. SUPPLE, *Commercial Crisis and Change in England, 1600–42* (Cambridge, 1959).

T. E. GREGORY, 'The Economics of Employment in England, 1660–1713', *Economica*, I, 1921.

C. H. WILSON, 'Treasure and Trade Balances: the Mercantilist Problem', *Econ. Hist. Rev.*, 2nd series II (2), 1949.

E. F. HECKSCHER, 'Multilateralism, Baltic Trade and the Mercantilist', *Econ. Hist. Rev.*, 2nd series III (2), 1950.

C. H. WILSON, 'Treasure and Trade balances: further evidence', *Econ. Hist. Rev.*, 2nd series IV (2), 1951.

W. D. GRAMPP, 'The Liberal Elements in English Mercantilism', *Quarterly Journal of Economics*, LXVI (4), 1952.

R. W. K. HINTON, 'The Mercantile System at the Time of Thomas Mun', *Econ. Hist. Rev.*, 2nd series VII (3), 1955.

J. D. GOULD, 'The Trade Crisis of the early 1620s and English Economic Thought', *Journ. Econ. Hist.*, XV (2), 1955.

D. C. COLEMAN, 'Labour in the English Economy of the Seventeenth Century', *Econ. Hist. Rev.*, 2nd series VIII (3), 1956.

H. F. KEARNEY, 'The Political Background to English Mercantilism, 1695–1700', *Econ. Hist. Rev.*, 2nd series, XI (3), 1959.

J. SPERLING, 'The International Payments Mechanism in the Seventeenth and Eighteenth Centuries', *Econ. Hist. Rev.*, 2nd series, XIV (3), 1962.

M. BLAUG, 'Economic Theory and Economic History in Great Britain, 1650–1776', *Past and Present*, No. 28, 1964.

R. DAVIS, 'The Rise of Protection in England, 1668–1786', *Econ. Hist. Rev.*, XIX (2), 1966.

France

P. BOISSONADE, *Le socialisme d'état* (Paris, 1927).

C. W. COLE, *French Mercantilist Doctrine before Colbert* (New York, 1931).

C. W. COLE, *Colbert and a century of French Mercantilism* (2 vols., New York, 1939).

C. W. COLE, *French Mercantilism, 1683–1700* (New York, 1943).

L. ROTHKRUG, *Opposition to Louis XIV* (Princeton, 1965).

Germany

A. W. SMALL, *The Cameralists: the pioneers of German Social Policy* (Chicago, 1909).

L. SOMMER, *Die Österreichischen Kameralisten* (Vienna, 1920).

A. TAUTSCHER, *Staatswirtschaftslehre der Kameralismus* (Berne, 1947).

I. BOG, *Der Reichsmerkantilismus* (Stuttgart, 1959).

Holland

J. G. VAN DILLEN, 'Beteknis van het begrip mercantilisme voor de economische en politike geschiednis', *Tijdschrift voor Geschiednis*, 1959.

W. D. VOORTHUIJSEN, *De Republick der verenigde Nederlanden en het mercantilisme* (The Hague, 1965; English summary and detailed bibliography).